THINKING SMALL

THINKING SMALL

THE UNITED STATES AND THE LURE
OF COMMUNITY DEVELOPMENT

Daniel Immerwahr

Harvard University Press

Cambridge, Massachusetts
London, England

First Harvard University Press paperback edition, 2018
Second Printing

Library of Congress Cataloging-in-Publication Data

Immerwahr, Daniel, 1980–
Thinking small : the United States and the lure
of community development / Daniel Immerwahr.
pages cm
Includes bibliographical references and index.
ISBN 978-0-674-28994-9 (cloth : alk. paper)
ISBN 978-0-674-98412-7 (pbk.)
1. Community development—United States—History.   2. Community development—
Developing countries—History.   3. Economic assistance, American—Developing
countries—History.   4. Rural development projects—United States—History.
5. Rural development projects—Developing countries—History.   I. Title.
HN90.C6I44 2014
307.1'40973—dc23
2014011215

For my father

CONTENTS

.

MODERNIZATION, DEVELOPMENT, AND COMMUNITY

This is a book about poverty and the ways in which people have made sense of it. It is also, therefore, a book about contested concepts, about terms whose meanings have been up for grabs. It may help to say something up front about three of those terms.

The first is *modernization*. It is a confusing word, for the same reason that *modern* is confusing. Does it refer to a time period or to a condition? Do we become modern merely by living in the "modern" period (whenever that was or is—opinions vary widely), or must we adopt some particular practices or worldview? In the past, enthusiastic users of the word *modern* and its cognates tried to have it both ways, by insisting that the passage of time carries societies inevitably toward the "modern" condition. But the notion that there is a single destination upon which all societies will ultimately converge now seems implausible.

In this book I avoid talk of the modern and of modernity. I do, however, use *modernization* to refer to a political vision: the desire to achieve a particular social configuration in which institutions are oriented toward industry, governed by urban norms, shaped by bureaucratic practices, and centralized to a significant degree. I use the term in that way because that is how the people I am writing about used it. Or, in many cases, they pointedly avoided the language of modernization because they were trying to refer to something different.

Another term that can cause confusion is *development*. It is often used as a synonym for modernization. In this book, I use it in a broader sense, to refer to the increase of social capacity. Modernization is one form of development, but it may be possible to improve people's lives without centralizing their institutions. Many of the subjects of this book thought they had found one such way. That does not mean that they wanted to return to the past. It rather means that they had mapped out an alternate route forward. They sought development—but development without modernization.

A final confounding keyword is *community*. Here the problem is not the definition—a social unity bound together by face-to-face ties—but the connotation. A warm, glowing aura surrounds the word. As I have learned, it is nearly impossible to tell people that one is writing a book about community development without their assuming that the book is a celebration of it. After all, why mention community if not to praise it?

Why, indeed? As the reader will discover, this is a book that tries to take the concept of community seriously, not as a vague source of inspiration but as a historical project. It asks what happened when societies tried to solve their problems by encouraging communal solidarity. The results were not always happy. The intimate scale can be just as oppressive as the large scale, and not every village is a garden of fellowship. But if it turns out that community—just like religion, science, and the market—was an imperfect vessel for the highest hopes of humankind, should that really be such a surprise?

THINKING SMALL

IN 1958, the *Saturday Evening Post* published serial installments of an unorthodox novel. It had no love story, little action, no single protagonist, and not much by way of a plot. Set in a fictional country in Southeast Asia, it dwelled mostly on embassy life, the relationship between nationalism and communism, foreign aid, and what Asians thought of the United States. But despite its unusual form and arid content, *The Ugly American,* by William J. Lederer and Eugene Burdick, shot onto the bestseller lists and remained there for seventy-eight weeks; by 1959, it was outselling even Vladimir Nabokov's sensational *Lolita.* In all, the book has sold over six million copies and gone through fifty-five printings.[1] Marlon Brando starred in the film adaptation, which appeared in 1963, and the phrase "ugly American" became a familiar shorthand reference for the sort of cultural insensitivity criticized in the book. By any measure, then, Lederer and Burdick's book was a major triumph—the biggest policy novel since Upton Sinclair's *The Jungle.*

The novel was so successful because it touched a nerve. The United States, it argued, had spent millions on aid to Asia, but with little to show for it. The problem was that "most American technicians abroad are involved in the planning and execution of 'big' projects: dams, highways, irrigation systems," projects that were often unwanted because they did not meet the requirements of the villages they were supposed to benefit.[2] What was needed, instead, was to focus on "little things" and "tiny battles."[3] The reduced scale of operations would allow rural people to participate in and shape aid projects themselves.

That participatory approach was showcased by Homer Atkins, the closest thing the novel had to a hero. In it, Atkins is a retired engineer who, upon arriving in the fictional country, grows disgusted with the technical experts who inhabit the capital and sets out for the "boondocks." There he meets a villager, Jeepo, and the two set out to develop a pump capable of carrying water from one rice paddy to the next. Such pumps are widely available in the United States, but Atkins refuses to import them. "It has to be something right here, something the natives understand," he explains. "If the pump is going to work, it has to be their pump, not mine."[4] Indeed, it is Jeepo who comes up with the crucial innovation that makes the pump a success, an innovation based not on technical knowledge of mechanical engineering but on social knowledge of the ways of his neighbors. Together, Jeepo and Atkins start a cottage industry that brings mild prosperity to the village. As Lederer and Burdick make clear, it is through such local knowledge of rural villages and democratic deliberation within them that development must happen, not through large plans forced upon those villages from Washington.

Could such an approach prevail? Lederer and Burdick doubted it. Homer Atkins was, in their view, "a wild exception to the rule."[5] Historians have agreed and have written numerous books making essentially the same complaint. The United States, they explain, was at the time in the grip of modernization theory, which called for the replacement of a locally rooted world of tradition-bound small communities with a cosmopolitan world of industrialized mass societies. Modernization theory was a complex body of thought, drawing on the work of economists, political scientists, sociologists, and anthropologists. But it was more than just an academic theory. It was, in the telling of historians, an "ideology," an all-encompassing worldview held instinctively and uncritically throughout U.S. society, particularly but not exclusively in the 1950s and 1960s.[6] The tendency of policymakers to draw on the tenets of modernization theory—even when they had read little of its scholarly underpinnings—explains why the United States placed such faith in experts and in top-down, large-scale transformations, while engaging so rarely with the historical and cultural particularities of the places in which they operated. It also explains why Homer Atkins was such a "wild exception."

Yet Homer Atkins was not all that exceptional. As a literary figure, at least, he had clear precursors. One was Victor Joppolo, the hero of *A Bell for Adano* (1944), reporter John Hersey's novel about the United States' wartime occupation of Italy. The book was a series of staged encounters between Joppolo, an Italian-speaking, democratically inclined major from the Bronx, and his authoritarian, efficiency-obsessed commanders in the village of Adano, where Joppolo is stationed. Although Joppolo's commanders display a callous disregard for local conditions in Adano, Joppolo spurns the brass and heroically unites the town by restoring a symbol of its traditional culture, a church bell. The book was a runaway hit. It won the Pulitzer Prize, the Council on Books in Wartime labeled it "Imperative" reading (a designation enjoyed by only five other books), and Franklin Delano Roosevelt chatted excitedly about it over dinner.[7]

Hersey also inspired a copycat, Vern Sneider, who set his *Teahouse of the August Moon* (1951) in occupied Okinawa. Yet again, a sympathetic protagonist arrives in a foreign village with orders from on high to transform it according to some central plan. But instead of building the schoolhouse that the Army has commanded him to build, he defers to the will of the people and pitches in with the community to build a traditional teahouse—another bell for another Adano. This book, too, found an appreciative audience, and within five years it had become both a Broadway play and a movie. Like the film of *The Ugly American,* the film of *Teahouse* featured Marlon Brando, although this time in yellowface, as the obliging native Sakini.

There was, in other words, a great appetite for the notion that the United States might engage with the rest of the world not as a broadcaster of some monolithic culture but as a sympathetic enabler of village-level democracy, plurality, and local knowledge. And that hunger was felt not just by book buyers and moviegoers, but at the highest levels of government. If *A Bell for Adano* had captivated Roosevelt, then *The Ugly American* won itself an ardent fan in John F. Kennedy. After the book came out, he had copies sent to every member of the Senate. He based the Peace Corps—itself one of the most popular initiatives ever undertaken by his administration—largely on its model, and Lederer was put to work training Peace Corps volunteers.[8]

The Peace Corps was not the U.S. government's first brush with village-level development. Lederer and Burdick based their book on their experience in the Philippines, where the United States and Philippine governments had launched a nationwide community development program designed to achieve precisely the sort of small-scale successes celebrated by *The Ugly American*. The Philippine program was, in turn, part of a much larger campaign by the United States to promulgate such community-based tactics globally. In 1954, the U.S. government established a Community Development Division within its foreign aid agency. By 1956, two years *before* Lederer and Burdick's novel appeared, that Division was providing aid and staff to forty-seven community development programs in twenty-three countries.[9]

Once we acknowledge the extent of these programs, we can better see that modernization has never been the whole of U.S. foreign policy-making. Instead, the urge to modernize has been in constant conversation with a rival inclination, what sociologist Robert Nisbet called the "quest for community."[10] Broadly defined, the quest for community was an effort to shore up small-scale social solidarities, to encourage democratic deliberation and civic action on a local level, and to embed politics and economics within the life of the community. Its adherents preached the values of grassroots democracy and recognized the ways in which traditional institutions could protect their members from the economic and political shocks of modernization. Communitarian values claimed many adherents in the age of Homer Atkins. Even the ostensible chief agents of modernization, such as Kennedy, were not immune to them.

Why don't Lederer and Burdick just say that? Why do they portray Homer Atkins as lonely prophet rather than as part of a widespread and popular campaign to address poverty on the level of the village, building on local knowledge and culture? And why have historians been so quick to endorse Lederer and Burdick's portrayal of U.S. foreign policy during the period?

Because if the urge to modernize and the quest for community alternated as point and counterpoint in the postwar period, there was also a marked asymmetry between them. In the war for the national psyche, they were evenly matched. But in their institutional expressions, they were not. There was, especially in the middle of the twentieth century, a structural momentum favoring industrialization, bureaucratization, standardization, commodification, secularization, urbanization, mechanization, specialization, and quantification—the related processes that we collectively call "modernization." On the whole, people moved toward cities rather than away from them, organized their lives around industry rather than around agriculture, and witnessed the growth rather than the diminution of state power. Those trends were more the result of economic and social forces than they were of conscious policy choices. Yet their effect was to make it look like the modernizers were winning the argument and the communitarians were losing it. It was a tug-of-war on a steep slope: the victors may not have been stronger, they may have just been the ones who had the good fortune to be pulling downhill.

Modernizers had gravity on their side. As such, it is easy to exaggerate their influence, just as it is easy to understate the influence of communitarians. It is easy to look at the twentieth-century world and see the guiding hand of "high modernists" or the effects of an all-pervasive ideology of modernization. And that makes modernization seem to be a more inexorable process than it surely was. Our tendency to inflate the influence of modernizers and diminish the role of the opposition has had serious effects on how we talk about both the past and present. One of the most popular genres of academic writing today is a type of narrative that I'll call "Modernization Comes to Town." It tells story of how a world that was once rooted in local, heterogeneous, informal, flexible, pluralistic, and, above all, small-scale institutions was lost. It was bureaucratized, mechanized, quantified, commodified, and all the rest. Such multisyllabic forces yielded efficiencies of a certain kind, the story goes, but they did so at the cost of some essential human element.

Modernization Comes to Town stories turn up everywhere, once you start looking for them. They operate on different terrains and on different time scales, but they follow the same plot. They tell the story of how some phenomenon was distorted, flattened, dehydrated, or frozen—choose your metaphor, really—as it was transformed from a viable local practice into something that could be known and managed from a distance. And so we learn how we went from communal borrowing and lending to money-center banks that were too big to fail, from a healthy diversity of agricultural practices to endless amber waves of genetically modified grain, and from bustling, mixed-use neighborhoods to superhighways and office parks.

Narratives such as these correctly identify an important trend. They note how new technologies and new forms of social organization have allowed for the projection of power with greater force and over longer distances than ever before. Implicitly, Modernization Comes to Town stories call for a reversal of that trend. Yet they give little reason to think that such a reversal would be possible. It is easy enough to find examples in these narratives of people and communities who have resisted modernization. Those people and communities, however, are nearly always cast as tragic figures, doomed to failure. There is a certain romantic despair that hangs over them. Genuine alternatives to the institutions created by modernization are frequently celebrated but just as frequently dismissed. They are foreclosed possibilities, inspiring might-have-beens, bubbles of freedom, Paris Communes—rocks that floated briefly before succumbing to gravity's inevitable pull. Or they are located in other places, other societies that are at furthest remove from the vortex of modernity (but, of course, they too will be sucked in). The trail of Goliath is thus strewn with the corpses of would-be Davids.

These themes can be seen clearly in the work of the anthropologist and political scientist James C. Scott, whose writings over the decades have dealt principally with the collision of large-scale systems and small ones—giant edifices of economics and politics versus local ways of making do. Scott forcefully captures the tension between the two in his *Seeing Like a State* (1998), which bears the ominous subtitle *How Certain Schemes to Improve the Human Condition Have Failed*. It tells how "high modernist" leaders, seeking to reform societies by making them more orderly, instead undermined them. Scott suggests that the societies in question would have been better off had they entrusted reform to local communities, whose vernacular practices and ways of knowing have invariably proved to be more sure-footed guides to the management of human affairs.

Yet Scott is no more optimistic than Lederer and Burdick were. The local forms of knowledge and practice he valorizes "depend on key elements of preindustrial life" for their transmission and are therefore becoming extinct.[11] In a later book, Scott offers a celebratory account of upland Asia—in his telling, the last major remaining zone of refuge from large, hierarchical institutions—only to conclude at the end of the book that its autonomy has now mostly vanished.[12] More recently, Scott has published a slim volume of political theory, *Two Cheers for Anarchism* (2012). Yet there is no sense in it that the decentralized world of old can be reclaimed. Contemporary anarchist practice has been, in Scott's telling, reduced to "petty acts of insubordination"—resisting but not dismantling the outsize institutions that surround us.[13]

There is something grim in the thought that modernization has so thoroughly transformed the world that the very grounds for opposition are crumbling away. But for localists, there is also something convenient in that thought. By relegating resistance to modernization to the past, to remote areas, and to "petty acts of insubordination," they preserve a utopian element in their vision. Localism becomes something to strive for rather than something to study. In that way, the localists of today are not unlike certain varieties of twentieth-century socialists who, dismissing the catastrophic record of the Soviet Union, grounded their faith by pointing to the short-lived Spartacist uprising of 1919 or the brief moment when the Republicans held Spain in 1936. Having never seen their preferred political configuration realized for any significant amount of time in the industrial world, they are free to freight it with the loftiest hopes without fear of contradiction. When the practice is nowhere to be seen, the theory can run wild.

Is modernization really such an unstoppable juggernaut that resistance to it can only be found in faraway times and places or in small acts of defiance? Again, it is important to distinguish structural forces from ideas and intentions. It is true that there has been a general—if not entirely steady or unidirectional—motion of human affairs in the direction of centralization, standardization, and so forth. But on that large river many people, from presidents to peasants, have rowed against the current. We cannot dismiss that upstream paddling as symbolic resistance, admirable but ultimately fruitless. We should see it rather as a purposive and—more importantly—consequential act of navigation.

AS THE reader will have gathered by now, this book sets out to take seriously the communitarian strain within contemporary thought and politics. Rather than seeing the Homer Atkinses of the world as "wild exceptions," it regards them as entirely normal. By the midcentury decades, *many* people had come to feel that social institutions had somehow grown too large to be managed. And some of them sought to do something about it. *Thinking Small* follows a generation of thinkers and policymakers who identified scale as a central issue and whose attitudes toward centralization fell somewhere between wariness and outright hostility. They include world leaders such as Jawaharlal Nehru, Mohandas Gandhi, Ferdinand Marcos, Ngo Dinh Diem, and John F. Kennedy. They also include a large number of midlevel functionaries— men and women who worked for the UN, the Peace Corps, the Japanese internment camps, and the CIA. Localism was for them not a fleeting fantasy. It was a plan of action, with powerful backers who put considerable resources behind it.

That many people would be interested in diminishing the scale of social life around the middle of the twentieth century should not come as a shock. The years 1935–1965, upon which this book focuses, saw global war, economic depression, famine, violent revolutions, the rise of totalitarian governments, and the threat of worldwide nuclear annihilation. It was hardly radical to propose that humans had somehow lost control of their own creations. "The trouble is that everything is too big," wrote the political theorist Dwight Macdonald in 1946, and he was not alone in that feeling.[14] Within the United States, the middle decades of the twentieth century were a time of newfound appreciation for small-scale social solidarities, from the small group to the faraway village. At times, that interest expressed itself as nostalgia or kitsch, as in the art of Norman Rockwell or the films of Frank Capra. But the mood also struck social scientists, who fretted about the perils of mass society and who launched countless inquiries into whether small communities might behave better than large crowds. Across the political spectrum, thinkers joined the quest for community, the attempt to re-embed social, economic, and political forces within small-group life.

The urge to modernize and the quest for community were not the doctrines of warring camps. They were rival impulses, felt sometimes by the same people simultaneously, coiled tightly around each other, often tangled together. The urge to modernize was the more prominent strand in the United States during the midcentury decades. It shaped the highest levels of policymaking while the quest for community operated as a respected dissenting tradition. In that, however, the United States was something of an outlier. It had made its way through both world wars relatively unscathed, reaping the richest rewards of the twentieth century while exempting itself from most of the horrors.[15] As the predominant power in the world, it had more to gain from modernizing processes than any other state. That did not prevent powerful people in the United States from favoring communitarian policies. But it ensured that such policies were usually overshadowed by larger forces, such as the industrial agriculture lobby and the imperatives of the war machine.

Things were different in the global South, in the lands scarred by poverty and by the legacies of imperialism. There, enthusiastic modernizers could certainly be found—and much has been written about them—but their enthusiasm was always tempered by an inescapable sense of the dangers that "modern" life might bring.[16] That skepticism provided fertile soil for communitarian strategies and shaped the way that the United States interacted with Southern countries. The community approach had made only a small dent in U.S. domestic policymaking during the Depression and war. And yet, when the United States began its postwar mission to exert some kind of control in the global South, it found a new use for its recently discarded methods. The keen interest in community strategies abroad both enabled and encouraged the United States to launch a global community development movement with the goal of winning the allegiance of Southern villages through small-scale, democratic, locally designed improvement projects—exactly of the sort that Homer Atkins undertook in *The Ugly American*.

The community development movement ran from the 1930s through the 1960s and touched much of the world. By 1960, the UN estimated that over sixty countries possessed large community development programs, about half of which were nationwide in their extent.[17] This book deals principally with three of those countries: the United States, India, and the Philippines. But those three were among the most important. After its efforts to implement communitarian strategies in the New Deal and World War II failed to get off the ground, the United States became the chief international bankroller of community development in the global South. India was an early and enthusiastic adopter, shaping both the ideological components of community development and many of its basic practices. The Philippines, for its part, served as a testing ground for community development as a form of counterinsurgency. Finally, these strategies were re-imported into the United States as part of the War on Poverty.

It was fitting that India should be the first overseas target for U.S. experiments with community development. As the acknowledged leader of the decolonizing world, India was of enormous importance to the United States, especially after the Chinese revolution in 1949 left it standing as the world's largest non-communist country. Yet India was not just a geopolitical prize. It was also, thanks mainly to the legacy of Mohandas Gandhi, a global beacon of communitarianism. So when an architect from the United States named Albert Mayer made his way to the subcontinent in 1948 to see what might be done to raise India from poverty, he quickly discovered great interest from all levels of Indian society in village work.

With the help of Prime Minister Jawaharlal Nehru, Mayer launched a pilot project in the north Indian district of Etawah. There, villagers were to attend to their own development, using local artisanal techniques and materials to collectively design and carry out improvement schemes, with financial assistance offered from the state. The project gained international fame. So when the U.S. government prepared its large bilateral

aid package to India in 1952, it placed at the center of it the establishment of a nationwide community development project, based on the
Etawah scheme, to be launched on October 2, Gandhi's birthday. Over
the next decade, the project grew, village by village, until it covered the
whole of rural India. By 1965, its national program serviced every village in the country—villages that collectively contained around one-
tenth of the global population.

Great hopes, and a great deal of money, were invested in India's community development program. And thus localism became not a utopian
dream but a legislated reality. The entire planning apparatus of the
Indian state was grounded in the community development scheme; for
many villagers in India, their community development officer was their
first and sometimes only point of contact with the central government.
As the program expanded, it carved out room for itself within the structure of the state. While Nehru's government sought to create the rudi-
ments of large-scale industry in India, it undertook a campaign it called
"democratic decentralization," intended to counter the centralizing
forces at work by devolving power to the community development projects. Local elections were established, village-wide council meetings were
called, and the decisions made by those councils were sent upward and
used as the basis for India's national five-year plans. The political system
came to be known as *panchayati raj*—the reign of the village councils.
As Nehru repeatedly insisted, community development was by "far the
most revolutionary thing we have undertaken."[18]

Revolutionary it may have been, but its benefits were elusive. Although
villagers proved willing to compose local development plans when
prodded by government officials, those plans were strikingly modest in
their ambition: wells, market roads, community centers, and other minor
improvements, often benefiting the well-off members of the village.
Conspicuously absent from community council deliberations were any
measures that might address some of the structural issues most obviously responsible for the depressed conditions of the lower orders: debt,
unequal land tenure, caste, and patriarchy. The community councils, it
turned out, were easily captured by landlords, village headmen, and
caste leaders, which virtually guaranteed that attempts to address the
problems of inequality on the local level would meet with quick and
severe social and economic sanctions. After a careful study of the Indian
community development program, Swedish economist Gunnar Myrdal
concluded that its "net effect" had been "to create more, not less,

inequality."[19] As an anthropologist who worked in India put it, to simply turn matters over to elite-dominated villages and then expect any kind of democratic social change was "even more unrealistic than to expect rapid, orderly integration of the schools in the southern United States to result from putting responsibility for school integration in the hands of local school boards."[20]

That community development favored landlords over peasants was a disappointment to many in India. But in the Philippines, where a rural rebellion threatened to topple the government, it was—at least in the eyes of the U.S. government—a boon. Acting on the advice of legendary CIA officer Edward Lansdale (who appeared in the pages of *The Ugly American* as the amiable man of the people Colonel Edwin Hillandale), the Philippine government learned to use community development, like a drug prescribed for its side effect, as a form of counterinsurgency. By channeling local political energies through village councils, CIA operatives and Philippine politicians hoped to create vertical bonds linking the tillers of the land to the owners of the land, and crowd out the dangerous horizontal ties that might connect peasants across space. This was off-label use, to be sure, but the treatment appeared to work. After the Philippine rebellion subsided, the CIA eagerly sought to export this weaponized form of community development to other troubled spots in the Cold War: Latin America and, most notably, Vietnam. The readiness of the United States to fund village-based strategies there, including the Strategic Hamlet Program, had a clear precursor in its support of Philippine community development.

The exportation of community strategies from the United States to the global South should be a familiar story. As the world's superpower, the United States often imposed its practices and policies on the rest of the world. But historians are increasingly coming to see that the traffic was not only one-way. Programs designed for other countries had a way of creeping back into the United States.[21] In the case of community development, the reversal of flow was particularly pronounced. By the early 1960s, policymakers in the United States realized that the postwar affluence that they had been so confidently seeking to export to the rest of the world had not fully taken root at home and that the tide that had lifted so many boats had caught others in its undertow. Casting around for solutions, they found that the functionaries in government best prepared to address the problem were the ones who had been honing their craft on the villages of the global South for the past decade.[22]

Could the localist approach that had been used in the countryside of Asia, Africa, and Latin America work in the "urban villages" of U.S. cities? The designers of the War on Poverty thought so, and they placed at the center of their program a controversial initiative called the Community Action Program, which they openly admitted was based on overseas community development. But inner-city neighborhoods were not the same as Third-World villages. Whereas in the rural parts of the global South community development shunted power to the landlords and local potentates, strong residential segregation in the United States had turned urban neighborhoods into revolutionary tinderboxes, with few powerful local figures around interested in or capable of preventing an explosion. Community action in the United States thus became a vehicle for a sudden rebellion, with close ties to the increasingly militant civil rights movement. Politicians rushed to shut down the program and put in its place more politically palatable versions of "community-building"—ones that worked, or failed to work, more like the Indian program. Fire, not ice, had destroyed this iteration of community development.

IN INDIA, the Philippines, and the United States, the quest for community came to different ends. It very rarely turned out as advocates imagined, though: the simple balm of community was not the cure-all that it had seemed. Yet even if community development programs did not always hit their mark, they had consequences. They permanently altered the political structures of the places they touched. They also quickly entangled themselves with top-down modernization programs, the very programs they were designed to balance out. Community development was, in other words, neither a utopia nor a panacea. It was a complex undertaking encompassing a mix of hope, disappointment, and unintended consequences. Just like any other policy effort.

These pedestrian realities of actually existing localism are worth reflecting upon because today there is, once again, a palpable interest in the local. One reason Modernization Comes to Town stories are so popular is because of a widespread dissatisfaction with centralization. There is now a pronounced effort under way to reverse it—to move, as the environmentalist Bill McKibben has put it, from "the world of few and big to the world of small and many."[23] We eat locally, ride bicycles, build political movements from the bottom up (whether they be occupations or tea parties), invest in startups, and fight wars by winning over the villagers one cup of tea at a time. Those various impulses are not all the same, of course, nor are they all effective. But behind each stands a suspicion of large-scale processes. It takes a village, Hillary Clinton famously observed.[24] She lost the Democratic presidential nomination to a man who spent the early part of his political career as a community organizer and whose electoral victory was said to demonstrate the power of grassroots mobilization.

The new localism has colonized the world of international development, too. Over the past decade, the World Bank has spent some $85 billion on something it variously calls community-based or community-driven development.[25] Although there are a few new twists, most notably a focus on women, it is essentially community development reanimated, accompanied by the same paeans to the power of grassroots participation and to the importance of vernacular knowledge and local ways of doing things. The strategy appeals both to the left and the right, since it draws upon both a faith in local cultures and a suspicion of the regulatory state. With it has grown up a whole host of small-scale techniques, such as microfinance. In all of this, though, there has been almost no acknowledgment that such strategies have been tried before. The new wave of communitarianism has been carried out in near-total ignorance of the global community development campaign that preceded it by only a few decades.

The inability to remember what was once a major policy initiative that affected dozens of countries, including the United States, is not an accident. It is a consequence of our knee-jerk Weberianism, our tendency to see the past since the nineteenth century solely in terms of centralization, bureaucratization, urbanization, industrialization, and similar processes. It is true that, overall, there has been a momentum in favor of those forces. And yet that trend has been far from uniform and, more importantly, has been challenged with force and frequency. The proponents of alternative social arrangements, based on decentralization and community life, have not just been marginal figures; they have been serious thinkers and persons of influence. They have shaped our world, if not always as they would have hoped.

Our challenge today is to understand the present moment as one rooted in the history of the twentieth century. But to do that, we must allow ourselves to see that our past contains not just the urge to modernize but the quest for community as well. When we relegate communitarianism and decentralism to the realm of the impossible—when we treat them as only utopian or no longer viable—we not only blind ourselves to significant episodes in our own past, we also rob ourselves of the tools required to analyze such phenomena in their fullness. Having caricatured our past, we impoverish our ability to think clearly, and critically, about our present.

1

THE FUTURE looked bright from Anaheim in 1955. There, Walt Disney opened his long-awaited theme park, Disneyland, with its five "lands." In one, Tomorrowland, Disney offered "a vista into a world of wondrous ideas."[1] Forecasting the future of 1986, its attractions included the Flight to the Moon, Autopia, and the Hall of Chemistry. Disney accompanied it with a series of television programs—"Man in Space," "Mars and Beyond," and "Our Friend the Atom"—that U.S. military advisers and prominent technical consultants, such as the famed rocket scientist Wernher von Braun, had helped to write. The message of Tomorrowland and the television programs was very much the official one: government, scientists, and corporations were extending the frontiers of human striving. That lesson was conveyed by the space rides and also by the Disneyland exhibits showcasing everyday technology, such as Monsanto's House of the Future, added to Tomorrowland in 1957.

But Tomorrowland was not the only attraction in Disneyland. Visitors entered the park via Main Street, U.S.A., a re-creation of a small, turn-of-the-century midwestern town. It was modeled on Marceline, Missouri, where Disney had lived as a child. "I feel so sorry for people who live in cities all their lives and don't have a little hometown," Disney explained. "I'm glad my dad picked out a little town where he could have a farm."[2] The word *little* was not an accidental verbal choice. In contrast to the imposing Tomorrowland, with its Moonliner cresting the horizon, Main Street, U.S.A. was purposefully diminutive. At substantial cost, Disney had "every brick and shingle and gas lamp" made at five-eighths of their ordinary size.[3] As an avid model trainman, Disney had an affinity for such scale models, yet there was something more to it. Disney yearned for, as one of his later exhibits would famously put it, a "small world"—

a world of the neighborly sociability he associated with Marceline. That desire showed itself frequently in his films. It grew even stronger toward the end of his career, which he dedicated to an attempt to create his own town, the Experimental Prototype Community of Tomorrow (EPCOT).[4]

Disney was simultaneously fascinated by technological transformations and obsessed with small-town life. It is easy to see where the first of those two allegiances came from. The midcentury decades are often regarded as a golden age for technological optimism in the United States. World War II, which gave so many Europeans reason to question the very basis of industrial society, was for the United States an astonishing triumph of technical expertise and mass-production techniques. It also catapulted the country into a position of unassailable economic supremacy, which in turn released a flood of cheap consumer goods. And so the war set a pattern for the United States. It was to be a mass society, managed by experts, promising widely available rewards. When Jonas Salk embarked on a highly public campaign to find a vaccine for the devastating polio virus, *Time* put him on the cover. He was a fitting symbol for the age: a benevolent technocrat in eyeglasses, a lab coat, and a tie.[5]

But Tomorrowland brought dangers as well. Two weeks after Salk's appearance in *Time,* the magazine's cover showed an ominous black-and-white photograph of a mushroom cloud, with small text at the bottom of the page reading "H-Bomb over the Pacific."[6] The test of the hydrogen bomb on Bikini Atoll was the largest human-made explosion in history to date. It summoned reminders of industrialism's dark side, to which the middle of the twentieth century had been no stranger. Even in the Arcadia of the United States—perhaps the most fortunate nation on earth in that period—economic depression, decreasing autonomy for workers, the deterioration of rural life, the emptiness of consumerism, the horrors of combat, the unbounded growth of the warfare state, the possibility of nuclear catastrophe, and the threat of totalitarianism stalked the land.[7]

For Disney, such issues were personal. Despite all his mythologizing of his "little hometown" of Marceline, he had only lived there for three and a half years. His family had been forced to leave when his father, who refused to use chemical fertilizers or market his crops through middlemen, could not keep pace with agricultural mechanization. The farm went up for auction, and the Disneys moved to Kansas City.[8] For the rest of his life, even as he experimented boldly with new technologies, Disney could not give up the vision of the community life that Tomorrowland had imperiled.

Disney's ambivalence about the prospect of a technology-driven mass society was not unusual. Even the most zealous boosters of Tomorrowland appear to have felt it, their hypercharged optimism seeming at times to be a sort of the-lady-doth-protest-too-much-methinks attempt to "ward off the ghouls" of anxiety, totalitarianism, and nuclear obliteration, as Nils Gilman has put it.[9] Yet less noted is how many thinkers and artists sought to escape those same wraiths by a different route, one that took them through Main Street, with its promise of life lived on a small scale. That cultural turn can be hard to see because it is easy to assume that the United States has *always* had a soft spot for the small town, that it is a chronic form of nostalgia and a timeless cliché. And yet it is remarkable how many of the images of small-town life that are now stock elements of U.S. culture were generated during the middle of the twentieth century—and how few were generated before that. Rather than being an always-longed-for point of origin, the small town in the United States was an "invented tradition," and a tradition that was invented particularly to express a growing discomfort with industrial society.

THE SUDDEN interest in the small town in the 1930s is best understood in contrast to what came before. Skepticism about the benefits of technology was, of course, not new to the United States. A tension between the pastoral ideal and the industrial one runs through the whole of U.S. thought and literature. In the nineteenth century, expressions of pastoralism could be found in sentimental celebrations of village life, promotion of the home environment as a sort of familial community, and the intentional communities that utopians built for themselves.[10] Not all pastoralism was communal, though. Among the most enduring visions of agrarian and non-industrial life in literature are Hector St. John de Crèvecœur's *Letters from an American Farmer* (1782), Herman Melville's *Moby-Dick* (1851), Henry David Thoreau's *Walden* (1854), and Mark Twain's *The Adventures of Huckleberry Finn* (1884).[11] Notably, those books associate the world of nature not with the rural community but with the individual.[12]

Throughout the nineteenth century, pastoral thought increasingly favored the individual over the community. That trend reached its climax with Frederick Jackson Turner, who captured the pastoral revolt against industry in what became the single most potent hypothesis that has ever been offered in the field of U.S. history. In his vaunted "frontier thesis," Turner held that, contrary to the heady celebrations of industry that were so audible in the Victorian culture of his day, it was the frontier—the border between savagery and civilization—that was the true source of U.S. democracy and political character. But what was it, precisely, about the frontier that was so important? It was its "anti-social" character: "frontier individualism."[13]

By the end of the nineteenth century, the rugged frontiersman had become the counter-image to industrial society. Writers continued to discuss the small town but rarely in positive terms. Rather, what one critic described as a "storm of literary abuse" descended on small-town living starting in the 1880s.[14] Novelists saw the small town not as a place of rustic peace and neighborly cheer but of punishingly constrained horizons. The torrent of invective grew to a flood by the 1910s, in what the scholar of literature Carl Van Doren called "the revolt from the village."[15] Novels such as Edgar Lee Masters's *Spoon River Anthology* (1915) and Sherwood Anderson's *Winesburg, Ohio* (1919) and *Poor White* (1920), under the guise of literary realism, chronicled the narrow-minded pathos of provincial life.

Sinclair Lewis—the first U.S. writer to receive the Nobel Prize for Literature—offered the archetype of the genre with his bestselling novel *Main Street* (1920). Writing about a fictionalized version of his hometown, Sauk Centre, Minnesota, Lewis laid out his complaint: "There was no dignity in it nor any hope of greatness."[16] It contained only "a savorless people, gulping tasteless food, and sitting afterward, coatless and thoughtless, in rocking-chairs prickly with inane decorations."[17] Better people were to be found, no doubt, in the cities. Or at least that was the message conveyed by two new magazines, H. L. Mencken's *American Mercury* (founded 1924) and the *New Yorker* (1925), and by Mencken's sardonic coverage of the Scopes Trial in 1925.[18]

The 1930s, however, saw a series of stunning reversals. A cadre of intellectuals, swimming against the demographic current, moved away from cities to small towns. One member of that group was none other than Sinclair Lewis. After a career made on eviscerating provincial ways, Lewis moved to Barnard, Vermont. From there, he wrote two new novels: *It Can't Happen Here* (1935), pitting small-town values against Hitlerism, and *The Prodigal Parents* (1938), pitting them against Bolshevism.[19] Remarkably, Sherwood Anderson followed a nearly identical path. He moved to Marion, Virginia, and took up the editorships of the *Smyth County News* and the *Marion Democrat*.[20] "Our only hope, in this present muddle, was to try thinking small," is how Anderson explained his logic.[21] He made that point in a book called *Home Town* (1940), which defended small-town ways with as much vigor as *Winesburg, Ohio* had attacked them two decades earlier.

The exodus continued. Surely it meant something when, in 1938, the *New Yorker*'s fiction editor and the longtime author of its "Notes and Comments" section—Katharine Angell and E. B. White—nearly wrecked the magazine by catching the "decivilizing bug" and decamping together for North Brooklin, Maine (where White wrote *Charlotte's Web*).[22] Of course, by that time, the *New Yorker*'s architectural critic, Lewis Mumford, had been writing his regular "Sky Line" column from the hamlet of Leedsville, New York, for nearly two years. Even the solidly Marxist literary journal *The New Masses* found itself vulnerable. Its literary editor, Granville Hicks, abandoned New York City for Grafton, New York. Within a few years he had quit his post, resigned from the Communist Party, organized a community league, joined the PTA, become the editor of the Grafton town bulletin, and begun to publish a series of books and articles in praise of localism, including the widely read *Small Town* (1946).

What made small towns, for so long the targets of derision, suddenly attractive? "It would be hard to put my finger on one thing," wrote E. B. White. "Rather it was an accumulation of things," a gnawing feeling that the forces of modernization had somehow overshot their mark.[23] That feeling arose sharply, and for obvious reasons, during the Depression, a time when the enormous technical and industrial capability of the United States seemed to have ruined rather than enriched the nation. But it continued through the war and into the postwar period. "The trend is toward bigness," wrote Paul Appleby in his 1945 overview of the political scene.[24] That observation, in various forms, animated a great deal of social criticism of the day. From all angles, social critics considered how best to achieve what Lewis Mumford called "the restoration of the human scale."[25]

Of course, reducing the size of human affairs would not in itself solve longstanding problems of politics and economics. But perhaps it might render them tractable. There were forces alive in small towns—improvisatory adaptation, informal negotiation, and widespread participation—that were not to be found on the larger scale. And just as surface tension can

GOOD NEIGHBORS in the country, says Hicks, are not impersonal like city folk but help each other. Here Hicks comes into the kitchen of Mr. and Mrs. Clifford Agans with mail and groceries he has brought them from town.

Granville Hicks, formerly the premier literary critic of the Communist Party, showing off small-town life in Grafton, New York, for a *Life* photographer in 1947. Kosti Ruohomaa, photog. (Black Star)

hold together a drop of water but not a gallon of it, perhaps those tiny forces could overcome challenges that, when encountered in enlarged form, were insurmountable. The "twin gods of Bigness and Sameness" must be brought to heel, wrote Granville Hicks, and the spirit of "personalized, face-to-face community" allowed to flourish.[26]

Hicks's attitude was a far cry from the gee-whiz optimism of Tomorrowland. But how common was it? A closer examination of some expressions of small-town pride in popular culture may give some sense of its surprising extent—and of how antagonistic it was to the incursions of mass society.

A good place to start is with Norman Rockwell, possibly the most popular artist in the twentieth-century United States. Although he is remembered today for his glowing portrayals of small-town life, Rockwell came to that theme only late in his career. In his early years, he was an urban artist; he lived in or near his birthplace of New York City, dressed in Brooks Brothers, and belonged to the Larchmont yacht club, north of Manhattan. His work in that period was that of a caricaturist, depicting stock characters—young boys, small dogs, benevolent grandfathers— against blank backgrounds.

It was only after an artistic crisis and a failed quest to Europe in search of a new style that Rockwell set his sights on the small town. He did so first when he took a commission to illustrate Mark Twain's *The Adventures of Tom Sawyer* in 1936 and traveled to Hannibal, Missouri, on an energetic search for the "authentic details" of Twain's boyhood home.[27] Three years later, Rockwell moved with his family to Arlington, Vermont. "It was like living in another world," Rockwell reminisced. Enchanted by the "great neighborliness" there, he "settled into the life of the community," befriending his neighbors and attending weekly square dances.[28] Rockwell's small-town residency, which lasted until his death in 1978, dramatically changed his painting. Details colonized the formerly blank backgrounds, details largely drawn from the places Rockwell lived. His famous *Freedom of Speech* (1943), showing a young man courageously rising to speak in a crowded assembly, was not just an illustration of a generic scene but a richly detailed painting of a Vermont town meeting—based on Rockwell's experience attending meetings of precisely that sort.[29]

A particularly illuminating example of Rockwell's small-town oeuvre is *Shuffleton's Barbershop* (1950), one of his most technically accomplished works (and one of his most beloved—it is the basis of a 2013 made-for-TV movie). In it, Rockwell presents a barbershop in East Arlington, as seen through its front window. Posters and a rack of comic books hint at the intrusion of mass media into the modest shop. But the focus is on the back room, where Shuffleton and his friends have gathered for a night of music. The back room had been a place of great concern for Progressive-era reformers anxious to remove from politics the taint of informal associations. In Rockwell's rendition, however, the back room appears not as the site of sordid deal-making but as a warm space where neighbors join in common purpose. Furthermore, in the "cozy implication that at the back of every small-town barbershop lurks

The revalorization of the back room in Norman Rockwell's *Shuffleton's Barbershop* (1950). (Printed by permission of the Norman Rockwell Family Agency. Copyright © 1950 the Norman Rockwell Family Entities)

a bunch of music-loving old men," as John Updike somewhat derisively put it, one can find a plea for holism.[30] The demands of urban and commercial society may have subdivided skills and dehumanized labor, but in East Arlington, the barber can still be the bandleader.

Playwrights and screenwriters took up the small-town theme, too.[31] The indisputable classic of the genre was Thornton Wilder's *Our Town*, a play in 1938 and then a film in 1940. Wilder fretted that the vaunted

22

frontier spirit of the United States was actually an "American loneliness," depriving the people of any ties to "human community."[32] *Our Town* was the antidote: a modest play following the rhythms of life in the fictional Grover's Corners, New Hampshire, over the course of twelve years. The long duration allowed Wilder to explore the ways in which everyday interactions, iterated year after year, form durable edifices upon which lives are built. Humdrum details that a writer of the 1920s would have found suitable for derision are invested with deep existential significance. That theme is compounded at the end when one of the characters dies and, as a ghost, reflects on the precious joy contained within every moment. *Our Town* has since reigned as one of the most treasured plays in the national theatrical repertoire—as of 2011–2012, it was the third-most-performed full-length play in U.S. high schools.[33]

Our Town's enduring popularity on the stage is matched in cinema by Frank Capra's film *It's a Wonderful Life* (1946), a perennial television favorite and "the most inspiring movie of all time," according to a jury of 1,500 artists and critics organized by the American Film Institute.[34] The two works are strikingly similar. Like Wilder's play, Capra's film takes place over a long duration, in this case the life of George Bailey, a seemingly unexceptional resident of the fictional Bedford Falls, New York. George is eager for travel, but his obligations to his family and neighbors keep him in Bedford Falls. And so, also as in *Our Town,* the action focuses on the minute aspects of small-town lives.

Some drama is added to the film by the presence of the malevolent Mr. Potter, a callous banker whose reckless pursuit of profits nearly drives the community-minded George to kill himself. But George's suicide is interrupted when an angel (clutching a copy of *The Adventures of Tom Sawyer*) appears and shows George how the town would have been if he had never lived. It is a nightmare vision of chaotic urbanization. George's counterfactual absence has turned the quiet Bedford Falls into Pottersville, where "wailing hepcat music" (as the screenplay puts it) blares on a street filled with nightclubs, bars, burlesque halls, and pawn shops.[35] And thus, in a final similarity with *Our Town,* George's encounter with death teaches him the meaning of all of the tiny moments that composed his life. He returns joyfully to Bedford Falls, and the film ends with George's neighbors gathered around him, repaying his kindnesses, one by one, by giving him the money he needs to keep his family-owned building and loan business afloat.

Capra hinted at the tension between mass society and the small community in George Bailey's terrifying glimpse of Pottersville. But he dealt with that tension—his great theme—more explicitly in another film, *Meet John Doe* (1941), starring Gary Cooper and Barbara Stanwyck. The film begins with a version of the Bailey/Potter confrontation: a small-town newspaper has been bought out by an oil tycoon, D. B. Norton, who fires every writer unable to produce sensationalistic copy. One such writer, Ann Mitchell (Stanwyck), publishes in her parting column a fabricated letter from "John Doe," in which Doe threatens to commit suicide in protest of all the ills "of what we laughingly call a civilized world." The hoax sells papers, so Mitchell is rehired and recruits a down-on-his-luck migrant worker (Cooper) to assume the role of John Doe. On Mitchell and Norton's prompting, Doe delivers a series of speeches against the loneliness of mass society, exhorting his listeners to get to know their neighbors, tear down the fences that separate them, and unleash "a tidal wave of good will." The message catches on. Soon, towns across the nation create "John Doe clubs" to solve their problems informally, without the help of politicians. As neighbors meet for the first time, they are overjoyed to discover how easily their difficulties are overcome—work is found for jobless men and longstanding feuds are revealed to be based on simple misunderstandings.

Norton observes all this with cynical pleasure. He plans to use the media to build the John Doe clubs into a national organization, which will serve as the basis of a fascistic "New Order." When the two principles of social organization—bottom-up small communities and top-down mass society—collide, Doe breaks free of Norton's control, and the ruse is exposed. But the members of the John Doe clubs are undaunted. They continue their community organizing, this time as truly grassroots organizations, without the help of any central office.

The movie was a hit and landed Gary Cooper, as Doe, on the cover of *Time*. Yet there is reason to think that it was more than just a popular film. The Frank Capra archives contain numerous letters from moviegoers demanding that Capra launch a real-life John Doe movement. A few of those letters reported that such clubs had already been formed.[36]

The John Doe clubs never got far, but something similar sprang up around Elmore McKee's celebrated radio program *The People Act* (1950–1953). McKee had taken part in the postwar reconstruction of German society and, while there, became disgusted with German devotion to technocratic leadership. Eager to combat that mindset at home, McKee secured funding from the Ford Foundation to document and encourage "the vast number of Americans who realize that local community is the testing ground of a free society."[37] The result was a four-year series, which Margaret Mead called "one of radio's great achievements," each episode chronicling the successful efforts of some town to solve its problems through communal action.[38] The series was so popular that it provoked nearly ten thousand letters and visits to the program's central offices, requests for use of scripts and recordings from over four hundred educational institutions, and the establishment of a National Committee for *The People Act,* chaired by Milton Eisenhower.[39] It provoked an imitator as well, *The Whole Town's Talking,* also funded by the Ford Foundation.[40]

IT IS TEMPTING to dismiss this outpouring of enthusiasm for small-town life as decorative nostalgia—compensatory comfort for a nation lurching toward Tomorrowland. But scale-diminishing aspirations were not limited to artists tugging on the national heartstrings. Just at the same time as small towns bubbled up from the wells of popular culture, social scientists developed a keen interest in "small groups": sets of unrelated individuals connected by face-to-face social ties. In sociology, anthropology, political science, psychology, social work, and other fields, the small group became a central unit of analysis. It was, as Edward Shils wrote in 1951, "a focal point, toward which have converged the hypotheses and investigations of a variety of scholars working on widely different concrete problems and subject matters."[41]

No person better illustrates that convergence than the psychiatrist, sociologist, and dramatist Jacob Levy Moreno. Today he is hardly remembered, and even in his own day he was a curious figure. A flamboyant character given to grandiose and often baffling pronouncements, Moreno believed himself to be living in the social scientific end of days, an epoch that—building on the contributions of Anton Mesmer, Mohandas Gandhi, and Moreno himself—would "reach a climax with a scientific Christ."[42] There was something of the crank in Moreno, but something of the prophet, too, for his ideas had a surprising way of finding their mark. Moreno's influence despite his oddities can be taken as an indication of just how receptive U.S. thinkers were to the idea of the small group.

Moreno began his career in Vienna, studying the psychology of prostitutes. He found them intriguing, he explained, because "they were not acceptable either to the bourgeois or to the Marxist"—they stood on the margins of society but not as part of some large dispossessed class.[43] Upon arriving in the United States in 1925, Moreno moved on to studying a new set of troubled young women: the students of the New York State Training School for Girls. Had Moreno been a typical sociologist, he might have inquired into the causes of their delinquency and measured their attitudes or average characteristics. But what interested Moreno and his collaborator Helen Hall Jennings had nothing to do with who those delinquent girls were or how they had ended up at the school. He wanted to know about the patterns of their social interactions. Who knew whom? Who talked with whom? Those were novel questions, and their answers took the form of a novel artifact, the "sociogram," which diagrammed the "networks" of social relations between individuals. Moreno and Jennings identified local leaders, relative degrees of social cohesion in different friendship networks, chains of information sharing, and the level of "emotional expansiveness" for the community as a whole.[44]

At the heart of the project lay Moreno's view that a person's identity derived from his or her immediate group context. Standard sociological approaches such as the sample survey, in asking about individual characteristics or preferences in isolation, made the error of ignoring the context, of treating the individual as "the mass man, the functional man, the man who can be *exchanged*."[45] Such methods could yield an understanding of the characteristics of the population in aggregate—in the way that one could study a human by placing him in a meat grinder and finding out how much nitrogen, calcium, and magnesium he contained—but they could not show how the society was strung together, how it operated as a system. Hence Moreno's insistence on studying individuals as embedded within social space. He hoped that by mapping that space, the sociologist would not only be able to diagnose communal failings but identify ways to fix them, to encourage more social cohesions through the cultivation of spontaneously formed groups.

The approach that Moreno and Jennings pioneered, which Moreno called "sociometry," made an immediate splash, and the "sociograms" they invented were widely reproduced. Moreno's ideas made such an impression on Rev. Frank Wilson of the Episcopal Church at Hyde Park that Wilson delivered a sermon on sociometry and introduced Moreno to the most famous member of his congregation: Franklin Delano Roosevelt.[46] Presidents aside, when Moreno began his own journal,

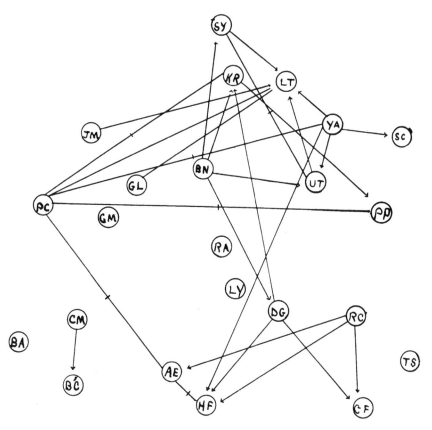

Mapping social space: A sociogram by Jacob Moreno representing relationships among a group of delinquent girls. (Courtesy of the American Society for Group Psychotherapy and Psychodrama)

Sociometry, in 1937, he was able to elicit the participation of a startling number of leading social scientists. In the eighteen years that *Sociometry* ran under Moreno's supervision, the roster of contributing editors and editorial board members included ten presidents of the American Sociological Society, four presidents of the American Psychological Association, and such luminaries as Margaret Mead, George Gallup, and John Dewey. Less than a decade after Moreno debuted sociometry, the American Sociological Society established a section on sociometry (1941), and in 1942 Moreno opened the Sociometric Institute in New York. The journal, meanwhile, had gained enough of a following that the American Sociological Society took it over in 1956 and continued to publish it for over twenty years. In time, network analysis—the field that Moreno and Jennings had invented—became an established subfield within sociology.[47]

Had Moreno stopped with sociometry, his legacy would have been secure. But for Moreno the theory was always intended as a prelude to practice. Thus Moreno began investigating therapeutic techniques for the cultivation of small groups. Here he ran up against the growing influence of Sigmund Freud, who believed psychiatric disorders to be the result of traumas within the life history of the individual, and for whom therapy meant analysis of that history. In Moreno's understanding, by contrast, most disorders were essentially problems of group integration. Thus, in place of the psychoanalytic couch, Moreno offered the "psychodramatic" stage, on which a group of patients would explore their relationships by improvising short scenes. This style of therapy aimed to be more democratic (it recognized no major role distinction between therapist and patient), participatory, and social. And it enjoyed some influence. The American Psychiatric Association sponsored the first conference on Group Methods in 1932 and engaged Moreno to give an address. By 1942, Moreno had formed the American Society of Group Psychotherapy and overseen publication of the first journal of group therapy, the quarterly *Bulletin of Psychodrama and Group Psychotherapy*.[48]

What Moreno and his contemporaries had discovered was a new scale of social space. As they saw it, eighteenth- and nineteenth-century thought had focused on the rational, profit-seeking individual: *homo economicus*. That understanding of human behavior had undergirded a massive generation of new technologies and the founding of an industrial order. Yet as industrialism grew, it threatened to break apart the old ties that bound men and women together in a society. New "social" philosophies emerged to combat this, to restore the social element to human affairs. But by the 1930s, thinkers like Moreno had concluded that such attempts to re-create society within an industrial milieu had failed. The social philosophies—of which socialism and the social sciences were examples—had misconstrued "society" as a large-scale phenomenon, operating on the order of the nation, the class, or the race. The problem was that centralized sources of identity, reinforced by industrial technologies, could not create organic unities. They could only create agglomerations of unconnected individuals—counting chips pushed into a pile.

The sinews of society, Moreno argued, were to be found in small groups and in face-to-face relationships. Only with those intact could a crowd become a community.

Where earlier thinkers had seen only individuals and an overarching "society," Moreno's generation saw something else: a thick middle layer of informal institutions, folkways, and cultural norms that accounted for the bulk of social coordination. Such institutions were not governed by the command of despots or by impersonal market forces. They were instead negotiated, day after day, by members of small groups and communities.

Of course, the group was not an entirely new category of social thought. As the thinkers of the midcentury decades would soon recall, nineteenth-century social theorists such as Alexis de Tocqueville, Sir Henry Maine, Frédéric Le Play, Ferdinand Tönnies, and Emile Durkheim had written about small groups and their relation to the forces of modernization. And in the Progressive era, a coterie of U.S. thinkers including John Dewey, William A. White, Charles H. Cooley, Robert E. Park, and Jane Addams grew interested in the idea of "community" and its place within industrial society. The Progressives were particularly enamored of urban neighborhoods and imagined that participation might scale up from them to what they called the "Great Society."[49] That vision was on full display in Mary Parker Follett's *The New State* (1918), which proposed "group organization" as the "basis of our future industrial system."[50] Once democratic participation had been established on the level of the neighborhood, Follett argued, it could be expanded to the city, to the nation, and to a world government. The local, in other words, was the precursor to the global, to the "Perfect Society" consisting of "the complete interrelating of an infinite number of selves knowing themselves as one Self."[51]

The problem is that, by the 1930s, the notion of a great political chain stretching from the neighborhood to the "Perfect Society" had become harder to envision. The global economy and the international system lay in ruins, and the idea of a "Great Society" had acquired new totalitarian overtones. And so, although midcentury theorists shared with their Progressive-era forebears an interest in small groups, they saw the matter in a new light. The centralizing tendency that was so distinctive among turn-of-the-century thinkers and that reached its climax in Follett's *The New State* had become anathema. If for Follett's generation small communities were the building blocks of a global order, Moreno's generation celebrated them as *defense* against remote centers of power. Plurality, not unity, motivated the new interest in the small scale.[52]

The difference was not just qualitative; it was also quantitative. Simply put, the small group commanded far more attention after 1935 than it had before. In 1954, a massive survey of small-group research in sociology, psychology, psychiatry, and related fields revealed an explosion of scholarly activity. Whereas up to 1920, articles pertaining to the small group came out at the rate of under two per year, by the last half of the 1940s, there were more than fifty-five articles per year, and by the early 1950s there were more than 150 per year.[53] By the 1950s there were also a few journals dedicated principally to small-group research *(Autonomous Groups Bulletin, The Group, Human Organization, Sociometry)* and numerous book-length surveys of the field published by major presses.[54] "A very curious thing has been taking place," noted *Fortune* in 1952. "In a country where 'individualism'—independence and self-reliance—was the watchword for three centuries, the view is now coming to be accepted that the individual himself has no meaning— except, that is, as a member of a group."[55] Sociologist David Riesman agreed. Summing up the trends of his times in 1951, he concluded, "the pendulum has swung toward groupism."[56]

IN THE MIDDLE of twentieth century, the small group was the key that could open nearly every lock. Particularly telling was its use in the field of history, where Frederick Jackson Turner's "frontier thesis" had long been a dominant paradigm. In 1954, a team of historians curious about the accuracy of the frontier thesis concluded that Turner had been right to see a link between the frontier and democracy but wrong about the mechanism. It was not "frontier individualism" that gave rise to democratic habits, argued Stanley Elkins and Eric McKitrick, but the small, strong, and participatory communities of the frontier.[57] If the original Turner thesis explained democracy by pointing to rugged frontiersmen who lived half apart from society, the revised one explained it by reference to groups of people whose common hardship and small numbers endowed them with extraordinarily rich social bonds. In a telling coincidence that points to the power of the intellectual Zeitgeist, the same reformulation of Turner was offered simultaneously and apparently independently by Lewis Atherton, who attributed U.S. democracy to the "togetherness" of frontier towns—togetherness arising from "informal community life."[58]

30

But it was not just historians. The small group made its way into nearly every field of inquiry. In 1935, social workers began to supplement individual casework with something they called "group work," which they hoped would "provide a very essential antidote to the mechanical, passive, conforming habits of industrialized communities."[59] Sociologists started to take a new, sympathetic interest in gangs, understood not as bastions of criminality but as sustaining social networks in a destabilizing urban environment.[60] Anthropologists turned away from the family as the locus of acculturation and toward the tribe, the group, and the village.[61] In political science, Paul Lazarsfeld and his colleagues used sociometric methods to revise their understanding of how political participation and persuasion worked. Rejecting the view of "the omnipotent media, on one hand, sending forth the message, and the atomized masses, on the other, waiting to receive it—and nothing in-between," Lazarsfeld emphasized the importance of the "face-to-face influences" and "local 'molecular pressures' " that determined how people voted.[62] Even architects, previously interested in erecting great glass skyscrapers, felt the magnetic pull of groupism. The 1940s saw Frank Lloyd Wright pleading for "decentralization and organic reintegration" while Walter Gropius, alarmed that city streets had become "mere traffic channels for lonely strangers," called for a "community rehabilitation" in which "*everyone* took part as a member of a *group*."[63]

The task of community rehabilitation might have seemed daunting, especially given the extraordinary militarization of U.S. society during and after the war (the military had grown to ten times its 1939 size by the early 1950s).[64] Yet even in an archetypal mass organization such as the military, social scientists insisted that they could discern the outlines of the small group. Military psychiatrists fastened on group ties as the keys to servicemembers' mental health.[65] Indeed, the centrality of small groups arose as a persistent theme in the War Department's two-volume study of the Army, *The American Soldier* (1949)—at its time one of the largest social scientific research projects ever conducted. The study made much of the groups that emerged spontaneously within the military hierarchy and concluded that soldiers persevered in combat not mainly for God or country but for the fellow members of their small groups.[66] As a special commission of psychiatrists studying the U.S. soldier under fire put it, "the group life *is* his inner life."[67]

The economy, too, was a plump target for revision. Victorian understandings of capitalism had located the roots of the system in the rational, autonomous individual, freely choosing the most profitable course of action. On the shop floor, that theory found its highest expression in the managerial practices of F. W. Taylor, who, with careful time–motion studies, devised incentives, punishments, and task-standardization so as to draw the most work out of each employee. Workers found Taylorism exhausting and exasperating. Midcentury group theorists also found cause for objection, although along slightly different lines. For them, the problem was not capitalism's exploitation of workers so much as its obsession with the individual.

Groupist criticisms of prevailing notions of capitalism came out first in the Hawthorne Studies, conducted between 1924 and 1933 by researchers from the Harvard Business School. The purpose of the studies was to solve the riddle of "industrial fatigue," a polite euphemism for turnover, absenteeism, inconsistent output, and the other signs of workers' alienation that were so common in the age of Taylor. In the most prominent study, the experimenters proceeded by removing a group of women from the main floor of the Hawthorne Works plant to a small room, where they could be studied under semi-laboratory conditions. They systematically altered every variable that they could think of. They offered wage incentives, took away wage incentives, added and removed rest breaks, provided food, modified the lighting, and changed the workers' schedules. What surprised the researchers, however, was that nearly *all* of the changes increased output, even the ones that had merely reversed previous changes. Their conclusion, heavily publicized throughout the 1930s, was that the productivity gains had nothing to do with Taylorist variables such as wages. The women worked better because they had been removed from the factory floor, where they had been proverbial cogs in a machine, and placed in their own room, where they could talk freely and become friends. The experimenters noted with interest that the women had begun inviting each other over to their homes. Without intending to, the Hawthorne experiment had created community in the factory.[68]

Industrial anomie could be cured by small-group interactions: that was the triumphant finding of the Hawthorne Studies. It was encouraging, at least to the managers of corporations, since it suggested that their labor problems could be easily solved by a liberal application of the "human element"; no concessions to unions were necessary. It was flattering to managers as well, since small-group methods were ostensibly democratic rather than authoritarian, a point that the researchers

1940
John Smith in Conference

1620
Chief Big Feather
"in conference"

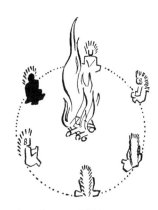

The anthropology of the corporation: Illustrations from a 1945 management theory book, originally bearing the caption "Individuals Change, Problems Change, but the Ageless Small Group Goes On." (George B. de Huszar, *Practical Applications of Democracy* [1945])

mentioned frequently. Thus began a cottage industry in "human relations," the study of group dynamics within corporations.

Whether such interventions improved life on the shop floor is unclear. But they undoubtedly transformed the upper echelons of corporate life, imbuing it with an entirely new self-understanding. Corporations were not just profit-seeking leviathans, their managers now maintained, but democratic sociocultural institutions. Each had, as if it were some anthropologist's tribe, its own "corporate culture." Older concerns with efficiency and profits were partially displaced to make way for probing explorations of group life within the corporation and questions about whether employees were truly being "team players." If they were not, there was help. The National Training Laboratories for Group Development, established by the psychologist Kurt Lewin in 1947, ran an increasingly popular series of workshops designed to train corporate executives in group methods. Across the next three decades, over a hundred other organizations in North America would offer similar training. Group dynamics became the new religion of corporate life.[69]

That shift in industrial practice was accompanied by an even larger shift in thinking about capitalism. In the midcentury period, some still defended capitalism as a system of individual profit-seeking. Ayn Rand received an enthusiastic reception for her forceful promotion of that Victorian ideal in her novels *The Fountainhead* (1943) and *Atlas Shrugged* (1957), and Milton Friedman found a similarly engaged audience for his *Capitalism and Freedom* (1962). But in the three decades between 1935 and 1965, Rand and Friedman were the exceptions, not the rule.[70] Far more common were theories that stressed the social foundations of the market. The economic individualism that had rooted so much of social thought in the Victorian period appeared by midcentury to be a mirage, vanishing upon close inspection.[71]

Even F. A. Hayek, the author of *The Road to Serfdom* (1944) and the most celebrated individualist of the period, subscribed to a form of individualism that was surprisingly unlike those of Rand and Friedman. It was not enthusiasm for the unfettered individual that drove him to valorize markets, but suspicion of the state. Thus his version of individualism invoked the importance of traditions and of other informal mechanisms of social coordination. True individualism, as he called it, would nurture "all the common efforts of the small community and the group." The problem with centralized planning in Hayek's understanding was that it would "dissolve all these smaller groups into atoms which have no cohesion other than the coercive rules opposed by the state."[72]

If capitalism had to be reconceived to accommodate the small group, so did socialism. For when thinkers such as Moreno complained about the Victorian tendency to see the world only in terms of unconnected individuals and abstract society, they were talking about Karl Marx just as much as they were talking about Herbert Spencer. Neither Lenin nor Stalin had helped matters. Their vision of communism, with its emphasis on a revolutionary vanguard and mass institutions, was inimical to the small group. Nevertheless, a band of socialists gathered around Max Shachtman proposed a new understanding of things. Shachtman himself was a minor figure, and his followers were never numerous. Yet that handful of activists contained some of the most fertile political minds of the generation. The list of those who counted themselves as Shachtmanites at one point or another includes C. L. R. James, Dwight

Macdonald, Irving Howe, James Burnham, Grace Lee Boggs, and Michael Harrington.

Shachtmanites were erstwhile Trotskyists who broke with Trotsky over the question of Stalin. Whereas Trotsky believed the Soviet Union to be a "degenerated worker's state," i.e., the right idea in the wrong hands, Shachtman and his followers insisted that the rot ran deeper. The problem was not that the Soviet Union had "degenerated" under bad leadership, it was that its fusion of socialism with mass forms of organization had created a pernicious new pattern, "bureaucratic collectivism."[73] James Burnham offered the diagnosis most forcefully in *The Managerial Revolution* (1941), a book that is best known today as the basis for George Orwell's *Nineteen Eighty-Four* (1948). Burnham argued that both socialism and capitalism were growing unmanageably large and, in their scale, coming to resemble each other. Their philosophical differences and different bases in property, Burnham contended, were increasingly irrelevant as both became top-heavy, all-consuming bureaucracies. Burnham himself had no solution to suggest, but other Shachtmanites did. "We must begin way at the bottom again, with small groups of individuals," wrote Dwight Macdonald.[74] Whereas orthodox Marxists called upon workers to organize large collectives capable of fighting corporations and seizing the state, Macdonald advocated "guerrilla operations": the formation of small, participatory political communities.[75]

By 1950, capitalists and socialists alike had significantly revised their ideological commitments to accommodate the small group. In doing so, they had shown it to be a tool that could be grabbed from the left or the right. It is in fact the political ambidexterity of groupism that has largely erased it from our historical memory. When we turn to the past in search of capitalism's discontents we look to the left, and when we search for opponents of the regulatory state we look to the right. The great midcentury enthusiasm for the small group, however, implied a different sort of orienteering. Arthur Schlesinger, Jr., recognized this in his most influential book, *The Vital Center* (1949): "The rise of fascism and Communism illustrated vividly the fallacies of the linear conceptions of right and left. In certain basic respects—the totalitarian state structure, the single party, the leader, the secret police, the consuming fear of political and intellectual freedom—fascism and Communism are more clearly like each other than they are like anything in between."[76] The familiar spectrum of left and right, Schlesinger suggested, should be replaced by a two-dimensional map.

Such a map, charting the traditional tension between states and markets on its horizontal axis but adding a new vertical axis to capture the tension between centralism and decentralism, would make a good guide to midcentury thought. We tend to think of that time, and particularly the postwar part of it, as being marked by an ideological consensus. Acceptance of the mixed economy and the welfare state appeared widespread enough by 1960 for Daniel Bell to declare the "end of ideology"—a final truce between left and right.[77] Perhaps there was a consensus of sorts, but the thinkers of the period were anything but content. *Crisis* and *anxiety* are two words often invoked, both at the time and retrospectively by historians, to describe their prevailing mood. Such anxieties had many sources: changing gender norms, paranoia fueled by the prospect of atomic warfare, the new imperatives of consumerism. But a large portion of that crisis had can be attributed to the newly visible vertical axis of politics. The fear that the United States might somehow slide into totalitarianism haunted the age.

That fear pervaded *The Vital Center.* To be sure, Schlesinger expressed opinions about the public–private divide, but he was more deeply moved by the transformations that affected the entire political arena. He devoted the final chapter to a shrill warning: "freedom has lost its foundation in community." Unbounded individualism would quickly lead to totalitarianism if not checked by the revival of "widespread and spontaneous group activity."[78] Readers of *The Vital Center* usually emphasize the "center" that is mapped out in the book. But it is equally important to notice Schlesinger's plea for "vitality," a vitality that he believed could be achieved only through the promotion of voluntary associations, group life, spontaneity, and community to combat the demons of mass society and atomized individualism.

The small group was not the whole of midcentury intellectual life, any more than the small town was the whole of midcentury culture. The same period saw the flourishing of fascist, communist, libertarian, statist, and technocratic approaches to the challenges of the twentieth century. But if the small group was not everything, it was also not nothing. It was a persistent theme throughout midcentury thought and a reminder that not all thinkers greeted the prospect of industrial mass society with enthusiasm. They sought to temper it, to "humanize" it—to use language current at the time. They proposed to do so in various ways, not all of which were compatible with each other. At its most basic, however, their approach was about size. If industrial society had brought with it institutions on a newly enlarged scale, then the correct response was to replace the big with the small, to reduce the size of affairs to the point where informality, improvisation, interpersonal understanding, and widespread participation were once again possibilities. Hence the small town and hence the small group.

"GROUPISM," AS David Riesman called it, did not endure forever. After a remarkably unchallenged ascent in the 1930s and 1940s, it began to encounter serious criticism by the 1950s. Then, a social scientific vision that had privileged communal belonging was partially displaced by one that instead emphasized dissent, struggle, and individualism. An early and important critic of the small group was Riesman himself, whose *The Lonely Crowd* (1950) and *Individualism Reconsidered* (1954) praised the virtues of the "inner-directed" individual as against "other-directed" members of a group. The problem with groupism, Riesman argued, was that it sought to erase conflict from daily life, whereas that conflict—both psychological conflict within the individual and the friction between the individual and society—were of supreme value to a dynamic society.[79]

William H. Whyte, Jr., took the logic further in *The Organization Man* (1956). The defining condition of the titular organization man, for Whyte, was the social ethic that governed his life. At his job and in his suburban home, he was engulfed by institutions that exalted belongingness and sociability over individuality and idiosyncrasy. "He is imprisoned in brotherhood," Whyte wrote.[80] Creativity at the individual level had been entirely subordinated to what Whyte pejoratively called "groupthink."[81] Community, in this revised understanding, was conformity.[82]

More striking still was Schlesinger's attack on the small group. In *The Vital Center* (1949), Schlesinger had called for the revival of "widespread and spontaneous group activity" as a matter of dire necessity.[83] By 1958, however, Schlesinger felt that things had gone too far. "One of the most sinister of present-day doctrines is that of *togetherness*," he warned, citing Whyte. The "cult of the group" was aggressively colonizing all of national life, "forever developing new weapons with which to overwhelm and crush the recalcitrant individual." What was required was to "recover a sense of individual spontaneity. And to do this a man must visualize himself as an individual apart from the group."[84]

Two things are worth noting about these revolts from groupism. The first is their prominence. Riesman appeared in 1954 on the cover of *Time* magazine—the first sociologist to be so honored. Both Whyte's *The Organization Man* and Riesman's *The Lonely Crowd* were period-defining works whose terms were quickly adopted into both social scientific and popular discourse. And Schlesinger was an indispensable policy intellectual. At the time he turned on groupism, he was just between running Americans for Democratic Action (which he had founded) and joining the Kennedy administration as an all-purpose Special Assistant to the President. The centrality and renown of groupism's detractors is an indication of just how far the norms of the small group had gotten.

The second thing worth noting about the attack on the small group is that it was largely an inside job. It came from critics who had a history with, and even continued sympathy for, groupism. Schlesinger, as discussed above, had regarded small groups as the salvation of mass society before he decided that they were the bane of it. Riesman, too, had been something of a groupist. As a young scholar, he had taken an interest in community studies and worked on one under W. Lloyd Warner, an anthropologist who had been a central figure in the Hawthorne Studies.[85] He was also an avid fan of Granville Hicks, the former communist turned small-town advocate. "I hardly know where to begin to set down my enthusiasm for *Small Town*," Riesman wrote after the publication of Hicks's book. Riesman visited Hicks frequently in Grafton, New York, and gave his friends so many copies of *Small Town* that he felt himself to be a "one-man Gideon Society" for the book.[86]

Tellingly, Riesman's criticisms of group life were always measured and, indeed, ambivalent. Although "groupism" in his judgment had "become increasingly menacing," he also felt that "the older brands of ruthless individualism are still a social danger."[87] The groupists had been right to criticize the Victorian mentality and its conception of the entirely independent individual. The trick, then, was to strike a balance. "We must skeptically question the demands for greater social participation and belongingness among the group-minded while, on another front, opposing the claims of those who for outworn reasons cling to individualism as a (largely economic) shibboleth."[88] If Riesman mainly emphasized the dangers of the group ideal, it was only because he felt that the ideological momentum was too much on the side of groupism. The tools to "escape from groupism" were thus more immediately needed, he felt, than those to escape from individualism.[89] In remarkably similar language, Whyte endorsed the basic insights of the groupists. "The side of the coin they have been staring at so intently is a perfectly good one, but there is another side and it should not be too heretical at least to have a peek at it."[90] What was needed was not an abandonment of groupism but a "middle way," Whyte argued—"individualism *within* organizational life."[91]

THAT EVEN the small group's strongest critics could not bring themselves to reject it entirely is worth remembering. It is a reminder that, even in a country rapidly urbanizing, industrializing, and in every other way becoming a mass society, the lure of decentralism persisted. That impulse in U.S. thought and culture—the quest for community—has not always been easy to see. It commanded no partisan faction, and thus has little place in our political histories. It was more like a field effect, a magnetic pull from which few were completely free. And it expressed itself not as a coordinated movement with a high command but as a general form of ambivalence and anxiety, although differently felt in different times and places.

How seriously to take that anxiety is open to debate. The tendency among historians has been to treat modernization as the reigning ideology and to regard any back-chatter as interesting (even admirable) in its individual manifestations but inconsequential when taken all together—a series of nervous twitches. But at a certain point, one has to ask how monogamously committed the United States could really have been to the ideology of modernization when so many of its central thinkers and artists bucked in the opposite direction. Walt Disney, Norman Rockwell, Thornton Wilder, and Frank Capra—it would be hard to produce a list of twentieth-century artists who touched closer to the core of the national psyche. Similarly, it would be hard to imagine midcentury social science without its fascination with group life. Small was big, and the quest for community was baked into the most fundamental and important patterns of thought at the time. It was that quest, carried into the realm of policymaking and applied to the problem of poverty, that begat community development.

2

THE AGE of development started big. In the valley of the Tennessee River, whose basin sprawls across eight states and is only slightly smaller than Guatemala, the U.S. government launched an enormous campaign of economic and ecological transformation. Starting in 1933, the Tennessee Valley Authority (TVA) hired tens of thousands of men to clear more than 175,000 acres of land, build more than 1,200 miles of highway, and excavate thirty million cubic yards of rock and earth.[1] At the center of this frenzy of construction stood a series of dams designed to irrigate the valley, generate billions of kilowatt-hours of electrical energy, and use that power not only to electrify rural homes but also to manufacture chemical fertilizers to rejuvenate the river basin's deteriorating farms.

In its marriage of state power and large-scale technology, the TVA seemed to herald a new age. "I believe in the great potentialities for well-being of the machine and technology and science," proclaimed David Lilienthal, one of the TVA's directors and its chief spokesman. For Lilienthal, faith in technology meant faith in "the experts—the technicians and managers"—who "have a central role to play . . . in every facet of modern living."[2] It also meant accepting the "fruits of bigness," of which Lilienthal was a prime expositor.[3] "I have no apologies to make to anyone that we do things in a big way," he said. "Why shouldn't we be proud that America has as many miles of highways as the whole of Europe, has half the world's trucks and three quarters of its automobiles . . . that this country accounts for more than half the consumption of energy on this planet?"[4] With a gleam in his eye, Lilienthal predicted the exportation of the TVA to "a thousand valleys over the globe."[5]

"The fruits of bigness": The TVA's Norris Dam. (Tennessee Valley Authority)

Lilienthal's prediction was not bad. Between his writing of those words in 1944 and the end of the twentieth century, the world's governments constructed around 40,000 dams, collectively redistributing enough mass in the form of water to measurably alter the rotation of the earth.[6] Many of those dams were built explicitly on the TVA model. For that reason, scholars of development have turned to the TVA as a point of origin for the top-down modernization schemes that were so common in the second half of the twentieth century. For James C. Scott, the TVA was a paragon of "high modernist social engineering"; for Paul Josephson it was an example of "brute force technology."[7] In David Ekbladh's rendition, it was a "grand synecdoche" for the U.S. approach to development, symbolizing the many large-scale, industry-centered modernization projects that the United States launched throughout the world in the twentieth century.[8] And the 125,000 residents of the Tennessee Valley forced by the construction to relocate were harbingers, too, though of a more ominous sort. By the end of the century, dams had displaced some forty to eighty million refugees worldwide.[9]

But the TVA had another side. Alongside its public worship of expertise and top-down industrialization came genuflections toward democracy and bottom-up participation. Indeed, when summing up the main contribution of the TVA on its twenty-year anniversary, Lilienthal did not name the importance of technicians or managers but of "self-government, of decentralized grass-roots administration, of local and individual participation in the valley's development."[10] Decentralized administration came in two parts. First, the TVA claimed autonomy from Washington, generating its own revenue and operating free from the typical Congressional oversight. Second, it committed itself to working with the "grass roots" and "people's institutions"—local groups and agencies in the region. It was this "democratic" side of the TVA that distinguished it in the eyes of liberals from the Soviet planning projects to which it bore an otherwise discomfiting similarity, such as the Dnieprostroi Dam or the steel-mining city of Magnitogorsk. As the eminent British biologist (and future director of UNESCO) Julian Huxley put it, the TVA's promise lay not in its material accomplishments but in "the possibility of obtaining the efficiency of a co-ordinated plan without totalitarian regimentation."[11]

Historians tend to read the TVA's decentralism as a mere distraction, a coat of sugar on an otherwise bitter pill. Indeed, for all of Lilienthal's boasts about democracy and decentralization, there is little evidence that the TVA practiced much of either. The planning still came from the top, and the "people's institutions" with which the TVA worked were highly conservative organizations representing large farmers.[12] But there *is* reason to think that the TVA's decentralist program was, at least, heartfelt. Lilienthal's paeans to the grass roots may have been empty talk, but that rhetoric was based on a comprehensive social vision. It was the vision of Arthur E. Morgan, the original chairman of TVA's board of directors—Lilienthal's boss. And if Lilienthal was an unabashed cheerleader for bigness, Morgan was, like so many others of his time, a champion of the small.

The two men were a study in contrast. Lilienthal was the child of Jewish immigrants and a Harvard graduate. Morgan had not graduated college at all. He was a strongly spiritual Protestant who identified closely with the agrarian Midwest and had been a charter member of the American Eugenics Society.[13] Lilienthal, a lawyer, moved smoothly within the halls of power, whereas Morgan, an engineer and educator, lacked both the ability and the inclination. More importantly, the two had entirely different visions for the TVA. Lilienthal emphasized the

The two TVAs: Arthur E. Morgan, left, and David Lilienthal. Granville Hunt,
photog. (Tennessee Valley Authority)

economic aspects of the project and sought to use his position at a large
government agency to discipline monopolistic utilities providers. Morgan,
by contrast, stressed the social side of things and sought to create a cooperative economic system featuring local currencies and based on small
and self-sufficient towns—all of which Lilienthal dismissed as "basket-
weaving."[14] The differences proved irreconcilable and, after a sensational
and highly public showdown, Lilienthal pushed Morgan out of the
agency.[15] Disgusted by what he took to be pervasive instrumentalism at
the level of federal policymaking, Morgan left public life and retreated
to Yellow Springs, Ohio, from which he wrote a series of books about
the perils of centralization. Their titles are revealing: *The Small Community: Foundation of Democratic Life* (1942), *Bottom Up Democracy*
(1955), *The Heritage of Community* (1956), and, at the end of Morgan's
life, *Dams and Other Disasters* (1971).[16]

The revelation that the leaders of the TVA disagreed with each other is perhaps not shocking. After all, the Roosevelt administration was notoriously eclectic and improvisational, frequently mixing approaches and rolling out contradictory initiatives. When asked about the political philosophy of the TVA, Roosevelt famously evaded the question, quipping that it was "neither fish nor fowl" but would nevertheless "taste awfully good to the people of the Tennessee Valley."[17] Still, the ingredients in the New Deal's political cocktail that receive the most attention from historians are the centralist ones: the bureaucratic accomplishments and technocratic aspirations. What Arthur E. Morgan's unsuccessful attempt to use the TVA as a vehicle for community life reminds us is that that there were other components, too. In fact, the 1930s saw not just the turn to the small town and small group in the realm of culture and ideas but the embarkation of a decades-long political experiment with communitarianism.

THE EMERGENCE of communitarianism within the New Deal apparatus has not escaped notice by historians. It is becoming common to separate the centralizers within the federal government from the decentralizers, or the "high modernists" from the "low modernists," as Jess Gilbert calls them.[18] Usually, this is motivated by a desire to resuscitate the low modernist vision, the vision that was less obsessed with production figures and more aligned with concerns that are of interest today: ecology, community, and participatory democracy.

Scholars in search of the communitarian elements of the New Deal have gravitated toward the Department of Agriculture's Bureau of Agricultural Economics (BAE), which by the 1930s served as an all-purpose research and planning arm for the government in agriculture. Although the USDA as a whole was, like the TVA, divided between centralists and decentralists, the BAE contained administrative pockets—particularly the highly active Division of Farm Population and Rural Welfare—that served as bastions of decentralism within the Roosevelt administration. That division, unlike the larger bureau of which it was a part, was populated not by economists but by rural sociologists, who brought into public policymaking a different set of preoccupations than economists did. If economists generally sought to increase production, sociologists tended to orient themselves toward the preservation of rural society in an industrializing world.[19] The BAE's Division of Farm

Population and Rural Welfare, in other words, was an entire agency stuffed full of Arthur E. Morgans.

Two social scientists were central to shaping the communitarian aspects of the BAE, M. L. Wilson and Carl C. Taylor. Wilson led the charge from his various posts as the Assistant Secretary of Agriculture, the Undersecretary of Agriculture, and the Director of Extension Work in the Roosevelt years. Wilson was a late convert to communitarianism; his early career as an economist had been dedicated to increasing agricultural production. In 1929, he spent six months helping to write the master plan of what he called "the largest experiment in mechanical farming in the world": a Soviet attempt to grow 400,000 acres of wheat as part of Stalin's First Five-Year Plan.[20] But in the 1930s Wilson moved "beyond economics" to what he called a "cultural approach," re-styling himself as a rural sociologist.[21] He concluded that the Soviet Union represented the "way of dictatorship" and that to escape the same fate, the United States must become "a nation built of local communities."[22] That was a welcome thought to Taylor, a rural sociologist who served under Wilson as the head of the Division of Farm Population and Rural Welfare. "Hundreds of thousands of local groups" would be necessary, Taylor contended, as a "democratic corrective to anything which may tend toward national disunity on the one hand, or national totalitarianism on the other hand."[23]

For those "hundreds of thousands of local groups" to become a force in politics, however, they would first need to be understood. What did the farm communities strewn about the countryside *want*? Taylor sent out teams of social scientists to find the answer. It was crucial, though, that the task be handled with care. "We are trying to avoid the difficulties which arise when the scientist or the expert comes down to the local area to tell the farmer what to do," explained Wilson. Such areas, he continued, "have customs, traditions, standards of living, folk lore, and values which they cherish and which should not be interfered with lightly. In some cases, modern scientific planning and action programs, based upon value systems foreign to the culture, may not only fail to promote the culture of the region, but actually serve to destroy it."[24]

So as to avoid the top-down method, BAE staff members convened small committees of farmers and local officials, with roughly two dozen members apiece. Those committees, not the researchers, would answer the most important questions. They mapped the borders of their communities, surveyed the use of land within it, and proposed actions. Although BAE employees were eager to provide assistance, they were cautioned to wait for invitations to help and to avoid determining the outcome of the committees' inquiries. "It is more important that social planning be democratic than that it be either comprehensive or logical," explained Taylor.[25] Decentralized, participatory planning, Taylor and Wilson hoped, would awaken a communal spirit in an age of industry and bureaucracy.

On paper, the BAE's short-lived communal planning program was staggeringly effective. It started in 1938 and, by 1942, nearly two-thirds of the agricultural counties in the United States had planning committees—with almost 200,000 people serving on them.[26] But Wilson worried that both committee members and the extension agents sent to help them were too committed to a narrow-minded producerist outlook that valued technical knowledge and profits over the flourishing of democratic life. To offer balance, he inaugurated a "Schools of Philosophy" program within the USDA, designed to acquaint rural leaders and USDA employees with the "social and philosophical aspects of agriculture."[27] Wilson also brought in major thinkers to address the USDA's graduate school in Washington. Academic luminaries such as Charles Beard, Thurman Arnold, George Gallup, and Ruth Benedict gave wide-ranging talks to USDA employees there, while thinkers such as W. E. B. Du Bois, Howard Odum, Eleanor Roosevelt, Milton Eisenhower, and Frank Knight addressed audiences throughout the rest of the country.[28] All of the Schools of Philosophy talks were to be followed, in proper democratic fashion, by discussions that would provide opportunities for audience members to mull over the topics in small-group settings.[29]

Not everyone, though, shared Wilson and Taylor's enthusiasm for the grass roots. It would be hard to find a better representative of the opposing camp within the USDA than Rexford Tugwell.[30] An economist rather than a sociologist, Tugwell played David Lilienthal to Wilson's Arthur E. Morgan. (In a nice symmetry, Tugwell and Wilson both served as Assistant Secretary of Agriculture and as Undersecretary of Agriculture at different times during the New Deal.) Tugwell saw little promise in the BAE's grassroots planning efforts. "If we look at the structure of American agriculture, we must see that grass-roots decisions are not likely to be democratic," he argued in an article written with Edward Banfield. Wilson and Taylor, rolling all farmers together into the "grass roots," had tended to see them as "equal sons of toil." But serious "class and caste differences . . . exist within most farming communities," Tugwell and Banfield argued. Those differences could not just be overcome with neighborly spirit; they were entrenched and would inevitably undermine any campaign for grassroots reform. "In the South grass-roots democracy can only mean the exercise of the powers of government by white planters. Elsewhere it must mean control by and for the prosperous farmers who have hired men to do their work while they go to committee meetings." True democratic administration, Tugwell and Banfield maintained, could only come from "organizing a central government strong enough to eliminate those conditions which make much of our national life grossly undemocratic."[31]

Was the BAE's grassroots orientation a "two-handed commitment to democracy," as Jess Gilbert has argued, or was it, as Tugwell and Banfield had it, "a make-believe" that papered over the fact that rural society was anything but communal?[32] It is hard to say. The sympathetic attention that the BAE has garnered from scholars has shed far more light on the Bureau's intentions than on its achievements. Such achievements are difficult to judge, since the longest-serving of the BAE's planning committees ran for only three years.[33] In 1942, a Congress hostile to the New Deal and fearful that the committees might threaten large industrial farms or white supremacy in the South shut them down and gutted the Bureau. The Schools of Philosophy continued until 1945 but mainly as instruments of war propaganda. Gilbert and others have lamented this as the dashing of the dream of participatory democracy against the stony cliffs of industrialization. Not only were worthy programs dismantled but "their very *ways of thinking* were lost," Gilbert has written. "Progressive leadership in rural policy and research circles disappeared. Alternative voices were silenced by the midforties and remained unarticulated for decades."[34] Modernization, it would seem, had come to town.

HOW "SILENCED" those "alternative voices" were after the 1940s is a question that will be taken up in a moment. Meanwhile, it is worth turning to another Roosevelt administration agency where men like Wilson and Taylor wielded some influence: the War Relocation Authority (WRA), which administered the Japanese internment camps. Although the scope of the WRA was far narrower than that of the Bureau of Agricultural Economics, the possibilities for action were greater. By rounding up some 30,000 Japanese families from the West Coast into ten remote camps, the government had essentially created a planner's

utopia: a blank canvas, where the population involved had no prior organization, little leverage, and no rights that the U.S. government was
bound to respect.

With such free rein, one might have expected to see the state launch
aggressive top-down schemes for social transformation. But that is not
exactly what happened. The removal of the Japanese from the West
Coast, handled by the Army, had of course been enormously disruptive.
Yet once they arrived in the camps, the internees fell under the jurisdic-
tion of the civilian-controlled WRA, which hoped to use the camps as
training grounds for democracy. And, much like Wilson and Taylor, the
heads of the WRA felt that the democracy depended on community. If
the Army had unraveled the social worlds of the internees, the War
Relocation Authority would try to knit them back together again.[35]

In its early months, the WRA took only a minimal interest in the
communal aspects of camp life. It had a Community Management
Division and hired an alumnus of the Bureau of Agricultural Economics,
the anthropologist John Provinse, to run it. But it was a division of one;
Provinse had no subordinates. Nevertheless, he brought his former
adviser from the University of Chicago, the anthropologist Robert
Redfield, to tour the camps and make suggestions. Redfield worried that
the authorities knew too little of the lives of the camp's inhabitants and
suggested of program of surveying, one that would incorporate "a great
deal of evacuee participation."[36] Provinse concurred. Drawing on his
own experience with the BAE, Provinse called for the establishment of
community councils.[37] As an example of the sort of thing he wanted, he
could point to the internment camp at Poston (on an Indian reservation),
where the Bureau of Indian Affairs ran a research bureau. The researchers
at Poston comprised both internees and non-Japanese anthropologists,
including another of Redfield's students, Edward Spicer.[38] Incorporating
internees into the research apparatus would, the Poston staff hoped,
allow the bureau to produce fine-grained "sociometric studies" that
went in greater depth than mere censuses and surveys.[39]

The value of such studies became clear after a riot in the Manzanar
camp, which killed two internees. Redfield's warning had been right: the
WRA knew little about its charges. Within the next month, the WRA
established a Community Analysis Section in Washington and posted
analysts to each of the camps. Most of the twenty-two social scientists
who served in the Community Analysis Section were anthropologists,

although a few were rural sociologists—the discipline that had dominated Taylor's division within the BAE. Only a small distance separated the two fields, anyway; both anthropologists and rural sociologists felt a strong attachment to small communities and worried about the threat that modernization posed to them. And so, the community analysts did precisely what Provinse and Redfield had suggested: they established councils within the camps and began an extensive campaign to encourage the formation of "communities" there.[40]

There was something bizarre about the WRA's obsession with communal life and participation, given the setting. Nevertheless, the community analysts managed largely to put the barbed wire and guard towers out of mind. Adopting a functionalist mode of analysis, they treated the camp populations as if they were small tribes, or at least tribes in the making.[41] In a fairly typical offering from the Community Analysis Section, the anthropologist John F. Embree set out to explain the causes of "unrest" in the camps. Although he acknowledged the "sense of disillusionment or even bitterness" that the experience of forced internment might have created, Embree fastened on a different explanation. The real problem was a pathological "lack of any integrated set of social controls as represented by family and community organization, public opinion and folkways." In Embree's analysis, then, the WRA should reestablish those communal mechanisms by working with community councils and paying respect to "traditional, (and useful) Japanese culture patterns."[42]

Their sense that the main thing to do was to inculcate a sense of community led the WRA's anthropologists toward a remarkably sanguine assessment of camp life. Poston was "rapidly becoming a community and will continue to be one," Conrad Arensberg boasted to his fellow anthropologists in 1942. "There is the strong neighborliness and the almost extraordinary cooperative spirit to be seen among the families of the blocks."[43] Spicer, who came to see the camps as "ideal cities" and "harmonious communities," felt that they had introduced "new stability and cohesiveness" into the internees' lives and speculated that the internees would be reluctant to leave.[44]

Not everyone agreed, of course. "The relocation centers are not normal communities," wrote the journalist Carey McWilliams. "They are institutions and they breed a type of 'prison complex.' "[45] But it is hard to find in the community analysts' reports any acknowledgment

A "harmonious community"?: Ansel Adams, Town Hall Meeting at Manzanar, 1943. (Library of Congress)

that there was something dysfunctional about the camps or something undemocratic about the undertaking as a whole.[46] For Redfield, even to call them "internment" camps was unfair; the camps were better understood as a "collective effort to build a new community."[47] As late as 1969, Spicer downplayed the "civil rights aspect" of internment and commended the "courage" of the men and women who worked for the Community Analysis Section. "The outstanding fact about the relocation centers was that the Japanese Americans did not remain aggregates of frustrated and confused individuals," he insisted. "The important fact to understand is that a certain kind of community life did develop."[48]

ON THE FACE of it, the Roosevelt-era adventures in communitarian statecraft do not look overwhelmingly impressive. There may have been decentralists within the government, but they lacked the power of their high-modernist counterparts. Thus, the Tugwells beat out the Wilsons and Taylors at the Department of Agriculture, just as Lilienthal had beaten out Morgan in the Tennessee Valley Authority. The War Relocation Authority's Community Analysis Section fared better but, of course, it was only a temporary program with purview over 110,000 people. The short-lived nature of such programs would seem to confirm Jess Gilbert's assessment that the localist "ways of thinking" found in the New Deal BAE were lost by the mid-1940s.[49]

The Department of Agriculture, TVA, and War Relocation Authority were not, however, the only places where policies were set. The United States had long been distinguished for its muscular "outward state," the portion of the government dedicated to handling the country's interaction with the rest of the world.[50] During and after World War II, when the United States ascended to the position of global superpower, that aspect of its government would come to take on enormous significance. And it was there, in the United States' dealings with foreign peoples, that the communitarian and localist vision shared by Wilson, Taylor, Morgan, and the workers in the WRA would find its fullest expression. Indeed, those men would all have a hand in carrying the quest for community overseas.

Why should communitarians have any more luck abroad than they had had at home? On the face of it, there is little reason to think that domestic and foreign policy would differ all that much in their values or approach. Yet a few factors distinguished U.S. activity in the global South, i.e., the impoverished countries that had been or were still colonies. The first was racism, in particular a subtle but pervasive form of racism that encouraged those in the United States to regard Southern peoples as particularly well suited to community life. Although modernization as an ideology contained a great deal of hubris and cultural chauvinism, it sprang from the conviction that humans were essentially the same and that, once they had mastered the right technologies, all could ascend the universal staircase to modernity.[51] Communitarianism, by contrast, was nourished by doubts about species-wide equality, usually in the form of a sympathetic Orientalism associating nonwhite peoples with tradition, community, and locality.[52] That "*Gemeinschaft* for them, *Gesellschaft* for us" attitude is no doubt one reason community strategies got much further in the U.S. government's dealings with Japanese internees than they did in its dealings with white farmers.

On the other side of things, leaders in the global South had their own reasons to question modernity, or at least the form of modernity with which they had thus far been presented. Technology, industrialization, and large-scale, state-centered processes of social transformation had come to the global South as violent disruptions. Were such forces to be emulated, ignored, resisted, or selectively accommodated? That was the great question facing the majority of the world's population in the nineteenth and twentieth centuries—the "one problem to the exclusion of all others," as the Meiji-era thinker Fukuzawa Yukichi put it.[53] It is remarkable how much ambivalence accompanied the answering of that question. To be sure, there were hard-core modernizers, just as there were immovable traditionalists. Yet many of the most influential thinkers managed to embody both positions or to slide from one to the other over the course of their careers.[54] In the early postcolonial period, even the most aggressive modernizers, the builders of dams and cities, retained a remarkable sympathy for tradition and community.

There was also an important material reason communitarians found safe berth overseas. The Second World War catapulted the United States into a position of global supremacy, but it did so at a time when the old mechanisms of international control, rooted in European empires, were quickly crumbling. Thus began a decades-long scramble on the part of the United States to find new ways to acquire influence in the global South. Some of the techniques it arrived at were standard geopolitical fare: diplomacy, trade negotiations, military aid, and covert warfare. But the quest for influence also propelled the United States into a new field of action: "development." The global South was conspicuously poor, the United States was conspicuously rich, and it seemed obvious that the price of influence would be to somehow address that imbalance. "We must embark on a bold new program for making the benefits of our scientific advances and industrial progress available for the improvement and growth of underdeveloped areas" is how Harry Truman expressed it the famous fourth point of his inaugural address.[55] That speech marked the entry of the United States into the business of supplying aid to poor countries not as an emergency measure but as a general policy.[56] What form that aid should take, however, remained an open question.

What international aid would look like depended on who oversaw the programs, and there the United States encountered a challenge. Dispensing aid was not just a matter of money, of which the United States had a great deal, but also of expertise, of which it had little. Its predecessor as the world's superpower, Great Britain, had a prominent colonial office and a cadre of specially trained colonial officials, many of whom worked in development after their imperial careers ended.[57] The

United States had an empire, too—the fifth largest in the world, containing nearly twenty million subjects by the war's end—but it ran it on an ad hoc basis. Its tiny colonial office was powerless, and the men who served in the territories had neither special training in nor a career-long commitment to colonial matters.[58]

The lack of colonial officials in the United States might have been compensated by the country's surfeit of anthropologists. Yet although anthropologists were prominent figures, few of them had experience in the places to which the United States would send aid after 1945. India, for example, had been entirely off-limits to U.S. anthropologists during the British *raj*.[59] "Empires do not want nosy busybodies snooping into their territories and business," explained W. E. B. Du Bois in 1945, lamenting the remarkable dearth of trustworthy social science on conditions in the world's colonies.[60] Over time, the United States would rely on its universities to train experts in "area studies," experts who would then hopefully staff government agencies. But learning languages and starting academic programs took time, and in the meantime, the shortage of "area" experts remained a constant bottleneck.

Because the United States lacked people who knew much about foreign places, it sought to recruit officials who knew about foreign problems. Thus, rather than fill its ranks with specialists in particular countries or regions, as the European powers did, it turned to specialists in the process of development itself.[61] Economics, political science, and theoretical sociology—the sorts of disciplines that gave rise to modernization theory—formed one important pillar of "development" knowledge. But for the day-in, day-out work of designing aid schemes, the United States depended on rural experts, for the obvious reason that much of the global South was agricultural. And so rural sociologists, often in the company of anthropologists, found themselves in positions of great influence within the foreign aid bureaucracy. Just at the same time that agricultural mechanization was diminishing the field of operations for rural experts at home, the United States' achievement of global supremacy opened up a much larger field abroad. And they brought to that field their distinctive sympathy for communities imperiled by modernization.

Rural experts found work at all levels of international development. Yet they were most needed in foreign countries, where they trained their foreign counterparts and oversaw agricultural improvement schemes. Since rural experts tended to be localist as a matter of philosophy, the prospect of working "on the ground" or near to it was not an unpleasant one. They often took great pride in their village work, seeing themselves as heroic Homer Atkins figures. A strange pattern thus emerged within the foreign aid apparatus. Modernizers gravitated toward the centers of power, communitarians toward the sites of implementation. The result was an unevenly balanced developmental state, with modernizers crafting policy from the top down and communitarians building it from the bottom up. That odd structure is one reason it has been easier for historians to register the influence of modernizers than that of communitarians. From the bird's-eye view, and from the archives in Washington, U.S. developmental policy looks modernist. It is only from the worm's-eye view, from the view of development as implemented in foreign countries and as registered in foreign archives, that the full extent of communitarianism can be appreciated.[62]

For communitarians accustomed to playing the underdog in the United States, the developmental field was a bonanza. Consider the case of Arthur Raper, a rural sociologist who worked under Carl C. Taylor at the Bureau of Agricultural Economics. Raper is mildly well known in U.S. history as the author of important studies of Southern tenant farming and of lynching. Yet his domestic career was easily eclipsed by his international one. Between 1947 and 1950, the Department of Agriculture released him to the Department of Defense, where he helped plan land reform in occupied Japan. The next year, still on loan from the USDA, Raper worked on behalf of the Mutual Security Administration in Southeast Asia on village welfare. Also in that year, he took a break from government service to work for a month for a private organization, the American Friends of the Middle East, in Iraq, Syria, Jordan, Lebanon, and Egypt. For the next fifteen years, Raper continued to travel, working for the State Department throughout Asia and Africa, three years of which he served as the International Cooperation Administration's Regional Community Development Adviser to the Middle East and North Africa. Raper also worked with two universities, Michigan State and the University of California, Berkeley, training other scholars in the field.[63]

Raper's trajectory was not unusual. In 1952, he made an informal count and found that he could name seventy-five of his fellow rural sociologists who had taken jobs abroad after the war.[64] That count would have included Raper's former boss, Carl C. Taylor, who left the BAE to become an international aid consultant. Taylor decided to abandon his domestic career when he "measured the declining opportunities" at home against the "possibilities of doing international work."[65] He soon became one of the world's leading experts on international development, serving as a consultant for projects in some twenty-one countries over the course of the 1950s and 1960s.[66] Taylor's collaborator within the USDA, M. L. Wilson, also became an international authority. And so, too, did John Provinse, Conrad Arensberg, and Edward Spicer from the War Relocation Authority.[67] Spicer, in fact, edited one of the most widely used casebooks on foreign aid, *Human Problems in Technological Change* (1952).

Raper, Taylor, Spicer, and the rest are not just interesting because they moved quickly from domestic activism to overseas work. They are interesting because, when they arrived in foreign countries, they—with their counterparts in the global South—converged on a program: community development. Just as they believed that the problems of U.S. farmers and Japanese internees could best be solved through small-group activity, they felt that global poverty could also be attacked via community councils, deference to local culture and tradition, and appropriate technologies. That vision, first tried on a country-by-country basis, received some coherence in 1954 when the Foreign Operations Administration (a precursor to USAID) established a Division of Community Development. Its budget was small—in 1956, a flush year, it spent only $18.6 million—but that is because its role was advisorial. And its advisers were posted around the world. In 1956, its staff worked on forty-seven projects in twenty-three countries.[68] Meanwhile, the real money came from other sources: U.S. bilateral aid, Department of Defense spending, the Peace Corps, the United Nations, Southern governments' planning ministries, and philanthropic foundations.

More than an item on a budget, community development was—much like modernization—an approach to the whole business of development aid. And by the 1950s, it had caught on. In that decade, it was easily the primary rural development strategy at the United Nations. Member nations were uniformly in favor of community development, remarked the director of the Bureau of Social Affairs, just in the way that they were "in favour of mothers and children, or in favour of peace."[69] In 1956, UN agencies sent out nearly four hundred community development experts to advise governments.[70] By 1960, the UN counted more than sixty nations with community development programs in Asia, Africa, and Latin America, about half of which were national in scope.[71]

"Along with a flag, an anthem, a seat at the United Nations, a university, and an international hotel," wrote two observers in the 1960s, "a community-development program is an essential part of the trappings of modern nationhood."[72]

WHAT *WAS* community development? Later chapters of this book describe community development as its proponents saw it: as an evolving practice. Unlike modernization theorists, whose interests in overarching patterns of historical change encouraged them to seize the commanding heights of theory, community developers had little interest in academic knowledge. As decentralists, they doubted whether the process of development could be comprehended as a single entity, from a single vantage point. Knowledge for them was both provisional and contextual; case studies carried greater epistemic weight than did grand strategies.

Nevertheless, there can be no practice without some theory behind it, even if that theory is implicit. The best place to look for the theory of community development is in the writings of the anthropologist Robert Redfield, of the University of Chicago.[73] Redfield never worked as a community developer, as many of the social scientists who studied the matter did, but he served as an *eminence grise* of the field. He had consulted for the Bureau of Agricultural Economics and, as described above, written a blueprint for the community program of the Japanese internment camps.[74] At the University of Chicago, he trained anthropologists who would go on to become leaders in the field.[75] His most important contribution, however, came as a thinker. For decades, Redfield explored the relationship between community, modernization, and development. In doing so, he laid bare many of the theoretical commitments that would come to define the practice of community development.

Redfield came of intellectual age in the 1930s, at the time when intellectuals and artists were beginning to take up the cause of the small group and small town. Anthropologists led the charge, turning away from family life, kinship structures, and cultural traits studied in the abstract toward research on integrated wholes, on "ways of life" sustained in village communities by face-to-face interactions. Despite the ostensible isolationism of the period, the 1930s were a decade when such village studies commanded a substantial audience. Popular portraits of non-"modern" or imperiled folk cultures from the time included Margaret Mead's *Coming of Age in Samoa* (1928), William and Charlotte Viall Wiser's *Behind Mud Walls* (1930), Pearl Buck's *The Good Earth*

(1931), Ruth Benedict's *Patterns of Culture* (1934), and even Margaret Mitchell's *Gone with the Wind* (1936).[76] Such books singled out places where non-industrial forms of life could be glimpsed intact, before they succumbed to what Ruth Benedict called the "massive universality" of Western culture.[77]

Redfield never shared his fellow anthropologists' interest in "pristine" or untouched cultures. He preferred to study cultural contact, particularly contact between non-industrial and industrial societies. In this, he owed a great debt to the Chicago school of sociology, led by Robert E. Park and Ernest Burgess. The Chicago school had sought to understand how rural migrants to cities became "urban," how they adapted themselves to the rhythms of a very different kind of life. Unlike anthropologists, however, they viewed that process with some approbation. (It helped that they were looking at migrants who had come to cities voluntarily rather than at villages plowed under by an encroaching industrial civilization.) Redfield appreciated the Chicago school's sympathetic sensitivity to change, although his connections to it were not just intellectual. Robert E. Park was Redfield's father-in-law and, for Redfield's early career, his mentor.

It was on Park's advice that Redfield launched his anthropological career not with a study of some faraway tribal community but by looking at Tepoztlán, a heavily trafficked town just south of Mexico City (the title of his resulting book, *Tepoztlan, a Mexican Village,* was misleading on this score). Tepoztlán had been in contact with European cultures for centuries, and its culture exhibited a complete "fusion of Indian with Spanish features."[78] On what Redfield would later call the "folk–urban continuum" that stretched from isolated villages to cities, Tepoztlán was somewhere in the middle.[79] And whereas Redfield's fellow village writers tended to regard the replacement of the folk with the urban as a catastrophe, Redfield saw something different. Tepoztlán *was* moving toward a more urban configuration but was "not breaking down," he wrote. It was merely undergoing a "gradual process of change."[80]

Redfield's interest in the urbanization of folk societies and his sense that such processes need not be catastrophic have led historians to see him as one of the first modernization theorists. Indeed, he was one of the first to use the term *modernization* in the way that it is used today.[81] But if the legacy of Chicago sociology drew his attention toward processes of change, his membership in the anthropological profession alerted him to the damage that such change might do to folk societies. And Redfield was not above playing up the benevolent aspects of those societies; his portrait of Tepoztlán was notable for its emphasis on harmony and its soft-pedaling of conflict. Thus, even as Redfield spoke of change and urbanization, it was not hard to read his book as a plea for the old ways. Stuart Chase, who popularized Redfield's research in his *Mexico: A Study of Two Americas* (1931), certainly understood it that way. "You have in your possession something precious," Chase advised the residents of Tepoztlán, "something which the western world has lost and flounders miserably trying to regain. Hold to it. Exert every ounce of your magnificent inertia to conserve your way of life."[82]

Redfield never went that far. But the tension between modernization and conservation defined his career. Like the village writers, he felt a romantic attachment to small-scale forms of life. Like the sociologists, he was interested in social change. His entire corpus can be seen as an attempt to answer a single question: is it possible for poor societies to improve their well-being by adapting to changing conditions without losing their traditions and distinctive forms of social organization? Can there be, in other words, development without modernization?

Tepoztlan established the parameters of Redfield's thought but did little to answer the question. The problem continued to fascinate Redfield as he studied a series of Mexican societies in transition, at different points on his folk–urban continuum.[83] He achieved a breakthrough of sorts in 1948, when he returned to Chan Kom, a village he had studied with a team of anthropologists in 1930–1931. In the intervening seventeen years, Chan Kom had developed individual property rights, a bustling commercial sphere, and rural industry. It was "a story of success," Redfield wrote.[84] Yet much of that success in Redfield's eyes stemmed from the striking fact that Chan Kom had appeared to enter a larger market society without losing its social solidarity. Family relations, religious rituals, basic thought patterns, and common traditions remained blissfully intact, and social stratification and commodification had been kept at bay. Chan Kom had gained the rewards of the new without paying the cost of moral or social upheaval. It had discovered a toll-free road to development.

Unfortunately, Redfield saw Chan Kom as more of an anomaly than a model. It had managed to develop without discarding its long-held values only because its long-held values, by a happy coincidence, turned out to be precisely those values known to promote economic growth:

industry, frugality, practicality, sobriety, clocklike punctuality, and a zeal for accumulating wealth even in the absence of any way to spend it. "These villagers," Redfield observed, "had much of the Protestant ethic before they ever heard of Protestantism."[85] Chan Kom showed that, with the proper traditional values, a community could develop without disintegrating. But how other cultural areas, lacking Chan Kom's native values, might do so remained unclear.

Redfield did not yet have a model for the sort of development he favored, but all the elements were in place. Tepoztlán had shown that, given time, a folk culture could incorporate aspects of metropolitan life (in this case, Spanish) without losing its cohesion. Chan Kom had shown that, given the right values, a village could even flourish without breaking apart. The trick was to find a way to embed development-enabling values within the Tepoztláns of the world via some gradual and nondisruptive process. Redfield called this "acculturation," or "culture contact without conflict."[86]

In 1954, Redfield wrote an article with his colleague Milton Singer that explained how such acculturation could be accomplished. There were, Redfield and Singer argued, two pathways along which a society might develop, which they called "primary urbanization" and "secondary urbanization." Secondary urbanization was straightforward modernization: traditional folkways disappeared as an urban (and often foreign) intelligentsia imposed new norms, norms that stood "in conflict with local folk culture."[87] But Redfield and Singer were more interested in the other pathway, primary urbanization. In that form of development, they explained, cities grew naturally from villages, and urban culture remained "still at bottom the same" as that of the villages.[88] The "little traditions" of the villages were given coherence and elaboration by urban (but emphatically not foreign) literati, who wove them into a "Great Tradition." The key, for Redfield and Singer, was that the Great Tradition connected organically to the little traditions, with each feeding each in a constant adaptation. In this vision, villages were not brittle holdovers from a premodern past but the taproots of a cosmopolitan, sophisticated, and dynamic society.

Ironically, Mexico—where Redfield made his career—was a poor place to study primary urbanization. There, an indigenous Great Tradition had been dismantled hundreds of years ago and replaced by a European culture. A more promising place to look for an intact Great

Tradition, Redfield felt, was on the Indian subcontinent. "Here, more than anywhere else, can the Western anthropologist hope to learn something about the interrelations of primitive, peasant, and urbanized life."[89] Redfield secured a series of grants from the Ford Foundation to study Great Traditions in 1951, and that study soon focused on India. Milton Singer traveled there in 1954, and Redfield went over himself in 1955.

Redfield and Singer's understanding of India, and consequently their understanding of primary urbanization, depended heavily on the work of an Indian anthropologist, M. N. Srinivas. Like Redfield, Srinivas was curious about the possibility that community and cosmopolitanism might sustain one another. And he felt that he had found such a way in the caste system. Modernizers, of course, had long criticized caste as an obsolete, oppressive, and backward institution. But for Srinivas it contained intriguing possibilities. On the one hand, it ensured social harmony within villages by assigning to each individual a clearly defined role within a complementary system. On the other, it connected villages to each other, and to cities, via the social ties that bound members of the same caste in different places. By opening two-way channels of communication between urban cores and villages, the caste system not only sustained folk societies but also placed them in conversation with a Great Tradition, which in turn allowed them to adapt to a changing economy.[90]

Srinivas gave a name to that process of adaptation: Sanskritization. It was a gradual process, he explained, stretching back "for over 2,000 years all over India," by which all Indians adopted the (changing) norms and rituals of Brahmin Hindus.[91] In Srinivas's understanding, Sanskritization had endowed India with a unified but flexible culture, in which new norms could be spread throughout the populace without disruption or coercion. In other words, Srinivas had identified an India-wide process that resembled Westernization in its best effects but that operated through indigenous traditions.[92] That was precisely the sort of development that Redfield had been searching for, and the Chicago School quickly adopted Srinivas as an honorary member.[93]

What Redfield had identified, with the help of Srinivas, was an alternative form of development, different from modernization. It proceeded not from the blueprints of a Western intelligentsia but from an ongoing, two-way conversation between the indigenous cultural elite and the many village communities. Its basis was therefore in traditional institutions, both in the villages and in the cities. To the degree that development entailed adaptation, the adaptation would have to come from those institutions.

For Redfield, a foreign power like the United States could not simply arrive bearing new technology and expect to see it adopted. He was a harsh critic of the "strong continuing faith in technology and material production" of both the United States and the Soviet Union.[94] He rejected the notion that poor nations should seek, in the course of their development, to emulate the United States and Europe. "The progressive spirit of Asia and Africa is not simply a decision to walk the road of progressive convictions that we have traversed," he contended, "but rather in significant part an effort of the 'backward' peoples to recover from their disruptive encounters with the West by returning to the 'sacred centers' of their ancient indigenous civilizations."[95]

THE POSSIBILITY that poor societies might profitably undertake a program of adaptation without discarding their cultures and without centralizing their institutions was at the heart of community development. It was because they saw things roughly as Redfield did that community developers privileged village work, allied themselves with local "leaders," and hastily deferred to vernacular customs and institutions. If they spoke of an intended end-state, it was only rarely and in the vaguest of terms. Notably, they tended to avoid the term *modernization* altogether, preferring the more neutral and open-ended term *development*.

The notion that community developers were pursuing "development without modernization" may sound strange, but that is because we still tend to use the words *development* and *modernization* as synonyms. That semantic identification is a holdover from the heyday of the modernization theorists, who not only advocated for a certain kind of development but insisted that it was the *only* kind. Today, however, the foundational axiom of modernization theory—that there is a single condition toward which all societies eventually converge—is difficult to maintain, and development practice has split into an increasingly complex tangle of models. Given that today we no longer assume that progressive change implies modernization, it is time to release ourselves from the assumption that it did in the past.

Community developers struggled with that assumption even in the 1950s. It could make their conversations with modernizers difficult. The two groups' mutual incomprehension emerged on full display in 1957, when MIT's Center for International Studies (CENIS) convened a conference on community development. CENIS, the home of W. W. Rostow, Max Millikan, Lucian Pye, and Daniel Lerner, was a bastion of modernization theory, and the meeting was modernization theorists' attempt to engage with community development.[96] Their camp included Millikan, Lerner, and Pye. The community development delegation, headed by Louis Miniclier, chief of the State Department's Community Development Division, included Carl C. Taylor and Conrad Arensberg. Redfield, invited, could not attend.[97]

Trouble began even before the conference did. Ernest E. Neal, who had worked as a community developer in India and the Philippines, wrote to Miniclier to express his "reservation" about the background papers circulated in advance of the conference. It was a small problem, but it signaled a deep epistemological divide. The CENIS organizers had sent out theoretical overviews of the topic, offering few details. Neal, however, felt that community development could be truly known "only from day-to-day contact with an evolving community development program."[98] The organizers, Neal explained, should thus have circulated reports from the field, not abstract reflections, which, in his judgment "showed a complete lack of knowledge about village life."[99]

One of those background papers had been written by Lucian Pye, a sociologist and a key figure in the development of modernization theory. Although Pye had sympathy for community development, it is not clear that he understood it. In his view, community development was a technique for creating "a modern nation—in which secular and industrialized modes of behavior will be secure and dominant—out of an earthbound society, predominantly composed of a population that is fragmented into tightly ordered village units."[100] It could accomplish that by bridging the gap between the modernizing elite and rural people. Yet Pye assumed that the bridge would allow one-way traffic only. Modernizing national leaders "could not possibly" accept "the outlooks of the village people." Were they to do so, "much of the political drive for change would be eliminated from these societies."[101]

Pye, in other words, had come out in support of community development but only because he had mistaken it for a part of the modernization apparatus—a way to guarantee village compliance with the dictates of the center. Community developers, Neal among them, saw it the other way around. The point of establishing a connection between national leaders and peasants was to teach the leaders about the needs of the peasants. Pye dug in: it was crucial for members of the elite to stand apart from the tradition-bound masses and to set their sights on modernity. That was what made them leaders.

The conflicts continued. One modernization theorist insisted that economic growth required a transition to mechanized agriculture—precisely the development that had pushed rural experts out of the United States in the first place.[102] The economists at the conference wondered what effect community development had on the gross national product and worried that it had none.[103] Community developers dutifully explained that the point of their practice was not to increase agricultural production or even GNP. It was to place power in the hands of villagers so that they could get the things they most needed, whether those things were economic or not. It seemed that the two camps had not only different methods but different goals.

The notion that villagers would shape their own destiny sat uncomfortably with modernization theorists. It sounded nice, Max Millikan conceded, but ultimately wouldn't communal decision making have to be sacrificed as a nation approached maturity and gained a Western-style government? The anthropologist Melvin Tumin expressed a deeper skepticism, accusing community developers of being "cultists about participation" and of assigning "almost magical properties . . . to group processes so that any decision reached by a group is by that fact rendered superior to any other decision." Carl C. Taylor shot back: the real thing to worry about wasn't that villagers would misconstrue their own interests, it was that experts making decisions on behalf of them would. Bureaucratic approaches to development made "building from the bottom up" impossible and guaranteed that technicians, rather than the poor, would set the agenda.[104]

The sociologist Wilbert E. Moore was aghast. Community developers were behaving like "peasant lovers, who have a somewhat distorted notion of peasant communities and certainly a distorted notion of the general level of health, material well-being, and general satisfaction on the part of the local people." Their approach, with its desire to "disturb as little as possible in the traditional social structure," would "confirm all the archaic elements in the traditional structure, bolster them, and effect what is precisely not needed with reference to long-term, continuing economic growth."[105]

The question, at bottom, was how well equipped poor people were to superintend their own development. Were their folkways intelligent accommodations of the conditions they faced or cultural pathologies that kept them poor? Community developers tried to explain that rural traditions contained an unseen wisdom. Such traditions would, of course, have to adapt to changing conditions, but adaptation should be piece-meal and experimental, with no *telos* in sight. Lawrence K. Frank described the aim of community development as "dynamic stability," a state in which institutions could "withstand changes . . . and roll with the punches and yet come back to maintain a continuous integrity of their social order."[106] The goal was not to replace tradition with moder-nity but to encourage flexibility within traditions, so that they could be extended and adapted without being lost. That was nearly identical to Redfield's ideal of primary urbanization.

In the end, there was little to build upon. The conference's recorder threw up his hands; the two camps spoke "at cross purposes" and were divided by "inherent disagreements."[107] "I did not anticipate the confu-sion or lack of communication," wrote Louis Miniclier to Max Millikan by way of apology after the event.[108] Neither did the CENIS scholars, who had expected community development to serve the ends of modern-ization. But, reaching for a weapon, they found that it would not point in the direction they had hoped. The two groups retreated into their separate spheres and, although Millikan hoped for a second conference, nothing came of it.

IN THEORY, then, modernization and community development were irreconcilable. Modernization theorists believed change should come through a Western-educated elite and that it should move societies through stages toward a predetermined endpoint. Community devel-opers believed that change must begin with communal deliberation and that its direction was up to the villagers themselves. They doubted, though, that such discussions would result in plans to jettison traditional institutions in favor of "modern" ones. It was more likely that villagers would seek to work through their existing institutions to accommodate the changing conditions they faced.

What community developers expected, however, is only part of the story. As they were the first the point out, the heart of their work lay in practice. So what happened when an aid apparatus populated by mod-ernizers at the center and communitarians at the periphery was set in motion? Could community development maintain itself as a distinct practice? Or would community developers simply become, as Pye had expected, the unwitting agents of modernization? And where would the foreign politicians with whom they worked fit into the program? Or the villagers themselves? The best place to turn for answers is to the place where community developers acted first and with the greatest consequence: India.

3

PEASANTVILLE

IN 1952, a staff member in the U.S. embassy in New Delhi named Ellery Foster wrote a series of memoranda about what he took to be a looming crisis in India. The crisis was not one of the sort usually discussed—a failure of the monsoon, an epidemic, or a famine. It was, rather, a more deeply rooted problem: the erosion and imminent destruction of the local community. Centuries of feudalism and imperial rule, Foster warned, had so strained the local community that it was on the brink of extinction.[1] In this regard, India was coming to resemble the United States, which had abandoned its own communities to "disharmony and waste" in its breakneck pursuit of economic growth.[2] Foster was therefore skeptical that the United States could provide "a ready-made answer" for India's crisis, since "it does not even have one for itself."[3] If the problem could be solved at all, Foster reasoned, the solution must be "a synthesis of the best wisdom of the East and West": the West's dynamism combined with the East's regard for communal welfare into a program of "decentralized development."[4]

What would decentralized development look like? Foster was clear that macroeconomic stimulation and the building of infrastructure—the main strategies that the United States had employed in the New Deal—were beside the point. What India needed was an "emergency scheme of *community* economics."[5] Government aid agencies should be augmented or outright replaced by community-run folk schools. Villages should be improved in order to stanch the flow of migrants toward cities. Developmental schemes targeting agricultural production should be broadened to make room for hard-to-quantify things like "laughter and song, poetry and philosophy, art and religion."[6] Where possible, Foster called for replacing money with a system of barter organized by local clearinghouses, which he hoped would prevent resources from escaping the countryside.

Those were bold ideas, but Foster took pains to clarify that they were simply suggestions, not a worked-out program. He had a profound suspicion of blueprints of any sort. "Whenever you attempt to have everything planned and directed by an organization you impose rigidity and bottlenecks that stymie progress and your efforts can too easily end in a dictatorship," he noted.[7] For community economics to take hold, it must proceed through "a grass-roots process of democratic planning and action."[8]

It would be easy to dismiss Foster as a utopian, hopelessly out of step with the imperatives of both foreign policy and economic development. Indeed, he eventually became disgusted with public life and retreated to the periphery of it, taking up countercultural causes such as organic farming, solar energy, recycling, cooperative living, yoga, and a Vedic celibacy practice known as brahmacharya.[9] But to write Foster off would be to miss important and central features of the United States' participation in Indian rural development. For, in many ways, Foster was not the exception but the rule. Community economics was only a slightly amplified version of the policies that both Indian and U.S. officials pursued under the name of community development. Community-run schools, improved villages, decentralization, and nonmaterial measures of welfare ("laughter and song") were, in fact, at the very heart of India's community development program. Even Foster's call for the abolition of money found some echo in the desire of the Minister of Community Development to protect villages from what he called the "evils of capitalism."[10]

Foster's views, in other words, did not disqualify him from holding a high-ranking office in the foreign policy establishment. Those views were precisely why he was hired. After years in the USDA's Bureau of Agricultural Economics and the U.S. Forest Service during the Depression and war, Foster became an in-demand international aid expert. In India, he helped to design the national community development program. But his work, which lasted into the 1960s, took him to Washington, Antigua, Puerto Rico, and the United Arab Emirates as well, all in the employ of the U.S. government.[11]

ELLERY FOSTER does not seem as if he should fit into the U.S. campaign to develop India. That is because historians have largely understood that effort to be an exercise in modernization. India was, in fact, a key reference point for modernization theorists. Large, well known, and of obvious geostrategic importance, it was the archetype of a developing nation.[12] Max Millikan and W. W. Rostow first formulated their stage theory of economic development in reference to it, and it was also the subject of Edward Shils's research into the politics of modernization.[13] India was, further, the point of entry for then-senator John F. Kennedy's preoccupation with "development" and what drew him to the modernization theorists as advisers.[14] But Foster's engagement with India is hard to explain in terms of the ideology of modernization. Like many of his fellow Bureau of Agricultural Economics alumni, he was a developer but not a modernizer.

The community development program that Foster helped to launch also fits uneasily with another, similar historical narrative: the one Indian historians tell about postcolonial India. In the same way that historians of the United States have interpreted the postwar decades of U.S. history as an era of modernization, students of Indian history have regarded policymaking under Prime Minister Jawaharlal Nehru (1947–1964) as profoundly modernist, dedicated to a faith in science, a technocratic style of politics, and a zeal for high-impact infrastructural projects. Historians are fond of quoting Nehru's description of dams as the temples of modern India.[15]

Scholars of India have put the matter in starker terms than historians of the United States have. Whereas U.S. historians treat postwar modernization as a strategy or an ideology, Indian historians, particularly those associated with the influential Subaltern Studies school, have characterized it as something more deeply rooted: an epistemology. For the most part, Subaltern Studies scholars have concerned themselves with the period of the British *raj,* which they have interpreted as an epistemic clash between native thought-systems and imperial rationality, the latter arriving with such totalizing force that the basic act of recovering indigenous perceptions becomes a delicate and at times impossible task. Yet in an influential account, Partha Chatterjee extended that analysis into the post-independence period. The problem with the postcolonial state, he charged, is that it inherited and then reproduced the same Enlightenment-derived mental habits of the British Empire. Thus whereas the Indian masses, for whom Mohandas Gandhi served as spokesman, occupied an "epistemic standpoint situated *outside* the thematic of post-Enlightenment thought," Nehru stood entirely within the framework of Enlightenment epistemology and regarded Gandhi with "a feeling of total incomprehension."[16] Science, rationality, and technology were

Nehru's bywords. They led him to favor a "supremely statist economy" dominated by "large-scale heavy industry."[17] Chatterjee's sense of things has been incorporated into the larger telling of Indian history. A major recent overview of the Nehruvian era has ascribed to policymakers in the period "an overwhelming consensus in favour of a heavy industry–oriented, state-supported model of development."[18]

Ellery Foster and community development do not fit easily into that "overwhelming consensus." They are better understood as part of a counter-tendency within Indian politics: a profound enchantment with the idea of the "village community." This, too, dates back to the days of the *raj*. Although the British Empire had long justified itself by the need to "civilize" India through good government, that had never been the only justification. Other, more conservative, imperialists emphasized the unbridgeable gulf between England and India, and they doubted whether India would ever fit the British model for it. The debate between the two forms of imperialism was largely decided by events, particularly the rebellion of 1857, a violent and widespread challenge to British rule. The revolt cast doubt on the idea that India was progressing smoothly toward British-style "civilization" and tipped the balance toward the conservative—and racist—strand of imperial thought. Indians were fundamentally unlike the British, imperialists concluded. So what *were* they like?

Sir Henry Maine's *Village-Communities in the East and West* (1871) offered an answer. Indian life was best understood not through its literature or law, as earlier colonial administrators had understood it, but through its customs as encountered in the village. There, Maine argued, one could glimpse a primitive form of social and economic life that was the true India. Maine was ultimately a modernizer; he seemed pleased by the "breaking to pieces" of village India that the advent of a liberal market order would require.[19] But his detailed description of India's villages was rendered with enough sympathy that most took him for a champion of them. J. S. Mill, Friedrich Engels, and Henry George all read Maine as having shown that traditional societies were socialist and, consequently, that socialism was practical.[20] The U.S. missionary William H. Wiser put a groupist spin on Maine's vision when, in 1936, he argued that the Indian village was more "socialistic than capitalistic" because it embodied "group and community concepts as opposed to individualistic concepts" and created "a balance in the community which makes for co-operation, satisfaction, and peace."[21]

The notion that the spirit of India resided in its villages and that those villages were essentially cooperative was by no means a conception exclusive to the colonizers. Drawing on both Indian and European sources (including Maine), Mohandas Gandhi used that portrait of the Indian village as the basis for a national independence movement.[22] It was an odd move. Most independence movements were led by urban and often Western-educated leaders who stressed the capacity of the colonies to modernize themselves. Yet in doffing his jacket and tie for a loincloth and staff, Gandhi tapped into a widely felt skepticism on the subcontinent toward modernization projects. It was Gandhi's leadership that turned the Indian independence movement from an elite-led affair into a mass movement. And although that movement was a machine of many parts, it maintained a prominent rural basis and deep appreciation for Indian customs and traditions.[23] That appreciation, Gandhi believed, endowed Indians with a distinctive approach to the problems of the industrial world. His followers called it "villagism."

Gandhi expressed his political vision most clearly in his slim dialogue *Hind Swaraj* (1909). In it, he complained not only of what doctors, lawyers, railroads, and other modernizing forces had done to India but what they had done to England itself. "Civilization is not an incurable disease," he commented wryly, "but it should never be forgotten that the English people are at present afflicted by it."[24] Gandhi therefore called for a polity of villages, a nation with no center—simply a collection of linked, organic cells.

Like many decentralists, Gandhi was more interested in practice than in theory. The task of filling out the political vision that he had sketched thus fell to others. The social theorists (and brothers) Bharatan and J. C. Kumarappa, with Gandhi's endorsement, elaborated his ideas into the theory of villagism. As the Kumarappas saw it, villagism was a third way between capitalism and socialism, both of which Gandhians criticized for their centralizing tendencies. "It is only in small groups," Bharatan Kumarappa wrote, "that the family tie of the individual to the group and of the group to the individual can develop, not in the huge nation-wide groups brought about through centralised large-scale production."[25] Villagism resembled the small-group turn in the United States. But here it was not a dissenting position; it was a national philosophy. If one were to draw a world map of communitarian thought, India at the moment of its independence would lie at the center.

The great puzzle of twentieth-century Indian history is making sense of what happened next, in the passage of leadership from Gandhi to Nehru with Gandhi's assassination in 1948. How did one of the largest countries in the world pivot so quickly from "civilization is a disease" to "dams are the temples of modern India"? The riddle becomes especially perplexing if, following the lead of the Subaltern Studies school, one sees the ascent of Nehru as signaling a shift not just in policy but in epistemology. Did non-modernist thought really abruptly vanish from the Indian political repertoire in the Nehruvian period? An emphasis on difference, on the incommensurability of different forms of "reason," might lead one to think so. But it is also possible that decentralism, Gandhism, and alternatives to modernization did not stand on the other side of an unbridgeable epistemological divide from high modernism. Indeed, a principal argument of this book is that the urge to modernize and the quest for community shared space, existing alongside or even within each other. To see how that happened, it is necessary to turn away from the hydroelectric dams and toward community development.

COMMUNITY DEVELOPMENT was not a new phenomenon in postwar India. Besides Gandhi's highly prominent village work, the Bengali poet Rabindranath Tagore pursued a scheme of rural reconstruction at Sriniketan, and there were about half a dozen other tentative efforts before independence to reform Indian villages.[26] The colonial state did little to develop such programs, though, so community efforts remained experimental, miniscule, and largely private.[27] Independence raised the possibility that the Indian government might adopt community development as an official doctrine and that the United States, seeking to purchase influence on the subcontinent, might fund it. Gandhi, who had proposed that the Indian National Congress disband after independence to devote itself to village work, obviously favored some sort of community scheme. The surprise is that Nehru appears to have agreed.

At the crossroads of India's communitarian plans and U.S. ambitions to bankroll development stood an unlikely figure: the architect and urban planner Albert Mayer.[28] As a New York–based professional, Mayer had little experience with either India or U.S. foreign policy. His only credentials to offer were as a communitarian. Mayer was best known as a member of a small but influential circle of regionalist planners in the United States that included Clarence Stein, Catherine Bauer, and Lewis

Mumford. The regionalists were alarmed by the commodification of land—the chopping up of living space into rectilinear, salable, privately held parcels—and its effects on social life. They lamented the effects of a market that served only the needs of individual sellers and buyers and made no provision for communal welfare. Keeping community in mind, Mayer believed, meant abandoning a concern for individual building and focusing instead on the neighborhood as a whole. Mayer planned "superblocks" in the city and, during the New Deal, Green Belt towns.[29]

Mayer first encountered India during World War II; he was sent there to build airstrips. It would have been an inconsequential posting had he not met Jawaharlal Nehru at the end of his tour. The two quickly established a bond and enjoyed "intimate talks until far into the night" about model villages and the possibility of applying Mayer's ideas to India.[30] Nehru was particularly taken by Mayer's notion that, rather than focus on one aspect of human welfare or another, a planner might conceive of "a whole with various aspects inter-linked" and thus "build up community life."[31] He invited Mayer back to India for an exploratory visit. What could be done in this regard with India's villages?

Clarence Stein and Lewis Mumford mulled over the question with Mayer. "We all began to see that you could not start with model villages," Stein recalled, meaning that the problem could not be solved merely with urban planning.[32] It was, rather, a question of sociology. Recognizing this, Mayer reached out to the communitarians of the Roosevelt administration. He read about the Japanese internment camps and met with rural sociologists from the USDA, including M. L. Wilson and Carl C. Taylor, who provided "both practical assistance and a sense of direction."[33] The most significant practical assistance, though, came from Nehru himself, who ensured that every door on the subcontinent was flung open for Mayer. Nehru introduced Mayer to Gandhi and other top politicians, discussed Mayer's proposals with Gandhi, and took an almost alarming interest in the mundane administrative details of Mayer's work.[34] Mayer, for his part, dove deeply into India, reading Indian sociology and Gandhian philosophy, particularly the work of J. C. Kumarappa.[35]

With Nehru's backing, Mayer gained permission to run a large pilot project in the villages of a a district, Etawah, in Uttar Pradesh. In some ways, the Etawah project was a standard development program. Project workers distributed seeds, rebuilt public spaces, vaccinated and inoculated villagers, ran hygiene campaigns, and provided superior livestock. But Mayer maintained that such accomplishments were of secondary impor- tance. He worried that an overemphasis on quantifiable material out- comes would lead developers to seek to maximize those outcomes by creating large bureaucracies run by specialized experts. Although Mayer conceded the occasional necessity of top-down structures, he believed that they usually came at the cost of "the deterioration of small commu- nities and face-to-face relationships." A better program would start on the small scale and favor the "folk-solutions" of the people over the advice of experts.[36] That bottom-up approach became Etawah's trade- mark. As one of Mayer's co-workers at Etawah quipped, "the only thing you can begin doing from the top is drilling a well."[37]

Eliciting the participation of Etawah's residents would require more than just having the right philosophy. For Mayer, opening development to the grassroots entailed a distinctive administrative approach. He began by creating the position of Rural Life Analyst, a "participant observer" with sociological or anthropological training who would report on "the People's habitual way of doing things."[38] It was a trans- posed version of the Community Life Analyst position from the Japanese internment camps. In a neat circle that illustrates how small the com- munitarian world could be, Mayer's first Rural Life Analyst left Etawah after two years to study at Cornell with Morris Opler, the former Community Life Analyst at the Manzanar camp (who then set up a research project on village life in India).[39]

More important than the Rural Life Analysts were the "village-level workers"—the backbone of the pilot project. Unlike the subject-matter experts who usually staffed agricultural projects, village-level workers had no particular technical aptitude. Their expertise lay in group dynamics, in eliciting the "felt needs" of the people through communal deliberation. Mayer treated these workers with a kind of reverence. He had them chair meetings attended by government officials who far outranked them, and he reserved ample time at those meetings for village reports. Those were democratic gestures, all the more pointedly so in a country that had been dominated for so long by a rigidly hierarchical civil service. The rural sociologist Arthur Raper thought it "highly probable" that Mayer's intro- duction of village-level workers would "go down in history as one of the great social inventions of the era."[40]

To observers, though, what was most striking about Etawah were its results. Someone visiting Mahewa block, Mayer's first site, at the

Albert Mayer (in center) talks as a worker lays bricks in Etawah. (Albert Mayer Papers, University of Chicago Library)

commencement of the project would have found Mahewa's hundred villages served by twenty mud schoolhouses, only a few easily flooded roads, open wells, and little local industry. The same visitor returning in 1954 would have found all the villages connected by roads with permanent culverts, nearly thirty brick schoolhouses, two high schools, and sanitary wells with hand pumps. Whereas in 1948 bricks would have had to be carried over muddy roads from the nearest city, by 1953 Etawah boasted 520 brick kilns, mostly run by cooperatives, employing over 42,000 workers. The kilns were "essentially a decentralized cooperative venture," Mayer explained with pride, since nearly all of the raw materials for the bricks were available cheaply and locally.[41] Agricultural outputs rose as villagers banded together to purchase threshers (which they eventually started to manufacture in Etawah) and villages established community centers and libraries. Best of all, Mayer noted, most of the labor and materials for the construction were donated by the villagers themselves, and hardly any new technology had been used. The achievement, just as he had hoped, was not material but sociological.

Etawah quickly became the international symbol for community development. The *Times of India* compared Mayer to A. O. Hume, the Scotsman who founded the Indian National Congress, and Etawah received frequent front-page coverage in the Indian press.[42] In the United States, Etawah appeared in *Time, Life* (a four-page spread), the *New York Times Magazine,* and *Ladies Home Journal.* President Truman mentioned Etawah in speeches, and Eleanor Roosevelt, who visited in 1952, praised it several times in her syndicated column "My Day."[43] Even the Harvard Business School paid tribute to Etawah by presenting the project to its students as a case study in democratic administration.[44]

MAYER BEGAN his work at Etawah in 1946, before Indian independence and before the Cold War. Etawah then was simply a pet project of Nehru's, an experiment. In July 1947, the ambassador George F. Kennan wrote his now-famous "X article" proposing that the United States adopt a doctrine of containment for the Soviet Union, and in August Nehru hoisted the Indian national flag above the Red Fort in Delhi. The Cold War had begun, and newly independent India was a valuable battleground in it—all the more so by 1949, when Truman announced a program of aid to the global South and, months later, the Guomindang government on the Chinese mainland fell to the communists.

By 1949, India's value to the United States was beyond question. Yet what precisely was to be done to maintain a non-communist India was far from obvious. After some delay, the question fell to Chester Bowles, a Democratic mainstay and, as of 1951, the ambassador to India. Bowles had no experience in foreign service. But he had sacrificed his governorship of Connecticut by backing Truman for reelection, and Truman owed him badly. Truman offered Bowles his choice of embassy positions and, to Truman's surprise, Bowles chose India.

Many regarded New Delhi as a hardship post, but in Bowles's eyes there was none more important. India possessed one-sixth of the world's population, commanded vast natural resources, and appeared to stand on the precipice of communism. In a confidential memorandum to Dean Acheson, Bowles rated India's odds of avoiding a revolution as "slightly better than 50–50."[45] If a Chinese-style revolution were to be forestalled, though, something must be done in the countryside. Within three weeks of arriving in India, Bowles toured Etawah. "That night I went to work with pencil and paper," he recalled. "How many village workers would it take to cover every village in India?"[46]

It wasn't an abstract question. The U.S. Congress had allocated $54 million in aid for India but offered little guidance in how it should be spent. Bowles met with Nehru and proposed devoting the entire sum to a multipronged program centered on a national community development scheme. In less than two hours of discussion, Nehru accepted the offer, and within weeks the aid agreement was signed.[47] Under the Indo-U.S. Technical Agreement of 1952, fifty-five pilot projects collectively covering 16,500 villages were established, with the understanding that the Indian government would expand the program and take on an increasing share of the financial burden over time. In the meantime, Bowles flew in rural experts from the United States, including Arthur Raper, Carl C. Taylor, Ernest Neal, and Ellery Foster. John Provinse oversaw the aid to India from Washington. With their guidance, Etawah was to become the new face of rural India.

Just as Bowles was laying the groundwork for Point Four aid to India, the Ford Foundation opened its own diplomatic relations with the newly independent government. Ford's director, former Marshall Plan Administrator Paul Hoffman, traveled to India in 1951. He arrived "with a completely open mind," determined only to do what was necessary to bolster Nehru's government against communism.[48] Nehru, by contrast, knew exactly what he wanted. India had tried top-down schemes, the prime minister explained to Hoffman, referring to an unsuccessful "Grow More Food" campaign launched in 1947. It hadn't worked because its monomaniacal focus on increased production ignored other needs. So Nehru proposed that Ford spend its money on community development. Hoffman proved a quick study, agreeing that "if democracy—political, economic, and social—was to be successful in India, it was imperative that a beginning was made to energise the roots from which the saplings could grow."[49]

The Ford Foundation had come to see its role in policymaking as that of an advance scout, running ahead of legislators to fund pilot projects, establish networks, and blaze the trail for government action. Thus, while the U.S. government supplied funds and expertise to India's national program, the Ford Foundation would commission studies, train experts, and launch policy experiments. For this, it would need its own specialists. On M. L. Wilson's recommendation, Ford hired the former head of community organization research at the Bureau of Agricultural Economics, Douglas Ensminger, to run its India office, which he did until 1971. Ensminger, a card-carrying communitarian, was the son of a tenant farmer. He held a degree in rural sociology from Cornell, and he had served in the BAE under Carl C. Taylor. He also came to his India post with significant prior exposure to Gandhism, having studied at the University of Missouri with a woman who had spent three months in India by Gandhi's side.[50]

Ensminger became the communitarians' man in India, and he brought nearly all of the leading lights in community studies out to India as consultants for Ford, including M. L. Wilson, Morris Opler, Milton Singer, and Robert Redfield. John Provinse, meanwhile, served as Director of Ford's South and Southeast Asia Overseas Development Programs. Ensminger's former boss at the BAE, Carl C. Taylor, visited India for a cumulative period of two years in the 1950s, alternating State Department stints with Ford-funded visits. By 1955, Taylor was reportedly fluent in Hindi.[51]

The "underlying goal" of community development, for Ensminger, was not to modernize agriculture but "to *recreate* a significant village culture."[52] Ford's focus was therefore on group dynamics. The foundation hired an expert from Kurt Lewin's National Training Laboratories for Group Development to explain the subject to Indian administrators. Taylor offered his own lectures on the subject, walking his Indian audience through all the social scientific research on the small group from the Hawthorne Studies to the findings of *The American Soldier*.[53] M. L. Wilson, for his part, assembled a library for the Ford Foundation's National Institute for Community Development and stocked it with the writings of John Dewey, Margaret Mead, Arthur E. Morgan, Kurt Lewin, and the BAE's rural sociologists.[54] Significantly, every lecture held at the National Institute was followed by a question period and then the breakup of the audience into discussion groups.[55] Ford also ran a series of seminars in democratic administrative methods, in which senior civil servants would practice small-group discussion techniques with their subordinates— corporate "human relations" for the Indian bureaucracy.[56]

THE COMMUNITY DEVELOPMENT PROGRAM began on October 2, 1952, Gandhi's birthday. As outlined in the bilateral aid agreement with the United States, the program initially covered 16,500 villages. But the program expanded with a rapidity that is hard to fathom. Within a decade, it had grown to thirty times its original size, covering 446,000 villages containing 253.2 million inhabitants.[57] By the beginning of 1965, it encompassed every village in India. In other words, in thirteen years, community development had gone from being a pilot

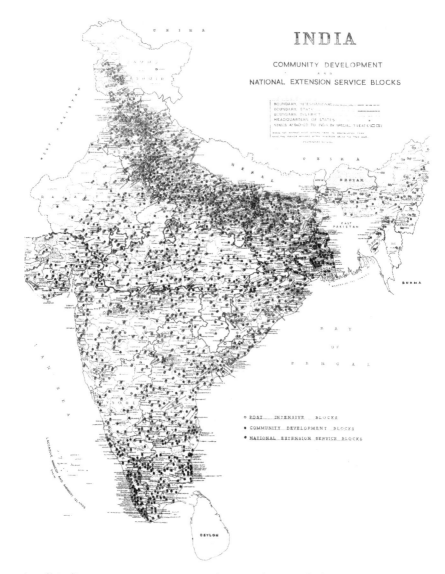

An all-India program: Map, c. 1956, showing the spread of community development blocks. (Jayaprakash Narayan Papers, Nehru Memorial Museum and Library)

project in one district in Uttar Pradesh to a development program covering, in India alone, over ten percent of the global population.

The sheer scale of the operation taxed the capacities of the Indian state. In Etawah, a single village-level worker might service four villages.

In the national program, exigencies of the national budget required workers to handle between ten and seventeen villages, with a combined population that could exceed ten thousand people.[58] That personnel strain redoubled community development's deference to the locality. Village-level workers made it their first order of business to identify and recruit "natural leaders" within the village who were sympathetic to the program and who could call meetings and initiate projects. It was the community leaders, then, who ran discussions and reported back to the village-level workers on the "felt needs" of the community. Those leaders had to supply material resources, too. Although state governments provided support at varying levels for seeds, livestock, technical guidance, and construction materials, the bulk of the resources were to come from the people themselves. Participation was the fuel that fed the system—both participation in meetings and in *shramdan,* volunteered labor for public service. That, too, was to be organized by the "natural leaders."

At the helm of the enormous but decentralized operation was the Community Projects Administration (CPA), run by the engineer-turned-community-organizer S. K. Dey. The CPA was an oddly shaped administrative object. In keeping with community development's holism, the CPA was not an independent ministry or department but rather, in Dey's words, "an organisation belonging to all the Development Ministries."[59] It commanded some funding to train its staff and hire village-level workers. But the village projects themselves, to the degree that they received government funding, were funded by the Ministry of Agriculture, state governments, and other ministries. The CPA was in principle a meta-agency, knitting together the strands of the developmental state into an unbroken fabric at the level of the village. On a more material level, this meant that the CPA wielded a very particular sort of power. It was, as the future president of India, Fakhruddin Ali Ahmed, put it, "virtually the only field agency for carrying out various development activities in the rural areas."[60] It was the only national development agency with boots on the ground.

Community development was thus central to the development apparatus of the Nehruvian state, although it has not always been recognized as such. Much more scholarly attention has been given to the high modernist aspirations of the Planning Commission, of which Nehru was the chairman. As a powerful but unelected arm of the Indian state, the Planning Commission was ideally positioned to circumvent the push and pull of politics and implement a technocratic vision of India's future.

Scholars have tended to focus on the second of the commission's five-year plans, the one that covered the period 1956–1961, as expressing the essence of Nehruvian state-driven development.

The visionary behind the second plan was P. C. Mahalanobis, a physicist and eager modernizer. Believing that India's "heavy industries must . . . be expanded with all possible speed," Mahalanobis pursued the development of the nation's manufacturing core with a zeal that baffled Western economists.[61] He brooked little criticism, though, and looked with undisguised envy toward the Soviet and Chinese models of industrialization. In those countries, the state had managed to shunt resources from the countryside toward large, state-controlled industries. Privileging industry over agriculture was never going to be a popular move in India, which remained largely agrarian, and so following the Soviet and Chinese models would require a certain degree of insulation from the will of voters. It required the concentration of decision-making power in the hands of a few far-seeing men: the men of the Planning Commission.

The imperatives of the Second Five-Year Plan, or at least the imperatives as Mahalanobis expressed them, seemed to leave little room for community development or any kind of decentralism. So how to make sense of the Planning Commission's simultaneous pursuit of Mahalanobis-style modernization and community development? The answer, as some scholars have recently begun to argue, is that the Mahalanobis moment was in many ways a limited affair. It was limited first by the resistance that the industrialization campaign met from rival ministries, dissenting economists, and wary politicians. But it was also limited in time. A full-fledged drive toward industrialization did not begin until the commencement of the Second Plan in 1956 and was quickly undermined by the foreign exchange crisis of 1957–1958.[62] In the third planning period, the Planning Commission restored the "first priority" to agriculture, which had been the focus of the First Plan.[63] An examination of the outlays for the first three plans helps put the Mahalanobis moment into perspective.

Indian plan spending

	First Plan (1952–1956)	Second Plan (1956–1961)	Third Plan (1961–1966)
Agriculture and community development	17.5%	11.8%	14%
Industry and mining	8.4%	18.5%	20%

It is not the absolute size of industry and mining that is so remarkable in the Second Plan so much as the sector's rapid rise between the first and second planning periods. That rise placed the industrial sector above agriculture and community development, but not overwhelmingly so.[64]

It is also useful to take an international perspective. The industrial dimensions of the Second Five-Year Plan are striking, to be sure, but mostly for how much they stand out against an Indian backdrop. From a global vantage point—one that includes South Korea, Indonesia, China, and the Soviet Union in its comparison class—what is notable about India is not how aggressive its modernization drive was but how committed it remained to decentralism, even as it undertook exercises in national economic planning. That had much to do with the legacy of Gandhi, who had been, after all, the leader of the Indian nationalist movement. Even during the Second Plan period, the ruling Congress Party remained the party of Gandhi and included Gandhians as well as hard-line statists. Nor were those Gandhians utopian thinkers, content to retreat from politics and occupy themselves with spiritual strivings. Economists and social theorists such as the Kumarappa brothers had translated Gandhi's prophetic vision into an actionable program, one based around a village economy, small-scale agriculture, and modest technology.[65] And that program clearly clashed with what Mahalanobis was offering.

Gandhians were not alone in their rural orientation. Across the political spectrum, politicians paid sincere tribute to village India. Their reasons were ideological but also practical: the villages were where the votes were. And so the manifesto of the Hindu right, K. R. Malkani's *Principles for a New Political Party* (1951), called for a decentralized landscape, drawing heavily on the same Anglophone regionalist intellectual tradition that had inspired Albert Mayer.[66] The Socialist Party, meanwhile, rejected the modernizing aspects of Marx and called for the establishment of village councils, proclaiming "a new era in village economy."[67] Leading socialist Jayaprakash Narayan elevated reverence for the village to a distinctive worldview, one that treated the individual "not as a particle of sand in an inorganic heap, but as a living cell in a larger organic community." Whereas the utilitarian conception of society championed individual welfare, Narayan's communitarian philosophy upheld "adjustment, conciliation, harmony and cooperation."[68]

Nehru, whose task it was to hold together the fissiparous Indian nation, was obliged to accommodate these many strands of thought, both within his party and to the left and right of it. It is likely, though, that on this issue his accommodation was not entirely reluctant. Nehru has been painted as an uncompromising modernizer, and it is not hard to find grandiose statements of his that would seem to confirm that description. But it is better to think of him as an eclectic thinker and subtle improviser, containing multitudes and given to exploring contradictory possibilities.[69] As Gandhi's named political heir, Nehru was perfectly capable of allowing his mind to wander down Gandhian pathways. Nehru's 1954 celebration of dams as the temples of modern India has appeared in textbooks in every Indian language.[70] But four years later, Nehru spoke out against the "dangerous outlook" that drove Indians to "want to show that we can build big dams and do big things." It was the "disease of giganticism," he charged, and it had infected developmental thought.[71] Even Nehru, in other words, could think small.

The big and the small wove together in India's five-year plans, which sought to industrialize India *and* to improve its villages, even if those two projects sometimes contradicted each other. Community development occupied a central position in the Indian plans. For Nehru, it was "the dynamo providing the motive force" of the first plan.[72] Although community development had started as a "tail attached to the Planning Commission," he noted in 1956—the year that the Second Five-Year Plan came into force—"the tail has begun to wag the dog."[73] In that year, he promoted the Community Projects Administration into the Ministry of Community Development, although he maintained its status as a meta-agency.[74] "Of course you want steel factories," Nehru explained to the Indian parliament in 1957. "But in the final analysis growth depends on the growth of rural India, that means the growth of the villager and the villager becoming self-reliant, self-dependent and cooperative—on the development of the village panchayat [i.e., the village council], on the development of the village cooperative. Both these things are included in the community development schemes."[75]

It is possible that the Planning Commission included community development as a sop to the Gandhians, a price reluctantly paid out of political necessity by men whose true priorities lay elsewhere. But that would not explain how personally the leadership of the Commission seemed to take the matter. Few key decisions in the Ministry of Community Development were made without Nehru's participation, and he directed the state governments to give the community projects "top priority."[76] "I was always amazed by the ease of getting an appointment to see Nehru," remembered Ensminger. "Never once was I asked what I wanted to see Nehru about, never once was I put off. . . . I had continuous entree to Nehru on community development."[77] V. T. Krishnamachari, Deputy Chairman of the Planning Commission from 1953 until 1960, had been another early and forceful advocate of community techniques and published a book on community development in 1958. He regarded it as the "largest single contribution the Planning Commission has made to the country."[78] Tarlok Singh, the Commission's Secretary, also took a "very strong interest" and was "forever championing the need for . . . village institutions," Ensminger observed.[79] Mayer, Dey, and Chester Bowles's staff found in Singh an eager interlocutor, one willing to enter into lengthy and probing discussions about the nature of rural development.

With the enthusiastic backing of the Chairman, Deputy Chairman, and Secretary of the Planning Commission and with the sympathy of Gandhians, Hindu nationalists, and socialists, community development advanced without facing any serious political opposition—a luxury that Mahalanobis's scheme of state-directed industrialization did not enjoy. Nevertheless, by its five-year mark, it was clear that the hoped-for "quiet revolution" in the villages had yet to materialize. A high-profile study by the Planning Commission named centralization as the problem. Too much of the program still remained in the hands of government officials who would never "adequately appreciate the local needs and circumstances" of the villagers.[80]

The study recommended "democratic decentralisation," a thoroughgoing restructuring of Indian government that would devolve decision-making power to the villages.[81] It was an elaborate three-tiered scheme of elected panchayats (councils) drawn from the villages, block councils drawn from the panchayats, and district councils drawn from the block councils. Development plans would originate with the "felt needs" of the villagers and flow upward through the councils to the Planning Commission. The system would, for the first time in Indian history, require the election of village officials and would, in theory, ground the entire planning apparatus in those village-level elections.

The proposal was a serious gamble, a frontal assault on the top-down planning model. Democratic decentralization challenged the authority of all appointed local officials and seemed to fly in the face of the industry-centered model of planning. There was some constitutional precedent for it: Gandhians had included in the Constitution an injunction to the states to "take steps to organise village panchayats and endow

Bottom-up planning: Cartoon from Ministry of Community Development's journal *Kurukshetra,* depicting village panchayats spinning parts of India's Five-Year Plan (December 1959). Courtesy of *Kurukshetra*, (Publications Division), Ministry of Information & Broadcasting, Government of India, New Delhi.

them with such powers and authority as may be necessary to enable them to function as units of self-government."[82] But that was a "directive principle," not a mandate, and it had idled unimplemented. What the study team now proposed was a reconfiguration of Indian government along those Gandhian lines. The plan acquired a name: *panchayati raj,* the reign of the village councils.

It would have been easy for the Planning Commission to stall and let community development wither on the vine. Nothing required the Commission to adopt the far-ranging recommendations of its internal report. But the records of the Planning Commission register great enthusiasm for democratic decentralization among the commissioners.[83] The Commission agreed that "the foundation of any democratic structure had to be democracy in the village."[84] And so, with Nehru's blessing, the Planning Commission directed the states to make immediate provisions for democratic decentralization.

On October 2, 1959, Gandhi's birthday, Rajasthan became the first state to transition to panchayati raj. Witnessing the ceremony in which appointed Rajasthani officials abdicated their posts to make way for elected officers, S. K. Dey reflected, "Never have I known people in the seats of power undertaking voluntary liquidation of themselves. As I watched the vast gathering under the rising and setting sun, I had a sense of history flowing in my veins."[85] By 1962, eight other states had implemented panchayati raj and the rest, save Jammu and Kashmir, were on their way.[86] In the era of the Second Five-Year Plan, the Planning Commission had decentralized the government.

THE "VILLAGE FETISH," as one U.S. observer called it, ran deep within postcolonial Indian political culture.[87] There was one thinker, though, who seemed immune to its magnetic lure. B. R. Ambedkar, the chief author of India's constitution and the political leader of the untouchables, never shared his country's enthusiasm for village life. Where caste Hindus (and sentimental U.S. observers) saw a miniature welfare state bound by ties of reciprocity and fellow feeling, Ambedkar saw a slave society. Village India was the place where caste ties were strongest and where untouchables were compelled to undertake the least pleasant tasks, live in poverty, and abase themselves daily through a comprehensive routine of material and symbolic humiliations. "The average Hindu is always in ecstasy when he speaks of the Indian village," Ambedkar observed, but only for the reason that white Southerners in the United

States praise Old Dixie.[88] "What is the village but a sink of localism, a den of ignorance, narrow-mindedness and communalism?"[89]

Ambedkar had a point. If the villages of India were communities, then they were inegalitarian ones. The caste system was the most notorious manifestation of that inequality, but it was not the only one. Landlords monopolized tillable land, forcing many cultivators to work as landless laborers or sharecroppers. The government's frequent land reform campaigns had done little to change this, since rural landholders wielded their considerable political power time and again to block any substantial redistribution.[90] One might also mention the crushing patriarchal system that condemned many women to live in ritual seclusion, which exerted its maximum force in rural areas.

Communitarians from the United States at times had difficulty registering the extent of India's rural inequality. The United States, for all of its own undeniable inequities, was unusual for how much equality it had achieved in its rural areas, particularly in the distribution of land. The historical conditions that had given rise to that rough equality had been far from just—a centuries-long history of warfare, Indian removal, and settler colonialism—but the result was that in many parts of the United States, smallholders enjoyed power and standing. For men like M. L. Wilson and Carl C. Taylor, both of whom were raised on family farms in Iowa, inequality was the consequence of the intrusion of commerce or other modernizing influences, not an inbuilt attribute of rural society.[91] Although rural sociologists and anthropologists were harsh critics of Southern racism and sharecropping, they rarely saw India as analogous to the U.S. South. Instead, their cultural pluralism—mixed with a healthy dose of Orientalism—inclined them to regard India's religious traditions with sympathy and to pass lightly over evidence of inequality or rural oppression. Confronted with peasants, they saw farmers.[92]

The disinclination of communitarians to consider village inequality, and indeed to dwell on *any* type of rural politics, could be seen in Albert Mayer's Etawah project. As a matter of principle, Mayer believed the villages of Etawah to be nascent communities, capable of solving problems cooperatively. This could lead Mayer to view the village through rose-colored lenses, as when he concluded that caste was a "calm and stabilizing institution"—a source of cohesion rather than, as Ambedkar saw it, a machine for producing "cruelties and atrocities."[93] Mayer enforced a policy of "complete impartiality and aloofness" among his workers when it came to divisive issues such as caste.[94] It was a strategic stance, but it also stemmed from Mayer's conviction that village-level conflicts were ultimately squabbles—"almost like the feuds in Kentucky"—rather than legitimate expressions of discontent.[95]

For all his interest in democratic participation, Mayer deferred easily to patriarchy, too. Women "don't take much part in village life," he observed, because of their ritual seclusion.[96] Noting that his male employees were "fearful of working with women colleagues or with village women," Mayer shrugged his shoulders—the project would just have to "do without" women.[97] When women in Etawah held meetings and even staged protests, Mayer took little note. His co-author McKim Marriott, a former student of Robert Redfield's, made even less of them. The protests, Marriott explained to Mayer, were merely the result of the "hysteroid or hysterical-like psychodynamics behind much feminine behavior."[98]

A similar attitude of deference to prevailing social arrangements marked the national community development program. Of course, development projects of all kinds tend to leave hierarchies intact, for the simple reason that the well-off and powerful are usually well positioned to benefit disproportionately from broad efforts to stimulate growth. But the "grassroots" orientation of community development exacerbated that tendency by turning the program directly over to local "leaders." "The wise gram sevak [village-level worker] will be always searching for leaders," advised Douglas Ensminger in the government's official *Guide to Community Development* (1957). "It needs to be said forcefully that only as the natural leaders of the village are effectively mobilized and the gram sevak has a firm, friendly working relationship with them, will the community and national extension programmes become and remain a people's programme."[99]

In 1957, the government codified that arrangement in the Gram Sahayak (village helper) program, by which non-officials were deputized into the community development apparatus. Within five years, it counted over four million Gram Sahayaks.[100] Unsurprisingly, those recruited were brought in because they were deemed "natural leaders," which usually meant that they owned property or held some other form of established power. A survey by the National Institute of Community Development found that 55.4% of those identified as "leaders" by the community development agencies were Brahmins, and fewer than one percent were agricultural laborers.[101]

Panchayati raj, which augmented that ad hoc recruitment of "natural leaders" with formal elections, seemed as if it might change things. The

Planning Commission study that had called for democratic decentralization had also suggested reserving seats for untouchables and women on the panchayats. Some localities did this, but reservations proved insufficient to unseat the rural elite, whose members deftly used their social power to engineer the outcomes of elections or simply to order the elected women and untouchables around. Morris Opler, the former community analyst in the Manzanar camp, made the following observation of an "old and respected" untouchable man who had managed to gain election to the panchayat:

> It soon became apparent that he was the messenger boy of the group, bearing notes from the headman to others and giving notice of meetings to members. When the group met he sat quietly on the bare ground to one side; he did not feel free to sit on the cloth with the others. Once when I was about to take a picture of some of the assemblymen, a discussion arose as to whether this man should be invited to sit on a cot with some others. It was finally decided that he should squat on the ground in the foreground, and there he appears in the picture.[102]

With untouchables habitually treated in that manner, the likelihood that the panchayats would serve as vehicles of democracy was slim.

Policymakers were well aware of clash between the democratic idiom of community development and the rigid hierarchies of Indian rural society. It would have been hard for them not to be since nearly every evaluation report on community development by the mid-1950s commented on it. Yet little was done. In 1961, the Ministry of Community Development commissioned a high-profile study of the "welfare of the weaker sections of the village community." It conceded the problem but did not recommend a change of course. Rather, it suggested a redoubling of effort—more participation, more power to the panchayati raj institutions, more thinking small. (E. F. Schumacher, the author of *Small is Beautiful,* contributed a report to the study.)[103]

That was the Ministry's general line: the problems of the villages were deficits of community and, if the village programs faltered, that was merely because decentralization hadn't been taken far enough. Its leaders rarely entertained the notion that something might be amiss with the communities themselves. When it was suggested to S. K. Dey that the plight of the "weaker sections" would be best explored not in community councils but by groups composed exclusively of members of the lower orders, Dey rejected the idea out of hand. History was made, he insisted, "not by representatives of the poor sections of the community but by members of the richer and privileged strata of society" who "took up cudgels for the poorer sections of the community."[104] A poor man "does not fight," explained Dey, "nor can he provide the leadership. He can line up for a cause. It is only the middle-class or the richer class that can champion a cause."[105] The domination of community development programs by a rural elite, in other words, was not a problem. It was, for Dey, the point.

COMMUNITY DEVELOPMENT was supposed to work through the social order of the village. If that meant placing faith in landlords, caste leaders, and patriarchs, community developers did not much mind. They saw villages as places of harmony, where the powerful protected the powerless and where hierarchy was sanctified by venerable traditions. Their vision was a fundamentally Gandhian one, stressing love over justice and communal duties over individual rights. At the heart of it was the notion that the village was a fully functioning micropolis, a self-sufficient society within itself, with its own forms of welfare and provision.

The Gandhian vision of the village contained both fictional and factual elements, and what was true and what was not depended on whom you asked. But there was one place in India where the Gandhian understanding of rural life seemed undeniably far-fetched: the southwestern state of Kerala. At independence, the area that would become Kerala (the state itself was not formed until 1956) experienced grinding poverty and a punishingly oppressive caste system. There was nothing unique in either of those, although Kerala's rural conditions were among the worst in India. What was unique about the place was that it lacked villages. It had them in the administrative sense but not in the sociological one. Common lands were rare, as were communal economic arrangements, and Kerala's extraordinarily dense population was spread out evenly across the countryside, like jam on toast, rather than clustered in villages like mounds of sugar. As its chief minister observed, Kerala lacked "the system of the village community" entirely.[106]

It is hard to say what role Kerala's unique patterns of habitation played in the state's political history because Kerala was exceptional in other important ways, too. It had an unusual family structure, a starkly unequal caste system (prompting Swami Vivekananda to conclude that

89

Keralites were "all lunatics"), extraordinary rates of cash-crop agriculture, large populations of Muslims and Christians, chronic food shortages, extreme population density, and a long tradition of political violence.[107] But nearly all of those factors pointed in the same direction: the bonds that tied the lower orders to their social betters elsewhere in India had been, in Kerala, severed. Rural inequality that usually came wrapped in finely articulated traditions and accompanied by some compensatory social protections appeared in Kerala as naked oppression. It was thus understandable when, in the elections of 1957, Kerala became exceptional in yet another way. It elected a communist government, the first democratically elected communist government of any significant size in world history.[108]

The Keralite communists took office in the midst of community development's expansion and just as the central government turned toward panchayati raj. Since both community development and the establishment of panchayats were matters for the states, it fell to the newly elected government to formulate a policy with regard to the communitarian institutions. The prospects, from the perspective of the Ministry of Community Development, were not good. Indian communists had taken a predictably Marxist line on community development, complaining that it glorified "the idiocy, the backwardness of village life as it is today," as one parliamentarian put it.[109] The Keralite communists largely agreed. E. M. S. Namboodiripad, the political theorist who became Kerala's chief minister with the 1957 elections, denounced the community development program as "a total failure" and "seriously defective" in its conception.[110] What is more, Kerala's communist party had been strongly influenced by the Soviet Union and had formed itself into what sociologist Patrick Heller has described as "a Leninist party, characterized by top-down organizational control over its mass organizations" and "wary of an autonomous civil society."[111]

Although Kerala's communists appeared likely to reject communitarianism in favor of state centralism, they moved in the opposite direction. On Republic Day in 1957, Namboodiripad announced that Kerala would undertake a massive program of administrative decentralization, not only devolving developmental responsibilities to the panchayats, as was standard in panchayati raj schemes, but also giving them significant responsibilities over revenue administration and regulation.[112] The key to this strategy, for Namboodiripad, was that Kerala was in the midst of a rural insurgency—which is how the communists had been elected in the first place. His support of decentralization, he explained, "arises from the fact that it helps the working people in their day-to-day struggles against their oppressors and exploiters."[113] Whereas S. K. Dey had believed that decentralization would strengthen village communities, in Kerala there were no villages to strengthen. And without vertical social ties binding peasants to landlords, decentralization would mean the strengthening of horizontal ties between members of subordinated groups, which could then be mobilized toward an assault on power holders. Namboodiripad's vision of community development was thus not about neutralizing partisan spirits within the village but about stirring them up. The panchayats were, for him, political bodies, and he welcomed the entry of peasants' organizations, students' organizations, and women's organizations into them.

Namboodiripad's politicized version of community control did not get very far. Although the communists had been elected democratically, their redistributive program alarmed their many opponents, who took to the streets. Violence flared up on both sides and Nehru, after a moment's hesitation, invoked emergency powers to dismiss the government in 1959, two years after its election. The incoming Congress government kept the panchayats running but diminished their powers. Nevertheless, communists had managed to push through some land reform bills during their brief tenure and, more importantly, continued for the next two decades to channel the political energies of tenants, wage earners, lower castes, and peasants toward agricultural reform, which Kerala achieved piecemeal.

By the 1970s, Kerala was still poor but, because of the extraordinary strength and persistence of its political activism, it had reversed many of the inequalities that had marred its economy in the early twentieth century.[114] Remarkably, it had transformed itself into the state with the highest life expectancy, lowest infant mortality, lowest birth rate, highest literacy rate, and most female-heavy sex ratio in all of India. Development experts took note and began to speak of the "Kerala model," characterized by the unexpected combination of high poverty with high welfare and equality. The Kerala model became an invitation to rethink how development itself was measured. The practice today of scoring development by factors other than simple per-capita income, for example by the Human Development Index, is in part the result of Kerala's anomalous history.[115]

*　　*　　*

91

THE KERALITE version of grassroots mobilization encouraged political action by large associations of peasants, students, workers, and
other subordinated groups. The results were largely positive, endowing
the inhabitants of the state with a surprisingly high quality of life, given
their severe poverty. The story was different in the rest of India. There,
men like Albert Mayer and S. K. Dey put a premium on grassroots participation, but with the understanding that the "grass roots" was the
village, and the village was a cross-class, cross-caste social unit in which
longstanding forms of social organization were upheld. As Mayer and
Dey would discover, their version of the grass roots implied very different developmental outcomes.

At the heart of community development was the imperative to elicit
villagers' "felt needs." Those needs would then determine the projects
undertaken and, since the villagers had expressed a desire for those projects, they could then be expected to donate labor and resources. The
whole thing depended, therefore, on getting villagers to express their
true desires, and that in turn depended on the implicit but fundamental
idea that village councils were the proper vehicles through which those
desires could be expressed. India's community development program, in
other words, had identified "what the people want" with "what the village wants," assuming the village to be a corporate body capable of
articulating and acting upon the general will. And although the tendency
of the spokesmen for the village to come from the powerful, landed
classes within rural life was widely acknowledged, Dey at least took such
men to be appropriate custodians of the villages they represented.

Shunting the will of the people through the village community had
serious consequences. It meant, first of all, that any "felt needs" that
threatened village solidarity—such as a desire for land reform, the abolition of caste hierarchies, or sexual equality—were immediately ruled out
of bounds by community development's refusal to tolerate "factions."
The development projects that village councils chose tended to be modest:
wells, roads, community buildings, and so forth. Some of these improvements were of general use, but much of the time their benefits skewed
toward the wealthy. Anything that increased agricultural output, for
instance, was of little interest to those who worked the land for wages,
since it only increased the wealth and thus power of their employers.
Community development programs targeting women or the "weaker
sections" of the village were rare and heavily circumscribed by the
implicit prohibition of anything that might challenge the authority of the

"natural leaders," on whom the entire program depended for its imple-mentation.[116]

Community development's bias toward the rural elite was not just a problem for the distribution of its benefits. It was a problem for the accomplishment of *any* of its goals. Lacking the ability to offer real incentives to most inhabitants of the village, community developers scrambled to generate the "grassroots participation" that the program fed on. The problem was particularly acute when it came to labor. In theory, it would come in the form of *shramdan,* voluntary labor donated to the commonweal. But the upper orders refused to work, for fear of what it might suggest about their status, and the poor worked only when forced. Shramdan drives became occasions for the upper castes to enlist their social inferiors into semi-coerced *corvée* labor on behalf of projects whose benefits clearly accrued to the rich.[117] Over the career of the com-munity development program, "donations" of labor and other resources by villagers steadily declined, leaving the government to shoulder more and more of the cost.[118] This was, as one group of social scientists put it, "grass without roots."[119]

As participation dried up, the program came increasingly to resemble the bureaucratic leviathan that Mayer and Dey had hoped it would never become. Lacking grassroots involvement, community development quickly fell prey to the desires of the few genuine stakeholders in the system, the officials in its employ. Mayer noted the descent of community develop-ment into bureaucratic ineffectiveness but blamed the problem on the national program's rapid growth. "This rate of expansion is altogether too fast for effective work or anything like effective work," he com-plained to Tarlok Singh.[120] Yet it is hard to imagine how slowing things down would have prevented the rural elite from hijacking the program, since even in Mayer's meticulous Etawah project, development had been limited to projects that kept the existing social relations intact. Indeed, it was starting to look as if the participatory zeal that Mayer had boasted of at Etawah had not been the result of genuine enthusiasm but of the extremely close supervision of some of the most powerful men in India.[121]

Hired to elicit the participation of the poor but unable to rely on it, community development officers found other ways of making do. Sometimes they fabricated results. One anthropologist noted how even a meeting that went entirely unattended could yield a satisfying report in the hands of the right village-level worker. "Every item of business was completed with some kind of action recorded or with appropriately filled-in lists of names, volunteers, or pledges of funds." What was an "utter failure" in developmental terms could still be—and often was— "a paper success."[122] Even S. K. Dey acknowledged that many of the community projects were mere "Potemkin villages" where forms were filled out but no meaningful action was taken.[123]

Community developers also found themselves relying on a sort of backhanded authoritarianism, designed to carry out government plans but under the sign of "participation." One social scientist observed this process in action at a village planning meeting. In principle, the village-level worker was supposed to elicit the "felt needs" of the villagers, guide them through deliberations until they produced a local plan, and then pass that plan up through the various levels of government. In reality, the worker "presented the programs in which the development departments were interested, explained their merits, and by some mixture of persuasion, bullying, smiles, and frowns, induced the meeting to pass resolutions adopting specific targets under at least some of the departmental programs." Having gotten the panchayat to sign off on the government's plans, he departed, leaving no copy of the resolutions and leaving the villagers with "only a vague memory of what they had agreed to."[124] Whenever villagers objected to this arrangement, the social scientist noted, the government would send an official to brusquely "answer" their objections.

That sort of backhanded authoritarianism could arise in implementation as well as in planning. An unusually candid field report from a community organizer working on a Ford Foundation project in Delhi overseen by Albert Mayer gives some sense of how. The organizer had been given the unfortunate task of eliciting local participation for a hygiene program in which residents would be vaccinated and have their homes sprayed with DDT. The female "participants," however, strongly objected; they believed DDT and the vaccines to be poisonous. Their fears were not irrational: the colonial state had a long history of violent and counterproductive "hygiene" campaigns and, as it turns out, the women were entirely correct that DDT was poisonous, as medical researchers were already beginning to learn. When the Ford Foundation's health officials moved to vaccinate the women's children, the women resisted, threatening violence.

As "felt needs" went, the Delhi women's determination to protect their children from vaccination could hardly have been more clear. And yet Ford's community organizer did not see it that way. Presented with

A village worker (in vest) leading health officials to local homes, as depicted in the Ministry of Community Development's journal *Kurukshetra* (June 1955). Courtesy of *Kurukshetra*, (Publications Division), Ministry of Information & Broadcasting, Government of India, New Delhi.

a conflict between what the women wanted and what the health officials did, she deferred immediately to the health officials. Addressing the women, she "explained to them the role of Government as well as [the Delhi Municipal] Corporation, and how they endeavored to protect the life of the people." She followed that up with further lectures on hygiene (stressing especially the importance of trimming nails) and by distributing DDT powder for the children's hair. As her report makes clear, she had sought enthusiastic participation in the DDT program but would settle for grumbling acquiescence. In this, as in many other instances, encouraging the "participation" of the community did not mean encouraging poor people to craft their own plans but rather eliciting their consent to the government's programs.[125]

The bureaucratization of community development reached a climax in 1962–1963, during India's border war with China. Wars are often times of centralization, and this war was no different. Despite their appreciation for decentralist principles, the members of the Planning Commission all agreed that the Chinese invasion called for the mobilization of a coordinated, regimented national effort. And having concluded that, their eyes turned toward the community development program, with its village-level workers posted throughout the countryside. Although the program was officially an instrument of democratic decentralization, Nehru and his fellow planners recognized its potential for a different use: top-down mobilization.

On Republic Day, 1963, the government established the Village Volunteer Force, a national guard ostensibly designed to protect India from Chinese invasion. The event was a remarkable display of all-India coordination. On the morning of that day, all village assemblies in India (with the exception of some in Punjab) convened. They took out "community listening sets"—radios that the Ministry of Community Development had distributed, many "pre-tuned" so that they could only be used to listen to the All-India Radio Station. At 9:00am, each village assembly listened to a speech by Jawaharlal Nehru. At precisely 9:30, each unfurled the national flag.[126] The entire day proceeded in that fashion, meticulously planned.

The government's schedule for the Republic Day rallies illustrates the tension within the Ministry of Community Development between its commitment to "bottom-up" methods and the importance it attached to achieving national goals. After the flags were flown, the schedule indicated that "a tentative programme of work will be discussed and an appeal will be made to the people to donate free labour for the minimum period of twelve days in the year."[127] But however "tentative" the program or open-ended the "discussion," the next steps were already laid out. A Village Volunteer Force and a Defence Labour Bank were to be established, a register was to be opened for community members to pledge their labor, and initial donations were to be taken. Next, all the members of the community were to take a prewritten pledge in which they expressed their "high appreciation of the valiant struggle of the . . . martyrs who have laid down their lives defending the honor and integrity of our motherland," conveyed their "firm resolve . . . to drive out the aggressor from the sacred soil of India," and promised the "mobilisation of all our resources, both human and material, . . . to the national effort."[128] Within a year, nearly 15 million had joined the Village Volunteer Forces, and villagers had "donated" 1.8 million rupees and 22 million days of labor.[129] Community development had become a handle by which the state could grasp its rural populace.

FOR THOSE most intimately involved with community development, the failure of the movement to inspire the grass roots came as a bitter disappointment, accompanied by much finger-pointing. But for many Indian policymakers, the real problem with community development was not its inability to nurture community participation but its inability to generate abundant harvests. By the late 1950s, the shortcomings of the program in that regard had become painfully clear. A sharp drop in food-grain output in 1957–1958—temporary, as it turned out—first drew attention to India's agricultural shortages.[130] In 1959, a pair of influential reports on community development, one by the Ford Foundation and the other by the United Nations, raised further alarms. India was facing a crisis of "overwhelming gravity" and must make agriculture the "top priority programme objective," declared the Ford commission.[131] The UN team, with equal urgency, warned that "all forces in India must be marshalled" against the "overshadowing danger of starvation."[132]

Taking these warnings seriously would mean a substantial reorientation of community development. In 1952, when he had unveiled the program, Nehru had explained that community projects were valuable "not so much for the material achievement they would bring about but much more so because they seem to build up the community."[133] Now, however, that material achievements were drastically needed, the government reconsidered the holistic nature of the program. In 1960, the Ministry of Community Development instructed its village-level workers to devote eighty percent of their time to agriculture.[134] Even that seemed too little for policymakers, and there were prominent calls for the workers to drop *all* other activities and work exclusively on agriculture.[135]

The tipping point came with Nehru's death in 1964, which robbed the community development program of its most devoted sponsor. The new prime minister, Lal Bahadur Shastri, lacked Nehru's appreciation for communal institutions. Shastri informed Dey that whereas Nehru had felt "full confidence in the people," Shastri himself did not "share his optimism."[136] To the Chief Ministers, Shastri announced that "the Community Development Department should for the next one year do nothing except concentrate on the question of increase of agricultural production."[137] Shastri's brief reign proved to be gentle in comparison to that of Indira Gandhi, Nehru's daughter. Upon becoming prime minister in 1966, Gandhi transferred Dey to the dead-end Ministry of Mines and Metals and brought Dey's Ministry of Community Development under the control of the Ministry of Agriculture, thus turning the panchayats and all the other programs of democratic decentralization into auxiliaries of the agricultural program.

Under Gandhi's production-centered regime, what remained of community development crumbled. She reduced the central government's community development grants to levels well below what was needed to run the programs, forcing development officers to go hat in hand to the state governments, which were rarely more generous.[138] The careful balance between centralization and decentralization that Nehru had cultivated gave way to stark authoritarianism when Gandhi declared a state of emergency in 1975–1977. The training centers for panchayati raj officials and for village workers were abolished or transferred to the states. What institutional presence community development retained on the ground had degenerated, in the words of one embittered development officer, into "a mere programme of distributing chemical fertilisers."[139]

WHEN THE community developers met the modernization theorists at MIT in 1957, they disagreed about many things. But one central confusion dominated the conversation. What was the point of community development? Was it to carry the demands of the people to the center or to carry the directives of the center to the people? It was an important question because the institutional apparatus that community development put into place could point in either direction. By establishing chains of communication between the villages and the government, community development could either decentralize the government or consolidate state power in the villages. Community developers in India hoped for the former but by the 1960s conceded that they had inadvertently accomplished the latter.

There are a few ways one might understand community development's transformation into an instrument for state penetration into the countryside. The first possibility is that community development had never been anything but a tool of modernization and central control—a hypothesis that has been developed, in subtle form, by Partha Chatterjee.[140] That reading is consonant with the tendency to read all forms of development in the 1945–1965 period as parts of a large modernization drive. But although interpreting community development as modernization helps make sense of some of the actions of the Ministry of Community Development, it is a less helpful guide to the intentions that stood behind them. It ignores what community developers had to say for themselves and the many ways in which they explicitly distanced themselves from modernization. It also ignores the deep-rooted ambivalence about modernization that could be found within the U.S. government and, to a much greater degree, within the Indian one.

A second hypothesis, proposed by Albert Mayer, S. K. Dey, and other architects of India's community development program, is that community development was genuinely decentralist but that, in the end, it was undermined by the modernizers and by an entrenched bureaucracy. This, too, is a Modernization Comes to Town story: it positions community development as a liberating alternative momentarily pursued before the forces of centralization took over. This reading captures the ideological nature of community development in the way that the previous one did not. Yet in pinning the blame solely on external forces, it declines to ask whether there might have been *reasons* the grassroots program withered and was reduced to a bureaucratic husk.

There is a third, more unsettling, scenario. Community development was genuinely decentralist in its orientation, and it commanded a surprising amount of support. When it appeared to falter, the government did not abandon it but reinforced it with panchayati raj. And yet the vision of the village community that was hardwired into the program proved to be its Achilles' heel. In channeling rural democracy through the village, it bolstered the power of the rural elite and circumscribed its own ability to meet or even comprehend the needs of most Indians. The contrast case is Kerala, where the village as an institution was noticeably weak and where decentralization therefore gave rise to important demands—for land reform, caste abolition, workers' rights—that simply never arose elsewhere. But because the larger all-India program proved both uninterested in and incapable of pursuing such reforms, it could not engage participation of most villagers. Without that participation, it ultimately turned into a well-funded partnership between the rural elite and government officials.

The tendency of community development to do little more than bolster the status quo in the countryside was, for those concerned with the fate of rural India, a tragic outcome. But by another calculus, it was an intriguing result. Development was not the only thing the U.S. government desired within the context of the Cold War. It also wanted political stability, particularly in rural areas. Thus, soon after community development debuted as a tool of development, it came into currency as a form of counterinsurgency, a weapon for putting down peasant rebellions. The United States would perfect that art in the Philippines, to which the Indian style of community development was exported.

4

ON MAY 24, 1943—the four hundredth anniversary of Copernicus's death—ten "modern pioneers of science" received citations for their contributions to "that democratic way of living which enabled such geniuses as Copernicus."[1] The ceremony was a regal affair, staged in Carnegie Hall and featuring a message from President Roosevelt. The honorees included Albert Einstein, Walt Disney, John Dewey, Henry Ford, and Orville Wright. Yet one honoree stood out from the group. Unlike the others, he was not a household name and did not live in the United States. He was Y. C. James Yen, from Sichuan, China.

Although not yet widely known in the United States, Yen was rapidly acquiring a devoted following of prominent U.S. liberals. Two years after his Copernican citation, the novelist Pearl Buck wrote an admiring book about Yen's work in China and made plans, before her death, to write his biography.[2] Supreme Court Justice William O. Douglas declared Yen to be a "Christ-like person," possessing "the same kind of personal magnetism that Saint Paul must have acquired in a blinding vision as he rode toward Damascus."[3] Nelson Rockefeller, Henry Ford, J. P. Morgan, Philip Morris, General Electric, and the Carnegie Corporation were among Yen's bankrollers. So was the Reader's Digest Association—to the tune of $600,000—and by the end of the 1950s Yen had become the single-most-profiled figure in the history of the *Reader's Digest*, including in an article drafted by William Lederer, co-author of *The Ugly American*.[4]

It was fitting that *Reader's Digest,* an instrument for bringing literature to the masses, would warm to Yen. For Yen had made his name leading a mass literacy campaign. By developing a simplified thousand-character system for Chinese writing and publishing the *People's 1,000*

Character Primer in it, Yen hoped to lower the bar to literacy among workers and peasants. Reliable numbers on how extensive this campaign was are hard to come by, although Yen reported to George Marshall that his movement had trained 27 million people in the simplified system.[5] "Mr. Yen, I like your idea," Henry Ford told him appreciatively upon cutting him a check for $10,000. "You go about mass educating people the way I go about mass producing cars."[6]

Ford was right. There was an unmistakable resemblance between Ford's assembly-line methods and Yen's mass education techniques. But in the mid-1920s Yen's concerns widened. His interest in the mechanics of literacy gave way to a much broader interest in the problems of poverty, disease, and ignorance, which he regarded fundamentally as questions of culture. He also moved his operations from the city to the countryside. By the time the Japanese invasion of 1937 ended his work in North China, Yen had developed a community-centered approach that emphasized the importance of existing folkways and starting "at the rice-roots, with the people."[7] Discarding Fordism, Yen embraced a brand of communitarianism not much different from that of New Deal agrarians such as M. L. Wilson, Carl C. Taylor, and Arthur E. Morgan.[8]

Liberals in the United States took note. Perhaps Yen's organization, reaching deep into the Chinese countryside, might serve as a counterweight to Mao Zedong's communist movement, which had also grasped the importance of a "rice-roots" approach. In fact, the connection between Yen and Mao was significantly closer than most of Yen's U.S. supporters knew. Mao had worked as a political organizer in Yen's mass education campaigns, writing his own, more radical version of Yen's *1,000 Character Primer* (and perhaps adapting techniques for his own later "campaigns").[9] But in the United States Yen was taken as a foil to Mao. Douglas introduced him to President Truman as the "one man who has done more to bring about a democratic front in the world than anyone else."[10] With the backing of both Douglas and George Marshall, Yen convinced Truman that ten percent of U.S. aid to China should be set aside for rural reconstruction.[11]

With Truman's blessing, the U.S. Congress wrote what was known as the "Jimmy Yen Provision" into the Economic Aid Act of 1948, earmarking ten percent of the $275 million in China aid for rural reconstruction, to be dispensed by a five-member board that included Yen. The Sino-American Joint Commission on Rural Reconstruction, as it was called, only managed to spend $9 million before Mao's communist revolution ousted it from mainland China.[12] Still, liberals claimed that it was in the provinces where Yen's program had gotten under way that communists had encountered the most stubborn resistance. "What a different story might have been told in China if this alternative to Communist strategy had been started a few years earlier," reflected Paul Hoffman, the former administrator of the Marshall Plan and president of the Ford Foundation.[13]

Mao's victory ended Yen's career in mainland China, but he did not have to look hard for work. The revolution had, if anything, increased Yen's standing in the United States by suggesting that village work could forestall communism. For anxious Cold War liberals, the question was simply how and where to put Yen to use. Prominent U.S. politicians formed an "international committee" of Yen's mass education movement to determine how best to deploy Yen. In its various incarnations, that committee would count as members William O. Douglas, Eleanor Roosevelt, Chester Bowles, Paul Hoffman, Walter Reuther, Marshall Field, Henry Luce, and Pearl Buck.[14]

At the urging of the committee, Yen toured Asia in 1952, searching for a country from which to build an international anticommunist movement for rural reconstruction. He visited India (meeting with Albert Mayer and touring Etawah), Indonesia, Thailand, Pakistan, Lebanon, and Syria. But Yen felt most drawn to the Philippines, where he met receptive civic leaders—men of the Rotary Club, the Lions Club, and the Junior Chamber of Commerce—who seemed eager to explore the possibilities of community development. The committee approved of Yen's choice, and Roosevelt suggested that Yen take Mayer's Etawah as his model there.[15] If Mayer had been the catalyst for a new approach to development in India, Yen was to be the catalyst for a new approach to fighting communism in the Philippines.

YEN ARRIVED in 1952 in a country on the verge of revolution. As in many other parts of the global South, the issue was land. Philippine land tenure had been drastically unequal since at least the sixteenth century, when the Spanish empire began to construct a hacienda system of large plantations. There was little in the colony's subsequent history to reverse that trend. The United States acquired the Philippines from Spain in 1899 but, lacking the will or capacity to govern in its own right, it subcontracted many of the state's powers to a Filipino elite, which handled much of the day-to-day collection of taxes and preservation of order.

The arrangement yielded some political stability, but its effect on the economy was disastrous. As the price of its cooperation with the colonial state, the Philippine oligarchy plundered the government's coffers, issued its members massive loans (bankrupting the Central Bank of the Philippines in the process), siphoned off government expenditures, and maintained a tax structure favoring landed wealth over the development of industry.[16]

The pronounced rural inequality of the Philippines depended on a complex feudal system of patron–client ties under which landlords offered tenants a minimal safety net in exchange for taxes, labor, deference, and—as the franchise extended—votes. But by the interwar period, those ties frayed as landlords turned away from their estates toward economic opportunities opened by the integration of the colony into global markets. Tenants' credit dried up, their share of the crop decreased, and the scant forms of protection they had for centuries depended on crumbled away. Peasant discontent emerged as a persistent theme in interwar Philippine politics, climaxing in the unsuccessful Sakdal uprising of 1935.[17]

An unstable situation became dramatically more so with the Second World War. The Japanese invasion of 1941 and subsequent occupation placed an enormous strain on the Philippine economy and society. Many of the elite Filipinos who had collaborated with the U.S. colonial government struck a similar bargain with the new Japanese colonial state. On the other side, the anti-Japanese guerrilla forces tended to be drawn from the ranks of the peasantry, which suffered the most from the occupation. It was a transformative moment in Philippine politics. Chronic rural discontent turned, in places, into outright warfare, with U.S.–armed peasants on one side and their former landlords on the other.

Of the large peasant armies, the most prominent was the Hukbalahap of Luzon. "The bearing of arms was thrilling," remembered the its leader Luis Taruc. "The only guns many of these people had ever seen before had been in the hands of the PC's [Philippine Constabulary officers] who threatened our picket lines. Now, standing in an armed group, running their hands down rifle barrels they felt more powerful than any picket line."[18] In the absence of both landlords (who had fled) and legitimate government, the guerrillas assumed the functions of the state. They ran elections, issued currency, tried war criminals, and redistributed lands. They also become indispensable allies in the U.S. reconquest of the Philippines, providing essential information, disrupting Japanese supply lines, and fighting alongside U.S. forces. It was hard to imagine, by the end of the war, a return to old ways.

However unfathomable that prospect may have been, it was precisely what the U.S. forces under General Douglas MacArthur insisted upon. MacArthur enjoyed close and longstanding ties to the Philippine oligarchy; just before abandoning the colony in 1942, he illegally accepted a personal gift of $500,000 from the Philippine president.[19] Thus, rather than use the occasion of the war to restructure the Philippine economy and politics, as he would later do in postwar occupied Japan, MacArthur essentially reconstituted the prewar government, overlooking the awkward fact that a number of those instated, including the new president, had served the Japanese during the war.[20]

Stuffing the genie back into the bottle was no easy task. The newly independent (as of 1946) Philippine government forcibly disarmed Huks, arrested Huk leaders, and shelled entire *barrios*—the Philippine term for villages—where residents were suspected of aiding the Huks. The fighting escalated, and by the 1950s, the Philippine Air Force was strafing villages and dropping U.S.-acquired napalm on Huk targets. That military offensive—which President Elpidio Quirino called the "mailed fist" approach—did little to persuade the Huks to surrender and in fact pushed the insurgency toward increasingly revolutionary goals. Quirino kept a motorboat tied outside the presidential palace so that he could escape if the Huks seized the capital. What might have been a peaceful social revolution had become a brutal civil war.[21]

The Huk insurgency placed the United States in a bind. The base of U.S. power had always been the Philippine oligarchy, and although the Philippines was no longer a U.S. colony, the United States still had stakes in the country, including a protected economic status and a string of bases that it held on 99-year leases. Were Quirino to lose control of the government, all that would be imperiled. In 1951, The United States sent over a team to study agrarian conditions, a team that included Robert Hardie, one of the key architects of Japan's postwar land reform. Hardie's recommendation was drastic: a clean sweep of existing laws and an energetic redistribution of land. It would entail, all understood, a frontal assault on Philippine landed interests, but what else was to be done? Over the objections of Quirino, who demanded that the report be suppressed, Secretary of State Dean Acheson declared the Hardie report to be "sound, feasible, and accurate" and "strongly recommended" its adoption as policy.[22]

*   *   *

THE U.S. government was facing a dilemma that it encountered frequently in the global South: its chosen allies lacked popular support. In the Philippines, the problem had become so acute that the State Department had come to accept the possibility of land reform, even at the cost of threatening its allies. But that course of action was desirable only in the absence of other options. Better would be some sort of middle path whereby the existing Philippine ruling class would gain legitimacy and the United States could proceed without losing old and valuable friends.

It was with the hopes of finding that middle path that Colonel Edward Lansdale, a former advertising executive and covert CIA officer, arrived in the Philippines in 1950. Although Lansdale was at the time an obscure figure, his work in the Philippines would eventually launch him to a sort of Cold War stardom. Lansdale was the man behind Operation Mongoose, the infamous serious of pranks (poisoned cigars, exploding seashells) designed to embarrass or assassinate Fidel Castro. He was also, more notably, the largest booster and one of the closest confidantes of Ngo Dinh Diem in Vietnam and a principal architect of the United States' political strategy there. Lansdale appeared prominently in the Cold War's two most famous novels. It was largely believed, including by Lansdale himself, that Lansdale was the model for the protagonist of Graham Greene's 1955 novel *The Quiet American*. (Subsequent research has suggested otherwise, although Lansdale did shape the message of the film version.)[23] In *The Ugly American,* the case was clearer: "Colonel Edwin B. Hillandale," who appeared alongside Homer Atkins as one of the book's few heroes, was undeniably Colonel Edward G. Lansdale. Lansdale also starred in a third major Cold War book, *The Pentagon Papers* (1971), which documented at length his covert meddling in Vietnamese politics.

Lansdale believed in the Cold War. But he did not believe it could be fought with the military tactics of World War II. The U.S.–supplied tanks and heavy artillery that the Philippine government was using against the Huks were in Lansdale's eyes just "noisy fireworks."[24] If it wanted to defeat the Huks, the government would need to understand them. To that end, Lansdale left his military compound for the mountains to camp on the Huk trail, playing Philippine folk songs on his harmonica and striking up conversations with anyone who would talk. From those conversations, Lansdale concluded that the Huks were winning because they had outflanked the government on the cultural front. He read Mao Zedong's writings on guerrilla warfare with appreciation. All of that confirmed for him that, to win, the Philippine government would need to become "a *brother* of the people, as well as their protector."[25] Lansdale applied that principle of familial affiliation to his own life by befriending and eventually marrying a Filipina reporter, who not only showed him "a lot of the backcountry the Huks went through" but was also, as Lansdale knew, a Huk accomplice.[26]

Lansdale's folksy manners, curiosity about the Huks, and complaints about "noisy fireworks" did not mean he disavowed violence. He merely sought a more discriminating use of it. One of Lansdale's more memorable stories concerned his routing of a squadron of Huks. Upon learning of a local belief in vampires in the area where they were operating, Lansdale's men planted stories that one had been living in the hills where the Huks were stationed. The team then ambushed a Huk and murdered him by puncturing two holes in his neck and turning him upside down to drain his blood, leaving the corpse in the hills to scare Huk sympathizers from the region.[27] It was not the only of Lansdale's many stories about mastering local culture that ended with him or his team members killing people.[28]

In Lansdale's understanding, the Huks had been provoked into rebellion not by the oligarchy's stranglehold over agricultural land but rather by the government's unsympathetic, autocratic style. To overcome that problem, Lansdale sought to cultivate a new ruling class, one that could carry out the designs of Washington while still commanding the allegiance of the peasantry. Lansdale believed he had found the man to lead that new class in Ramon Magsaysay, a former Congressman whom Quirino had appointed Secretary of National Defense in 1950. Unlike many other high-ranking members of the Philippine government, Magsaysay came from a middling family—he had been an auto mechanic—and had the common touch. He also took the unusual position that a rural peace could be more easily won by correcting "social evils and injustices" than by making war on the barrios.[29]

Lansdale and Magsaysay immediately fell in with each other. Learning that Magsaysay was in danger of assassination, Lansdale invited Magsaysay to stay at his military compound. "Every night we sat up late discussing the current situation," Lansdale remembered. "We grew accustomed to revealing our innermost thoughts to each other."[30] Together the two men developed a series of reforms, ranging from a sharp crackdown on

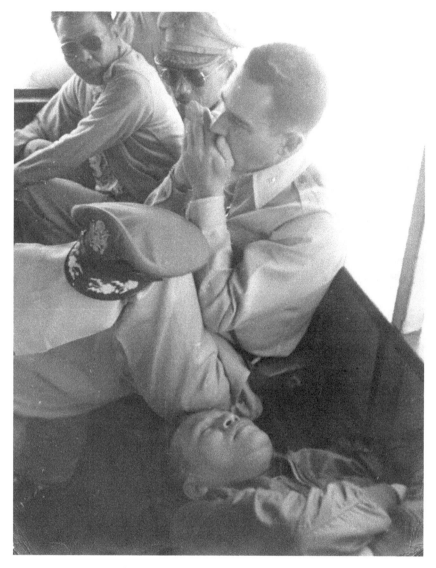

"We grew accustomed to revealing our innermost thoughts to each other": The CIA's Edward Lansdale playing harmonica while Ramon Magsaysay sleeps. (Edward Lansdale Papers, Envelope mCU, Hoover Institution Archives)

corruption in the military to the provision of lawyers to tenants hoping to sue their landlords. They opened the Civil Affairs Office within the Philippine Army, which posted to each unit men specially trained in "brotherly behavior": talking with villagers and intervening if Army officers treated them with disdain.[31]

By far their most prominent program was the Economic Development Corps (EDCOR), a much-photographed scheme by which ex-Huks were resettled to new farm communities. The program was itself miniscule—fewer than a thousand families were resettled, and only 246 were the families of reformed Huks—but those few Huks made for excellent propaganda, and Magsaysay did not hesitate to broadcast EDCOR's achievements via posters, pamphlets, and films.[32] The message behind the propaganda was clear enough: all that the rebels really wanted was membership in a well-rounded agrarian community and, if they got that, they would put down their guns. European empires sent observers to EDCOR, especially the British, who were fighting a guerrilla insurgency in Malaya.[33] Y. C. James Yen took an interest in the program as well, interpreting its popularity as evidence of Filipinos' dedication to village work.[34]

There were close resemblances between Yen's work in China and Magsaysay's and Lansdale's in the Philippines. Upon arrival, then, Yen quickly joined the Philippine counterinsurgency campaign. He established an organization, the Philippine Rural Reconstruction Movement (PRRM) and, on Magsaysay's invitation, launched its first pilot projects in Central Luzon, the heart of the Huk Rebellion. From the vantage point of the PRRM projects, Magsaysay noted, the Cold War appeared "as hot as the machine guns of the soldiers shooting Huks in their hideouts on Mount Arayat—towering on the horizon over there—the first thing you see in the morning and the last at night."[35] Magsaysay emphasized the proximity between the PRRM's village work and the government's military campaigns because he saw them as two fronts in the same war. While the army fought the Huks on the battlefield, Magsaysay explained, the PRRM fought on the "rice field."[36] To drive the point home, Magsaysay proposed that Yen establish another pilot project in San Luis, the hometown of Huk leader Luis Taruc, "to demonstrate to the dissidents . . . that it is possible for the barrio folks to enjoy freedom and abundant life."[37] Yen enthusiastically accepted.

All this community work generated excitement in the United States, and Lansdale seized on the opportunity to push Magsaysay up through the ranks of Philippine politics. Under Lansdale's direction, the CIA undertook a massive campaign to acquire the presidency for Magsaysay in the 1953 election. Few stones went unturned in the effort. CIA operatives created and covertly ran a "grassroots" organization, NAMFREL, to "reform" Philippine politics. Working through NAMFREL and other avenues, they planted articles about Magsaysay in the major newspapers; wrote speeches for him to deliver; illegally gave him at least a million dollars in cash; drummed up campaign contributions—also illegal— from U.S. corporations such as Coca-Cola; drugged the drinks of Magsaysay's opponent, President Quirino, before Quirino was scheduled to give speeches; and smuggled guns into the country for use in a coup in case Magsaysay was defeated.[38] The guns proved unnecessary. Magsaysay won the election handily, and Lansdale won a new nickname: "General Landslide." "This is the way we like to see an election carried out," President Dwight Eisenhower declared to the press—a wink to the CIA.[39]

Magsaysay's ascent coincided with the exhaustion of the Huk rebellion. Years of the carrot-and-stick approach—mild government reforms plus the continued use of napalm—finally wore down the rebels. Luis Taruc, the leader of the rebellion, surrendered in 1954, and most of the Huks slipped quietly back into agricultural life. The waning of the revolt did not put an end to calls for redistribution, though. The same year that Magsaysay took office, a Catholic-led peasant organization demanding "land to the tiller" formed, and it would press the issue for the next two decades. But the revolutionary moment had passed.[40] And from the perspective of the U.S. government, things could not have gone better. A major rebellion had been put down, a friendly and popular president had been installed, and the United States had been spared the prospect of its own soldiers dying for the cause.

The success of Lansdale's middle way also meant that the United States could abandon its hardline commitment to land reform, which it did in 1953. Robert Hardie, the author of the land reform recommendations that the State Department had previously accepted, resigned his post in disgust, leaving for a small farm and a teaching job in Missouri. Just as the Philippine oligarchy had hoped, both Hardie and his report disappeared from official memory. When a historian asked Lansdale about them decades later, Lansdale wrote back: "The name 'Hardie' does not ring a bell at all. Are you sure you have it right?"[41]

* * *

ON THE campaign trail, Magsaysay had made some promises about land reform, but it is not clear that anyone took them seriously. The agrarian reform laws he passed during his presidency were so riddled with loopholes that they barely made a difference.[42] Magsaysay's real commitment, plainly visible during his campaign, was to community development. Upon his election, "barrio fever" swept the halls of government. At the behest of Magsaysay, and often at the urging of the United States as well, politicians, government agencies, and private groups turned to community work. In 1953 alone, the Bureau of Public Schools established community councils, the Bureau of Agricultural Extension established barrio councils, and NAMFREL used millions to set up a string of community centers.[43] Meanwhile, Yen's PRRM continued its own high-profile pilot projects, much in the style of Albert Mayer's work in Etawah.[44]

But Etawah was not enough for Magsaysay. Just as Nehru had turned a pilot project into an all-India scheme, Magsaysay wanted a national program. In 1954, he established the Community Development Planning Council and placed a young man named Ramon Binamira in charge. Binamira had worked for NAMFREL's community centers and, consequently, with the CIA. Although Binamira was not himself an agent, he and other members of the planning council met regularly with the CIA's man in charge of community development, Gabriel Kaplan.[45] Binamira and his colleagues also had the advice of community development experts sent from the U.S. State Department and the United Nations. In 1954, Manila became the site of the UN's first regional conference on community development, which brought dozens more community developers from Burma, India, Indonesia, South Korea, Pakistan, the United States, and Britain to the Philippines.[46] The flurry of advice and planning culminated in 1956 with Magsaysay's establishment of a unified agency, the Presidential Assistant on Community Development (PACD), under Binamira's leadership.

When India launched its national community development program, four years before Magsaysay created the PACD, it had built upon a long-standing commitment to the "village community" that was an integral part of Indian political culture. The Philippines lacked any comparable tradition. It had landlords, of course—powerful men with a feudal social vision. But the ideology of nationalism had largely been crafted by an

Community development and the CIA: PACD chief Ramon Binamira (far left), CIA officer Gabriel Kaplan (second from right), and President Magsaysay's widow, Luz Magsaysay, at the dedication of the community development center at Los Baños in 1957. (Gabriel L. Kaplan Papers, Cornell University)

urban and educated elite, and there is simply nothing in the writings of José Rizal or any other major Philippine nationalist to match the communitarianism of Gandhi. The men who led the Philippines to independence were more likely to disparage rural ways than to celebrate them.

It wasn't an inbuilt sympathy toward barrio life that led the Philippines to community development; rather, it was fear of another peasant revolt. Yet if the motivations of Philippine leaders differed from those of their Indian counterparts, the results were notably similar. That was because the Indian program served as the model for the Philippine one, as indeed it did for nearly every community development program in Asia. And so, shortly after the PACD was formed, the UN's community development expert brought Binamira, a senator, and two provincial governors on a fact-finding mission that took them to India and Pakistan.[47] The U.S. government, meanwhile, sent over its own team of experts with pedigrees in international community development, one of whom, Ernest E. Neal, had served as the Chief of the Community Development Division of the Point Four administration's mission to India.[48] For a "bottom-up" program designed to incorporate local conditions and cultures, community development was displaying a remarkable modularity—a capacity to be taken from one context and slotted cleanly into another.[49]

As in India, the main purpose of the Philippine program was to sponsor thousands of small development projects in rural areas. Those projects were initiated by barrio workers: young men and women, usually college-educated, who had completed a six-month training course and who were then sent to the countryside. Upon arrival, they were to identify "natural leaders" and, with the help of those leaders, convene meetings in which barrio residents would discuss local conditions and identify "felt needs."

The point of those discussions was to generate community-designed development plans. If members of a barrio wrote a plan themselves, the PACD reasoned, then they should also be willing to carry it out. The PACD offered some assistance but adhered strictly to a "fifty–fifty" rule: at least half of the cost of the project must come from the locality itself, either as cash from the local government or, more frequently, in the form of labor, materials, and money donated by barrio residents. Generally, the PACD ended up paying around one-third of the costs, with barrio residents paying fifty-five percent and the balance coming from other sources, mainly other government agencies.[50] Although the official figures must be viewed with skepticism, in the first decade of its operation, the PACD recorded 31,109 small projects completed with government aid and—still more skepticism is necessary here—tens of thousands of even smaller ones undertaken entirely with local resources.[51]

The Philippine community development program, like similar efforts in India, led to political decentralization. A series of laws promulgated between 1955 and 1963 established elected barrio councils as the official organs of local government, funneled ten percent of local real estate taxes to them, and granted them their own limited powers to tax, collect license fees, and enact ordinances. From the PACD's perspective, the barrio councils were not just sources of aid for community development but—process being everything—valuable in themselves as bastions of local democracy and community life. In 1963, the PACD enacted the much-dreamed-of withering away of the state by declaring that it would reduce central funding for small-scale projects centrally and instead encourage barrio councils to superintend their own developmental programs. All PACD activities, the agency declared, would henceforth "revolve in and be anchored with the barrio council," not necessarily because the council was the most effective vehicle for development but because, by working exclusively through it, the PACD could "dignify and add prestige to the barrio council," thereby "building democracy from the grassroots."[52]

THROUGH THE PACD, Ramon Binamira sought to create a community development program like India's, without the benefit of India's distinctive native ideological investment in the village community. On a purely technical level, this proved simple enough, since the mechanics of community development had been worked out in India and were easily imported through the international network of community experts. Still, the national program required midlevel functionaries strongly committed to the village institution, and for that Binamira turned to the university system. A year after the PACD's establishment, Binamira and his U.S. advisers convinced the University of the Philippines, Diliman to establish an autonomous social scientific unit, the Community Development Research Council (CDRC). It was to be the intellectual arm of community development.

At first glance, a research unit within a university may not appear to be a major achievement—such programs are opened and closed often. But the CDRC was no minor undertaking. It had a significant budget, doling out research grants in its first year worth more than five percent of PACD's development grants to the entire nation.[53] And in a small and cash-strapped academic system like that of the Philippines, the money was an irresistible force. Scholars adjusted their topics of study and—according to one—their conclusions in order to receive CDRC funding.[54] By 1968, the CDRC had initiated sixty-three studies, many of them high-profile affairs involving multiple researchers.[55] But the dearth of social scientific literature on the Philippines was severe enough that any halfway-successful CDRC study, even if never published, would show up on the syllabi of sociology and anthropology courses.[56] Through the

CDRC, community development became *the* problem within Philippine social science from the 1950s through the 1970s.[57]

Yet community development was not only a problem, it was also a way of seeing the world, freighted with assumptions about democracy, poverty, and rural life. For the most part, that way of seeing was imported from the United States, the metropolitan center of Philippine intellectual life throughout the twentieth century. Many conduits carried the communitarian viewpoint from the United States to the Philippine academy, but none was more important than the anthropologist and sociologist Frank Lynch, who had, in the words of one historian, "the greatest impact on post-war Philippine social science" of anyone in any country.[58] A Jesuit priest, Lynch had taught in the Philippines since 1946, although it was not until 1959 that he acquired a commanding position within Philippine academia. In that year, he accepted a post at the Ateneo de Manila University and, in 1960, he became the inaugural director of the Institute for Philippine Culture.

Lynch first articulated his distinctive understanding of Philippine society in his dissertation, which examined social relations in Canaman, a town in Luzon. Lynch was at the time a graduate student at the University of Chicago, where he had fallen under the influence of Robert Redfield and other communitarians there.[59] Following in the footsteps of his mentors, Lynch wondered what held Canaman together as a community. He observed that the town's population was divided into two classes: "big people" who owned land and controlled the government and "little people" who depended on the big people. Yet although Lynch acknowledged the inequality between the two groups, he did not think it was an oppressive one. Landlords collected rents and crops, but they also offered "moral, medical, and economic assistance whenever they are called on."[60] It was an inherently cooperative relationship, he wrote: "the function of these classes is to complement each other socially, economically, and politically."[61] Canaman was thus "a community . . . where everyone knows just what and how much he can ask to the other fellow."[62]

Extrapolating from Canaman, Lynch delivered a paper in 1960, "Social Acceptance," which soon became the single most important article in Philippine social science. In it, Lynch argued that the entire lowland Philippines was bound together by a commitment to what he called "smooth interpersonal relations." He expressed this by comparing people from the United States to those from the Philippines. Whereas the former favored frank speech and a sort of cantankerous individualism, Filipinos tended to speak diplomatically and downplay contradiction in pursuit of reciprocity, unanimity, and harmony.[63] From the standpoint of a community developer, those were promising values, values that could be nurtured and drawn upon within the process of grassroots development.

In time, Lynch's influential thesis would gain detractors. F. Landa Jocano suspected that most of what Lynch perceived as smoothness in his interactions with Filipinos was merely a "front" strategically deployed by Filipinos "in dealing with strangers or with persons suspected of having certain government connections."[64] In other words, what Lynch had taken for harmony was not the consequence of cross-class fellowship but an artifact of the plain reality that "little people" were afraid of their superiors and could not afford to contradict them. But such criticisms only gained traction in the 1970s. During the 1960s, Lynch's view held sway, and the CDRC studies generally assumed both the possibility and the desirability of social harmony.[65]

Such an outlook may have seemed difficult to maintain in the face of the peasant rebellion that the government had recently suppressed, but Lynch was not bothered. In his analysis, the insurgency had not been caused by the exploitation of tenants by their landlords. He regarded it, rather, as the result of "dismay at landlords who had *failed* to function as traditionally expected. The 'good landlord,' who fulfills his paternalist obligations of patronage and assistance, is rarely considered exploitive by his tenants." When one of his interlocutors asked whether the landlord system didn't amount to a sort of "self-perpetuating tyranny," Lynch replied sharply. One could find injustices in the barrios, he conceded, "yet observation leads me to conclude that, *for better or for worse,* the two-class system *works.*"[66]

If the theory behind community development were to be reduced to a single sentence, Lynch's would not be a bad candidate: communities, despite their problems, *work.* Thus, as in India, the community development program in the Philippines sought to resolve the problems of the barrio not by reconfiguring social relations but by encouraging closer bonds between the classes. That emphasis came out clearly in the six-month training course that the PACD held for barrio workers. Rather than focus on technical skills such as soil analysis, animal husbandry, or agricultural economics, trainees learned how to sustain social harmony by using the tools of group dynamics, rural sociology, and community organizing. A central feature of that training was the formation of "T-groups"—contentless discussion groups that were meant to illustrate for their participants the dynamics of cooperation. T-groups had become a staple of corporate management training in the United States and would soon become the basis of the self-actualization movement there.[67] In the Philippines, they served a similar role, although with the barrio, rather than the corporation, as the object to be organized.

That therapeutic approach to rural problems came to dominate the PACD's work. It ran the Lay Leadership Institute, which many elected barrio officials attended as mandatory training for their new positions. On the first day of the four-day course, the village leaders were left alone in a room without instructions, inevitably falling into confused frustration. The trainers would return the next day and ask the leaders to reflect on that frustration and on their experience of dealing with others in the room. That discussion was meant to lead gradually to a more mature exploration of group dynamics and, eventually, into an examination of the various factors inhibiting the leaders from achieving their ideals. "Through this process," explained PACD chief Ramon Binamira, "they themselves realized that most of the problems in their villages could be met by them. They go home firmly determined to act on these problems themselves."[68]

That motivational training course was a major investment for the PACD, given widely throughout the country. In 1958, nearly the entire provincial government of Batangas—including the governor, the provincial board members, and 85 percent of the mayors and barrio officials—took leave of their posts and traveled to Los Baños to undertake the training together.[69] The PACD also offered motivational training to young people and women via an auxiliary program. Overall, millions of barrio residents participated in one form of PACD training or another; the PACD put the number of people trained between its inception in 1956 and mid-1967 at nearly five million.[70]

Within the barrios, too, the emphasis on social harmony governed all PACD dealings. This was especially true when it came to land, the issue that had provoked the rural insurgency in the first place. By design, community development was impervious to any scheme that might pit tenants against landlords. Out of the tens of thousands of local projects that the PACD sponsored, to my knowledge not a single one involved redistributing land or renegotiating the sharecropping contract. The barrio councils, at any rate, lacked the power to regulate tenancy agreements.

When the PACD addressed the land issue, it did so from the other side. The agency's 1957 handbook for barrio workers included a "Creed for Tenants and Landlords," under which both parties pledged to honor existing contracts (contracts weighted heavily in favor of the landlords) and under which tenants pledged to maximize production and care for their landlords' property.[71] To have sided with the tenants would have been nearly impossible, anyway, as both PACD and PRRM workers tended to live in the homes of barrio officials, i.e., with landlords and their families, often accepting free food and incurring complex social debts to their hosts.[72]

WITH ITS emphasis on harmony and deference to "natural leaders," the PACD program struggled to engage most Filipinos. The first sign of trouble was the stall-out of the barrio councils. Although they had been set up in the thousands under the various barrio acts, the available evidence suggests that they accomplished little. "Apathy is quite widespread in the matter of voting for the barrio council," commented one CDRC researcher in 1959, adding that nearly one-fifth of the councils failed to meet more than once.[73] Even when the barrios were given power to collect small amounts of taxes and license fees, few did so; property and business owners, it seems, were unwilling to pay the taxes, and the councils learned not to ask for them.[74] What few actions the councils took were generally accomplished, as one student of the matter noted, "through the established social and religious channels," i.e., through the same powerful men who had controlled rural society before the PACD came on the scene.[75]

When farmers *did* participate, they often wanted things other than what the PACD offered. The studies available describe Philippine agriculturalists as being far more technically and materially oriented than PACD workers expected. Surveys conducted by the CDRC revealed that barrio residents had little interest in cooperative processes. They consistently requested material aid, not the group dynamics training and democratic planning offered them.[76] A telling anecdote circulated among community development experts. A PACD worker, noting the lack of a bridge in a barrio, initiated a discussion about how the community might raise the resources to build one. A village leader asked the PACD worker how much he got paid. When the worker disclosed his salary, the leader paused, did some mental calculations, and then observed that if the village had just been given the PACD worker's yearly salary in cash, the village could have bought the bridge and skipped the group discussions altogether.[77]

A study of a multiple-barrio PACD project uncovered a similar dynamic. Farmers brought soil samples to barrio workers, hoping to have the soil analyzed. The PACD workers declined—they were not trained in soil analysis—but suggested, in textbook community development fashion, that the farmers set up field trials and controlled experiments in order to gain a better understanding of local agricultural conditions. The suggestion met with "shoulder-shruggings on the part of the farmers." If PACD workers are such experts, the farmers asked, why are *we* the ones who have to do the experiments?[78] Barrio residents did participate in PACD programs, of course, but researchers worried that they did so only as a way to please the workers or to gain access to PACD resources. At any rate, many projects folded soon after the aid workers left.[79]

As in India, apathy compromised developmental outcomes in the Philippines. This was a disappointment not just for the PACD but for the country as a whole, which had adopted community development as its chief strategy for ameliorating rural poverty. It was precisely in the period of the PACD's operation, 1956–1972, that the Philippines went from being one of the most promising Asian nations to being a regional laggard. During that period, population growth outpaced agricultural production, unemployment increased, tenancy increased, landlessness increased, and absentee ownership increased. More and more people, in both relative and absolute terms, slipped below the poverty line. Rural income distribution became more polarized, with the income share of the poorest fifth of the population slipping from 7.0 percent to 4.4 percent and the share of the richest fifth rising from 46.1 percent to 51.0 percent.[80]

The decline of the Philippine economy was a large and complicated phenomenon, depending on factors—such as pervasive political corruption—far beyond the purview of the PACD. Yet if community development was nowhere near being the sole cause of the Philippines' deterioration, there is little reason to think that it helped matters. One of the best sources of evidence for the effects of the PACD's programs is a longitudinal study of villages in Dumaguete between 1952 and 1966. Although some residents gained better access to things like drinking water and roads over the period, agricultural incomes and educational levels both dropped, and those surveyed in 1966 were less optimistic about future conditions than those surveyed in 1952.[81] "Community development had promised much," wrote USAID official David Korten, summing up the consensus in 1980, "yet delivered little."[82]

Lacking both popular support and measurable results, community development gradually withered in the Philippines, just as it had in India. President Magsaysay had been a staunch defender of the approach, but he died in a plane crash in 1957 (along with the head of Yen's PRRM), and by the time Diosdado Macapagal assumed the presidency in 1961, top politicians had lost interest in the program. Under Macapagal's indifferent watch, the PACD "quietly slid into limbo," according to the *Philippines Free Press*. "Some are wondering whether it still exists."[83] They had reason to wonder: Macapagal shrank the PACD's budget so severely that in 1963–1964, the agency completed only 475 grants-in-aid, down from 8,213 five years earlier.[84] By the late 1960s, the PACD's newsletter conceded, "demoralization" had "spread through the rank and file."[85]

The problem wasn't that Macapagal and his fellow politicians had given up on rural development. It was that they no longer thought community strategies up to the task. Macapagal's defunding of community development was part of a pendular shift, seen in India as well, away from approaches to development grounded in social networks and local culture toward ones concerned with technologies, infrastructure, and material resources. In the place of PACD aid to the barrios, Macapagal spent 100 million pesos on large-scale projects that sought neither the advice nor the participation of barrio residents. The United States' aid agency followed suit, pulling its funding from the PACD in 1966—a year ahead of schedule—in order to concentrate on an infrastructure- and agribusiness-heavy aid project called Operation SPREAD.[86] The Asian Development Bank ratified this shift in 1969 with its *Asian Agricultural Survey,* in which it rejected the possibility that production could be increased "by a judicial mixing of some aspects of modern science with the so-called traditional beliefs and methods." The "only valid route to sustained rural development," the surveyors declared, was "farming based on applied science."[87]

In both India and the Philippines, then, community development gave way to Green Revolution technologies in the 1960s, a movement away from communitarian strategies toward modernizing ones. Yet in the Philippines, the PACD did not vanish or find itself subsumed by an agricultural ministry in the way that India's Ministry of Community Development did. Although it had been nearly starved out of existence by Macapagal, the PACD gained a second life under Macapagal's successor, Ferdinand Marcos, elected in 1965.

Marcos is known as a devotee of the Green Revolution, but he was surprisingly enthusiastic about community development. His first act as president was to elevate the PACD to cabinet rank, granting it a long-sought measure of permanence within the government. He also changed the PACD's name from Presidential Assistant on Community Development to Presidential *Arm* on Community Development, signaling, he said, that the office carried "the prestige, the powers, and the capabilities of the presidency."[88] PACD employees received numerous presidential awards—so many that some joked that the true title of the agency should be the "Presidential Awards and Citations Department"—and Marcos declared the first week of every year to be Community Development Week.[89] As an answer to Macapagal's 100-million-peso fund for large-scale agriculture, Marcos established a 100-million-peso Barrio Development Fund, under which each barrio received a check for 2,000 pesos—a check that Marcos and his wife Imelda made a point of handing over personally when possible. "Were I to write my own epitaph," Marcos reflected in 1969, "this is what I shall choose: Ferdinand E. Marcos, who helped the barrios discover themselves and the power to change their lives."[90]

On the face of it, Marcos's adoption of community development seemed to indicate a resurgence of communitarianism. But Marcos's critics perceived an ulterior motive. Senator Benigno Aquino, Jr., the president's most formidable opponent, saw in the Barrio Development Fund "a huge pork barrel fund exclusively for President Marcos."[91] Aquino was not far off the mark. Having established barrio captains in every village, the PACD had unwittingly created a mechanism for a national politician to do something that no Philippine leader had yet been able to do: circumvent provincial and municipal powerholders and gain direct access to the villages. Marcos's 2,000-peso checks were his bid for the loyalty of village leaders, and the Barrio Development Fund was his tool for rewiring the circuitry of Philippine political bribery.[92] A partial and localized system of patronage, stuffed with middlemen, was to become a national one, with Marcos at the top and the barrio captains reporting directly to him. None of this was cheap; in Marcos's 1969 election, electoral spending by candidates equaled one-quarter of annual government expenditures.[93] It was no accident that the money for the Barrio Development Fund was released in 1968, just in time for Marcos's 1969 electoral campaign.

The 1969 elections were the last Marcos would ever face. In 1972, he declared martial law, arresting Aquino and concentrating the authority of the state under the office of the presidency. Although his 1973 constitution promised that the government would promote "the autonomy of local government units, especially the barrio, to ensure their fullest development as self-reliant communities," Marcos's actions pointed in the opposite direction.[94] He abolished the PACD in 1972 and replaced it with the Department of Local Government and Community Development, which became his instrument for supervising local politics. Barrio and barangay officials (in 1974, Marcos replaced the patchwork system of local government with a uniform barangay system) were directly answerable to the president's wishes. In 1975, Marcos converted all elective local offices to appointed ones, formalizing what was already an informal relationship of subordination of local government to national government. At any rate, politics under Marcos had become rife with vote-rigging, bribery, and outright terrorism. When, in 1983, an assassin murdered Aquino on the tarmac of the Manila International Airport—in daylight, in front of a security contingent of hundreds of soldiers and police—few doubted that the order had come from Marcos.

There is a palpable irony in Marcos's use of community development as a stepping stone toward a dictatorship. It was precisely the threat of centralized authority that had launched the quest for community in the first place. And yet, while the ideology that stood behind community development was staunchly decentralist, its institutional logic was intriguingly Janus faced. In grounding government in the decisions of small groups, community development opened up channels between the small scale and the large. Those channels might decentralize the government, but latent in them was the opposite possibility: that they might allow the tentacles of central power to reach further down into the localities. What looked to be an instrument of bottom-up democracy might serve instead as one of top-down control.

TO SOMEONE like Albert Mayer, the fate of Philippine community development would have come as a disappointment. Its deference to the rural elite, which drained away its participatory animus, prevented it from accomplishing much by way of development, and it turned into the tool of a dictator. But not every observer shared Mayer's philosophy and, for the men of the CIA, those outcomes were not entirely undesirable. After all, community development had helped to end the Huk rebellion.

In shoring up Marcos's power, it also had its uses. For Marcos, whatever his flaws, was a valuable ally of the United States: a strong anticommunist in a volatile region who controlled bases that were essential to the war in Vietnam.

Gabriel Kaplan, the CIA officer who oversaw Philippine community development, recognized the value of community development in protecting U.S. interests. Speaking to an audience of Dallas beef producers with investments in Latin America, Kaplan explained how community development created a bulwark "against the left extremist takeover of every hamlet in Latin America, Asia, and Africa":[95]

> Gentlemen, let's face it: your future, the future of the private elite sector, the future of the believers in the free enterprise system, depends on the ability of our societies to establish adequate systems of intercommunication and action between our economic and political power centers and the mass of our people. This is your insurance for survival. You can purchase this insurance through stimulating your national, regional and local communities to install appropriate techniques of mass organization and leader development and utilization. A generation of experience with such techniques is now at your disposal. . . . But the hour is so grave that it behooves us all to speak out, and to act in concert, in organization, and with dedication.[96]

A society with no vertical ties connecting the peasantry to their landlords or to their political leaders would quickly fall into revolution. For Kaplan, community development was valuable both for its cross-class character, which bound peasants and their superiors together in communal action and defused rural insurgencies, and for the access it granted rulers to their subjects in the provinces.

From the perspective of Cold Warriors such as Kaplan, Philippine community development was a tremendous success. The next step was to export it, and it was here that Y. C. James Yen proved his worth. Yen had always regarded his work in the Philippines as part of a larger international campaign against communism. He also saw eye to eye with Kaplan about the importance of including the "private elite sector" in community planning. The board of Yen's Philippine Rural Reconstruction Movement was largely composed of well-placed businessmen—the president of Republic Flour Mills, the president of the National City Bank of New York in Manila, the General Manager of the China Banking

Corporation, and so forth.[97] Its president had been a top executive at Shell before taking the job.[98]

In 1961, a glowing article about Yen's work in the Spanish-language version of *Reader's Digest* prompted more than 750 letters—mostly from businessmen, plantation owners, government officials, priests, and lawyers—expressing the hope that Yen would start a program in Latin America.[99] That year, Yen visited Guatemala, Colombia, Venezuela, Costa Rica, and Puerto Rico. In Guatemala, where Yen traveled on the invitation of the military junta government, President Colonel Enrique Peralta Azurdia "gave his blessing" to the Guatemalan Rural Reconstruction Movement, which Yen established in 1964.[100] In Colombia, Yen's invitation came not from the government but from U.S. corporations, which hoped to use community development to quell social unrest. Yen dutifully established the Colombian Rural Reconstruction Movement in 1962.[101]

By 1980, Yen had started rural reconstruction movements in South Korea, Thailand, Ghana, and India as well. At the same time, he used his International Institute of Rural Reconstruction, founded in 1960 in the Philippines, to train government officials from still more countries. Yen's institute took in officials from Colombia, Guatemala, Kenya, Ghana, Ethiopia, Jordan, Ceylon, Laos, Indonesia, Vietnam, and Papua New Guinea. Yen also contracted with the Peace Corps to train its volunteers, both those working in the Philippines and those destined for other countries. Although the nature of Yen's ties to the CIA is unclear, his work fell obviously in line with the CIA's mission.[102] As one CIA officer recalled, the prospect that the Philippine community development program might be exported in this fashion was one of the main reasons the CIA station in the Philippines had taken an interest in community development in the first place.[103]

For Gabriel Kaplan, taking the Philippine model abroad became a personal calling. Through his Community Development Counseling Service, he consulted with governments on the architecture of their national programs, often sending officials to the Philippines for training or to observe the PACD's work. Kaplan worked actively in Panama, Venezuela, and the Dominican Republic but had a particularly pronounced influence in Colombia. There, he served as a key adviser in the National Front government's establishment of a widespread program, which by 1966 had established more than eight thousand "community action boards" throughout the country. (Douglas Ensminger, chief of the Ford Foundation's field office in India, also advised the government.)[104] As Kaplan saw it, his main contribution to the Colombian program was to convince the government to "broaden" its conception of community development in order to accommodate the desires of "the private economic elite."[105]

ALTHOUGH YEN and Kaplan saw possibilities for Philippine-style community development in combatting rural unrest across the globe, there was one place where it seemed especially promising: Vietnam. The Philippines was already linked to Vietnam in the U.S. official mind. Since the Philippines was one of the few Asian countries that the United States knew well, it came up frequently as an analogue that guided U.S. navigation of the far less familiar terrain of Vietnam. When Franklin Delano Roosevelt proposed during World War II that the United States take over French Indochina, for instance, it was the Philippine model that he had in mind. "We were able to get together with the Filipinos and all agree on a date . . . when they would be ready for independence," he reflected. "There is no reason why it should not work in the case of Indo-China."[106] Similarly, after the Huk rebellion had been put down, some U.S. officials suspected that the same methods could be cleanly transposed to Vietnam.

It was with that easy analogy between the Philippines and Vietnam in mind that Edward Lansdale left the Philippines in 1954, with instructions to replicate his feats in Vietnam. Again, Lansdale sought a sympathetic politician, a Magsaysay figure, whom he found in Ngo Dinh Diem. And again Lansdale hoped that cultural sensitivity and small-scale approaches could succeed where heavy artillery had failed. With Lansdale's encouragement, Diem initiated in 1955 a campaign of "civic action," an adaptation of community development techniques to the military. Under its auspices, Diem's government sent its officials to train in villages, where they were expected to discard their uniforms, live among the people, and lead their neighbors in communal undertakings such as building houses.[107] At the same time, on Lansdale's urging, members of the Diem government traveled to the Philippines to meet Magsaysay and study Philippine counterinsurgency. The United States also brought Filipino advisers out to Vietnam, including Magsaysay's brother-in-law and various members of Lansdale's Philippine team.[108] As Diem put it to a New York audience, Magsaysay's Philippines had "set an inspiring example" for Vietnam.[109]

In Lansdale's highly influential version of things, Diem's adoption of community strategies—and in fact most of Diem's policies—resulted from Lansdale's influence. "South Vietnam, it can truly be said, was the creation of Edward Lansdale," is how journalist Neil Sheehan expressed the sentiment.[110] Historians today, however, doubt the extent to which South Vietnamese policies were Lansdale's doing.[111] In Lansdale's telling, he made Diem in the same way that he had made Magsaysay. Yet the analogy is hard to maintain; Diem was already the prime minister of the State of Vietnam before Lansdale met him. And not only did Diem manage to claim power without Lansdale, it also appears that his interest in village strategies developed independently of anyone in the United States. Diem, like so many other Southern leaders, had his own reasons for doubting the efficacy of high modernism.

Diem is often regarded as a Confucian or a Catholic traditionalist, but his social vision had a more recent origin. It was grounded in a twentieth-century philosophical movement, Personalism, that had emerged in French Catholic circles by the 1930s. Personalism bore a family resemblance to the groupist turn in the United States in the 1930s and to the Gandhian villagism that coalesced around the same time. Like both of those movements, it sought a middle ground between capitalism and communism in which both markets and politics would be embedded within the social group. The *person,* in philosopher Emmanuel Mounier's definition, meant neither the unattached individual nor the mass man, but the member of a community.[112] It was this element of communal belonging, the personalists insisted, that must be restored. Diem's brother Ngo Dinh Nhu took up the idea with zeal in the late 1930s and shared it with Diem. In 1954, Nhu founded the Revolutionary Personalist Workers' Party, known as the Can Lao, with the goal of undertaking a "personalist revolution" in Vietnam.[113]

Although Diem kept quiet about his desire for a personalist revolution while consolidating power, by 1956, his regime had adopted personalism as its official ideology, emblazoning the slogan "Personalism, Community, and Collective Advancement" on signs across South Vietnam.[114] Diem described this political vision as stemming "from an ideal conception of community life where the common good takes precedence over the good of the individual."[115] On a visit to Australia in 1957, Diem explained that the "extensive decentralisation" of precolonial Vietnam had been source of the country's strength, and that postcolonial Vietnam must decentralize again to recover the "moral cohesion" that it had lost in its confrontation with "weapons and ideas from the West."[116] Two months later, Diem toured India, where he spoke enthusiastically of Gandhi and singled out for admiration India's community development program. "India gives all the under-developed countries an instructive and encouraging example from the theoretical as well as practical point of view," Diem wrote after the visit.[117]

Facing a countryside in turmoil, Diem searched for ways to win a rural peace. Land reform held little appeal to him; he feared that redistributing land too broadly would threaten existing Vietnamese society. More appealing were resettlement schemes akin to Magsaysay's EDCOR program, by which he hoped to recast rural life in the personalist mold. Between 1956 and 1960, his government launched a series of experimental resettlement programs, the largest of which was the agroville scheme, which sought to move half a million people. The schemes were a blend of modernism and communitarianism. On the one hand, they were top-down campaigns to relocate hundreds of thousands of people. But at the same time, Diem insisted that settlers build their new homes themselves—he called this the "community development principle"—in order to inculcate in them a sense of communal belonging in their new villages.[118] Both aspects, unsurprisingly, provoked bitter resistance.[119]

The regime tried again in 1962, with the Strategic Hamlet Program, which discarded the previous emphasis on population movement and introduced village elections. This was to be at once a military strategy to create fortified bastions of regime support and a program of social transformation. It would be through living in the hamlets, Nhu explained, that "the people" would finally experience "the development of a new system of values concerning the duties, rights, and interests of the citizens."[120] But this, too, proved disappointing. The Viet Cong infiltrated the hamlets easily, and the program became a public symbol of the regime's inability to govern.

Although the Diem regime depended heavily on the United States for support, it kept the United States at arm's length when it came to its communitarian schemes. Nhu claimed that there was something authentically Vietnamese about them that must be preserved; he also doubted that U.S. developmental models based on the TVA or on Rostovian modernization theory would be compatible with personalism.[121] He needn't have worried. The United States had other cards in its hand besides modernization, and once the South Vietnamese government led with communitarianism, the United States followed suit. In doing so, it drew heavily on its experience with counterinsurgency in the Philippines.

Historians have not always fully acknowledged the communitarian items in the United States' Vietnam repertoire. The standard explanation for U.S. failure in Vietnam points to the war planners' technocratic faith and blindness to on-the-ground particularities. Brute force, overweening confidence, and bureaucratic rationality thus pulled the United States into Vietnam, kept it there, and ensured that, however many acres of forest it bombed or poisoned, it would never win the hearts and minds of the Vietnamese. Yet just as modernizers and communitarians coexisted when it came to development policy, they coexisted in Vietnam. In the upper echelons of strategy planning were modernizers like National Security Adviser W. W. Rostow and Secretary of Defense Robert McNamara. President Johnson, hoping to build a "TVA on the Mekong," went so far as to hire David Lilienthal to oversee it.[122] But closer to the ground, there were men like Edward Lansdale and his protégé in the CIA, Rufus Phillips, who believed that the war must be won in the villages, with sociocultural tactics rather than military or economic ones.

During the Diem years, the Lansdale approach seemed as if it might prevail. Kennedy had initially sought to appoint Lansdale as the ambassador to Vietnam, dropping the issue only after Dean Rusk threatened to resign over it.[123] And despite its exclusion from planning the Strategic Hamlet Program, the United States backed the hamlets fully, spending $10 million to support the program and establishing a new division within its overseas mission, the Office of Rural Affairs, with Rufus Phillips in charge. Meanwhile, a Lansdale brainchild called Operation Brotherhood, which brought Filipinos to work in South Vietnam, augmented its medical services by sending over community development workers.[124] In the Philippines, the U.S. and South Vietnamese governments used Y. C. James Yen's International Institute of Rural Reconstruction as a training center for Vietnamese village officials. Many of those trained came to hold high ranks in the South Vietnamese government upon their return.[125]

Lansdale's community strategy, however, depended on the ability of Diem's government to actually win the allegiance of the villages. This it could not do. Whatever interest Diem's subjects might have had in village democracy was easily eclipsed by their resentment of the regime's demands for forced labor and of the widespread imprisonment, torture, and execution of its political opponents. Faced with Diem's lack of popular support, the U.S. government removed its protection from Diem and acquiesced to a generals' coup that cost the president his life in 1963.

Lansdale retired on the day Diem died. The following two years saw General William Westmoreland's assumption of command over military activities in South Vietnam and the advent of the direct-action phase of the U.S. war there. From Lansdale's perspective, those developments marked a tragic blunder, the moment when a flexible, small-scale war turned into an affair of numbers, firepower, and command of the air.[126] There is still today a lingering, Lansdale-ian sense that the war was lost when modernization came to town.[127]

In reality, things were not quite so neat. The United States continued to deploy village strategies, most notably in its CORDS (Civil Operations and Revolutionary Development Support) program inaugurated in 1967; by the end of that year, the PACD newsletter complained of the "brain drain" that carried many of the Philippines' top community developers to Vietnam.[128] And Westmoreland, though known in caricature for his "search and destroy" tactics and commitment to a war of attrition, understood CORDS and village work more broadly to be an essential part of the U.S. military effort.[129] Nevertheless, the extensive work that continued in the villages of South Vietnam did not turn the tides of war. Between the napalm from above and the ineffective attempts to generate grassroots support from below, the United States lost its foothold. When an unnamed U.S. major, discussing the recently bombed Vietnamese town of Ben Tre, told a reporter that it "became necessary to destroy the town in order to save it," the statement seemed to many a fitting epigraph—or epitaph—for the U.S. war effort in Vietnam.[130]

THE CULT of Lansdale remains strong. The perception that U.S. counterinsurgency worked in the Philippines and would have worked in Vietnam, too, had it not been for the bureaucratically minded Westmoreland types, has adherents throughout the policy establishment. Most telling in this regard is the career of General David Petraeus, who, after years in Iraq, gained command of the International Security Assistance Force in Afghanistan and eventually became the director of the CIA. Petraeus's enormous popularity both within the military and within U.S. politics—during their first presidential debate, John McCain and Barack Obama appeared to be competing over who could claim him—had a great deal to do with his status as a counterinsurgency expert. In 2006, Petraeus oversaw publication of the widely reviewed Army/Marine Corps Field Manual 3-24, *Counterinsurgency*—a document downloaded more than 1.5 million times in the month it was released.[131] With its strong emphasis on cultural understanding and on-the-ground interaction (sample section titles: "Understand the Environment," "Build Trusted Networks," "Empower the Lowest Levels," "Most of the Important Decisions Are Not Made by Generals"), the manual could have been written by Lansdale himself. Perhaps in Petraeus's hands, his many supporters hoped, Iraq and Afghanistan might turn out differently than Vietnam had.

But how successful *was* Lansdale-style counterinsurgency? In Vietnam, although Lansdale and his followers presented U.S. defeat as a Modernization Comes to Town tragedy, communitarian approaches appear to have been just as complicit. Diem's community campaigns won him few followers and seemed no less prone to repressive violence than the helicopters above. More importantly, it is hard to imagine *how* the agrovilles and strategic hamlets could have succeeded. Diem's government had opposed land reform, cancelled the all-Vietnam elections mandated by the Geneva Accords, rigged South Vietnamese elections, and tortured and executed its opponents. Would the mere establishment of village councils be enough to convince Diem's rural subjects that they lived in a democracy?

A similar question could be asked of Philippine community development. On the surface, it appeared successful—it had helped to prevent a Huk-led revolution. But at the same time, it did little to alleviate the causes of that attempted revolution. By design, Philippine community development both blocked any effort to redistribute rural power and rendered the barrios more easily accessible from the center. That, plus napalm, was enough to hold the peasant insurgency at bay but not enough to make it vanish. In the longer perspective, what is most conspicuous about Philippine rural politics is not the quick "victory" of U.S.–backed government forces in the 1950s but the consequent delay of a rural settlement and the prolongation, down to the current day, of a cycle of rebellion and repression in the countryside.[132]

Social protests in the Philippines could have dismantled the oligarchy and brought about a redistribution of land. Had they done so, it is likely that the Philippine economy would have experienced something closer to the steady rate of economic growth that it seemed, in 1946, poised to achieve. It also would have laid the groundwork for politics based on voters' interests rather than on, as it is commonly said, "guns, goons, and gold." But that is not what happened. Instead, the carrot-and-stick combination of community strategies and violent repression continued, preventing revolution but also preventing reform. The Philippines has become an "anti-development state," in which resources are channeled not toward growth-enabling public investments but into the personal accounts of politicians and into bribing or threatening voters to continue to elect them.[133] The effect on the Philippine economy has been crippling. Today, close to ten percent of the country's large population lives abroad, and four out of ten Filipino students plan to leave the country after graduation.[134] It's not hard to see why. The Philippines today has the lowest per capita GDP in East and Southeast Asia—one-third of Malaysia's, one-tenth of Hong Kong's.[135]

5

URBAN VILLAGES

IN JUNE 1962, John F. Kennedy ascended the dais at Yale's commencement ceremony to deliver an address about the economy. It was more than an economic state of the union; it was a declaration of victory. Although previous generations had endured the "grand warfare of rival ideologies," Kennedy maintained, the United States had entered a new era. Economic problems had revealed themselves to be "subtle challenges for which technical answers, not political answers, must be provided."[1] The economy, in other words, was a math problem, and the economist John Maynard Keynes had largely solved it. Keynesian macroeconomic management and technological investment, overseen by a capable bureaucracy, could assure prosperity, Kennedy promised, as indeed they already had. In the preceding fifteen years, the already-enormous income of the average U.S. citizen had grown by more than a third, and the cornucopia appeared inexhaustible.[2]

Kennedy's Yale speech has caught the eye of scholars as representing the "ultimate triumph" of Keynesianism in the political culture of the United States.[3] But the Yale address can also be regarded as the last time a U.S. president could ever credibly speak with such confidence about the national economy. Three months earlier, Michael Harrington's *The Other America: Poverty in the United States* had appeared in bookstores. It was the first in a cascading series of books and articles— including Leon Keyserling's "Poverty and Deprivation in the United States" (1962), Dwight Macdonald's "Our Invisible Poor" in the *New Yorker* (1963), Harry Monroe Caudill's *Night Comes to Cumberland County* (1963), and Homer Bigart's reporting on poverty in eastern Kentucky for the *New York Times* (1963)—that forcefully reminded the nation of the intractable persistence of poverty, even in the world's largest economy. Harrington's book would eventually be listed by *Time* as one of the ten most influential nonfiction books of the twentieth century, ironically putting it in the company of John Maynard Keynes's *General Theory of Employment, Interest, and Money*. The editors of *Time* explained their reasoning: "Lyndon Johnson's War on Poverty was launched by Harrington's book."[4]

The Other America did not just note the existence of poverty. It challenged the prevailing notion that a rising economic tide would float all boats. Harrington described people who were "upside-down in the economy," for whom greater productivity meant worse jobs, agricultural advance meant hunger, and "progress" meant "misery."[5] It was, at the time, an unusual observation. Popular social criticism such as David Riesman's *The Lonely Crowd* (1950), David M. Potter's *People of Plenty* (1954), William H. Whyte's *The Organization Man* (1956), Vance Packard's *The Hidden Persuaders* (1957), and John Kenneth Galbraith's *The Affluent Society* (1958) had portrayed the United States as a land of hypercharged—perhaps dangerous—abundance.[6] Such books either ignored poverty or dismissed it, as Galbraith's book famously did, as "an afterthought," restricted to a few stubborn spots suffering from compounded bad choices or bad luck.[7]

What enabled Harrington to recognize, in the face of much insistence to the contrary, that the pockets of poverty in the United States were not vanishing? It helped that he had seen poverty firsthand through his work with Dorothy Day, a left-wing urban reformer who ran a soup kitchen and published the *Catholic Worker*. It also helped, no doubt, that Harrington counted himself among the Shachtmanites, that tiny but extraordinarily fertile off-Trotsky splinter group of socialists that had developed the notion of "bureaucratic collectivism." Like his fellow Shachtmanites, Harrington placed little faith in technocratic management, economic or otherwise, and it is telling that another key figure in the "discovery" of poverty, Dwight Macdonald, had also been a Shachtmanite. But both Day and Shachtman hailed from the Old Left, of the 1930s, and *The Other America* diverged from them in its analysis of poverty. For Harrington, the poor were not an oppressed proletariat. The problem, as he put it, was that "the United States contains an underdeveloped nation, a culture of poverty."[8]

The poor, in Harrington's eyes, constituted a foreign country. It was a striking claim, collapsing two categories that had often been kept separate—of domestic deprivation and overseas "underdevelopment"—into a single, unified field.[9] Nevertheless, there was something that made sense about it, given the United States' recent history of global engagements. By 1962, when people in the United States thought about poverty, they thought of it as a foreign phenomenon. "Underdevelopment" was a familiar category with an obvious Cold War significance. And thus, when poverty reappeared as a domestic issue, it became a way to comprehend the poverty now visible within the United States' own borders.

Harrington did not invent the concept of the "culture of poverty." Credit for that belongs to the anthropologist Oscar Lewis, one of the many globetrotting rural experts pulled from the New Deal into the global South. He began his career with a study of Tepoztlán, the site of Robert Redfield's first book. In the 1940s he found work in the USDA's Bureau of Agricultural Economics, where he examined rural community formation under the supervision of Carl C. Taylor. The next decade saw Lewis traveling to India for nine months, in the employ of India's Planning Commission, to evaluate the community development program. Lewis had been recommended for that job by another BAE alumnus: Douglas Ensminger, then in charge of the Ford Foundation's India office.[10]

But if Lewis traveled among community developers, he never was one. As a Jew, fifty-five of whose relatives were killed in the Holocaust, he lacked the community developers' faith in the wisdom of folkways. And among anthropologists he was best known for antagonizing Robert Redfield. In his restudy of Tepoztlán, he famously chided Redfield for mistaking the complex and conflict-prone town life there for that of a harmonious, premodern village.[11] In India, too, Lewis saw factions and divisions where Mayer and Redfield found social wholes.[12] That so much of Lewis's career was nevertheless spent following the tracks of community developers is a reminder of just how prevalent the practice was at the time, of just how much of the bandwidth of developmentalist thought it took up.

Lewis's culture of poverty thesis, which he debuted in 1958, didn't come from his revisionist studies of rural society but from his research on urban areas: Mexico City, San Juan, and New York City. Although it was notoriously imprecise and malleable, the gist of the thesis was that the poor suffered not only from material deprivations but also from a cultural and psychological malady that appeared with "remarkable similarities" across "regional, rural-urban, and even national boundaries."[13] That illness was "both an adaptation and a reaction of the poor to their marginal position in a class-stratified, highly individuated, capitalistic society," developing most frequently during moments of transition or "periods of rapid technological change."[14] In other words, it was a consequence of modernization's disruptive forces, a subject about which Lewis agreed with community developers. Where he disagreed was in his assessment of how much damage had already been done. For Lewis, trying to tap the latent energies of traditional communities was pointless; such communities no longer existed. Poor people had already been sucked into modernization's widening gyre. Lewis thus saw little difference between the "folk" societies in the global South and the urban slums of the global North.

Not everyone agreed with Lewis. But in positing a universal condition of poverty, he proposed a framework that would acquire enormous importance in the 1960s. If the earlier U.S. poverty strategy had been characterized by the assumption that what had worked in the Depression-era United States could work overseas, thinkers in the 1960s reversed the terms. What if the antipoverty strategies that had been honed for nearly two decades in the global South were brought back home?

THAT QUESTION would soon be answered. In 1964, in response to the storm stirred up by Michael Harrington and in the wake of the Kennedy assassination, President Lyndon Johnson launched an "unconditional war on poverty"—the centerpiece of his domestic agenda.[15] It was a large and varied legislative package, containing legal services, educational reforms, health care, and jobs training. But at its core was the Community Action Program, which sought to address poverty by placing control of reforms directly in the hands of the poor. It did so in a familiar way, through state encouragement and support for communal action, participation, and democratic deliberation.

The resemblance to overseas community development was nearly impossible to miss. Daniel Patrick Moynihan, who had been one of the principal architects of the War on Poverty, explained it in a six-page article in 1966. "From the time of the Point Four program the American government has been sponsoring programs of community development in backwards nations throughout the world," Moynihan wrote. "The program was and is a great popular success, and the idea of doing something of the sort through Community Action Programs with the 'underdeveloped peoples of the United States' came as direct and obvious carryover."[16]

If the carryover was obvious, it became less so with time. Three years later, Moynihan, then in exile from the liberal establishment and a member of the Nixon administration, published another discussion of community action, this time an influential, piercing, and witheringly critical book-length analysis titled *Maximum Feasible Misunderstanding* (1969). In it, Moynihan dwelled on the fact that many of the government-funded community projects had turned radical, merging with new political movements and feeding the social unrest of the 1960s. This Moynihan regarded as a disaster, and he blamed it on the place of social science in politics. In the postwar period, he complained, the "speed of transmission process" between the lecture halls and the halls of Congress had accelerated so much that politicians had essentially abdicated their positions, turning over the business of policymaking to intellectuals.[17] So when those intellectuals, acting on an idiosyncratic pet theory, proposed that poor communities be "empowered" to overcome poverty themselves, politicians hastily agreed without considering the political implications. The technocratic fusion of ideas and politics that had seemed so promising to Kennedy in 1962 was in Moynihan's eyes a reckless danger. And the Community Action Program was the baneful result.

Maximum Feasible Misunderstanding was a revenge book. Between the time of his short article and the book, Moynihan had fallen spectacularly out of favor with the liberal establishment—the result of the unexpectedly hostile backlash generated by the infamous "Moynihan Report." In that report, Moynihan had argued that the cumulative effects of racism had not only impoverished blacks but damaged their culture and family lives as well. Although civil rights advocates initially greeted Moynihan's argument with sympathy, the quickly shifting sands of mid-1960s racial politics buried Moynihan, who was widely accused of "blaming the victim" (a phrase, in fact, coined specifically in reference to Moynihan).[18] *Maximum Feasible Misunderstanding* neatly turned the tables, pinning the blame for community action's failures on precisely the groups that had abandoned Moynihan. In attacking participatory strategies, Moynihan was implicitly defending the thesis of the Moynihan report that black life had become pathological; in decrying the fecklessness of liberal politicians, he was implicitly accusing his former colleagues, who had allowed him to suffer, for being too cowardly to admit he was right.

Yet Moynihan's charges of intellectual laziness and cowardice made sense only if his readers understood the Community Action Program to be an untried scheme implemented by inattentive politicians. And for that interpretation to hold, Moynihan had to pass silently over the United States' extensive prior experience with community development. That prior experience had registered clearly enough in Moynihan's six-page article in 1966. Yet somehow, in expanding that article into a book, Moynihan managed to say *less* about community action's foreign precursors than he had in the article—almost omitting mention of them entirely.[19]

Not all historians agree with Moynihan that the fusion of community action with social protest movements was a disaster. Until very recently, however, they followed the empirical contours of Moynihan's influential account closely. The story of the War on Poverty was the story of social scientists developing a new, community-based approach to poverty and politicians adopting that idea without grasping its full consequences. Community action, in this narrative, popped onto the scene somewhere in the late 1950s and early 1960s and was to be explained entirely in terms of domestic politics and ideas.[20]

That dramatic out-of-nowhere arrival as described by the bulk of the scholarly literature bears an intriguing resemblance to the scholarship on the New Deal USDA's communitarian programs. Historians of that period, notably Jess Gilbert, have lamented the triumph of modernization and the rapid disappearance of participatory approaches to agricultural policy.[21] Historians of antipoverty campaigns in the 1960s, by contrast, have noted the opposite phenomenon: the sudden appearance of community strategies where none had been before. It is only by adopting an international frame of reference that we can fully explain either of these. The community strategies of the New Deal didn't disappear; they moved abroad. And the community strategies that became the centerpiece of the War on Poverty did not appear from thin air but rather were based, in large part, on overseas community development—the boomerang returning home.

Overseas community development was more than an inspiration for community action. It was also a training ground, in the sense that many of the architects of the War on Poverty had direct experience with community projects abroad. The reason was simple. Having spent so much time busying itself with the economics of prosperity, the U.S. government lacked domestic expertise in the area of persistent poverty. The people in government with poverty-fighting on their résumés tended to have accrued that experience in foreign lands. So, just as the hydraulics of expertise had once pushed rural experts from the New Deal out to the global South to become community developers, the discovery of domestic poverty reversed the flow and pulled foreign aid experts back to the United States as poverty warriors.

THE STANDARD account of the Community Action Program attributes its genesis to the collaboration of three related groups. The first, the Ford Foundation, established a series of pilot projects focusing on participatory approaches to urban problems, culminating in its celebrated Gray Areas Program in 1961. At the same time, a second group, the President's Committee on Juvenile Delinquency, led by Attorney General Robert F. Kennedy, funded a few other pilot projects along similar lines. After the publication of *The Other America* shone a national spotlight on domestic poverty, the Kennedy administration promoted the issue toward the top of its reform agenda, with President Kennedy's assassination a year later increasing the perceived urgency of the issue within the White House. Soon after taking office, Lyndon Johnson appointed Sargent Shriver, President Kennedy's brother-in-law, to draft an omnibus antipoverty bill. Shriver's team—the third group—worked closely with the Attorney General's staff and the Ford Foundation on the legislation that placed community action at the center of the War on Poverty.

That account is entirely correct, but it leaves out the international dimension, which historians have only recently begun to notice.[22] It leaves out the fact that Shriver, at the same time as he designed the War on Poverty, oversaw the Peace Corps, and it declines to mention the Ford Foundation's simultaneous work on the problem of poverty in India, where it was integral to that country's community development program. It now appears that many of the individuals and institutions involved in designing the War on Poverty came to it with direct experience in overseas aid. In fact, most of that experience was with community development.

Nowhere could the connections between community development and community action be more readily seen than in the Peace Corps. As a senator, John F. Kennedy had been inspired by *The Ugly American,* and as a presidential candidate, he proposed an agency dedicated to carrying out the ideals of the novel. The idea had proved to be enormously popular, so much so that Kennedy was obliged to follow through with it. "To those people in the huts and villages of half the globe struggling to break the bonds of mass misery," Kennedy promised in his inaugural address, "we pledge our best efforts to help them help themselves."[23]

After his election, Kennedy asked leading modernization theorist Max Millikan to craft a plan for the agency. Millikan envisioned the Peace Corps as part of "the broader U.S. governmental effort to assist the underdeveloped countries in building the institutions essential to self-confident and effective nationhood." It could do this, he proposed, by addressing the "serious shortages of educated and trained people" in the global South. Thus, the main job of Millikan's proposed Peace Corps would be to supply experts, "to use young Americans in filling the interim manpower needs of the underdeveloped countries," presumably as engineers, economists, and administrators.[24] Because he saw the Peace Corps as a weapon in the modernization campaign that he took to be the core of U.S. foreign policy, Millikan insisted that the Peace Corps be located within the State Department, as part of the International Cooperation Administration (ICA).

Historians have invoked Millikan's role in the early discussions of the Peace Corps as evidence that the Peace Corps was essentially an instrument of modernization.[25] But what is most notable about Millikan's plan is how thoroughly it was ignored. "No one wants to see a large centralized new bureaucracy grow up," exclaimed Shriver, whom Kennedy had tapped to head the agency.[26] Shriver thus rejected Millikan's suggestion that the Peace Corps become part of the ICA. Volunteers should not go abroad, he further argued, "as members of an official US mission to demonstrate or advise." They should go "to teach, or to build, or to work in the communities into which they are sent. They will serve local institutions, living with the people they are helping."[27] Whereas Millikan had envisioned the Peace Corps as a personnel bureau supplying experts to poor countries, Shriver's Peace Corps largely eschewed subject-matter experts in favor of "B.A. generalists" whose main training lay in fostering intercultural understanding and who were as eager to learn from foreign cultures as they were to reform them.

Shriver's antipathy toward Millikan's vision was no surprise, since Shriver had already displayed communitarian leanings. In the 1940s he had worked with his wife, Eunice Kennedy (who had completed graduate work at the University of Chicago, in Robert Redfield's department), on a program for "joint community action" against juvenile delinquency in Washington. In Shriver and Kennedy's view, anti–juvenile delinquency campaigns could not be "limited to the formal agencies" but must be waged "by the people themselves, in their own communities, striking at their own local problems."[28] It was that anti-bureaucratic, localist, and communitarian orientation that Shriver carried into his work in the Peace Corps.[29]

But Shriver was not alone in thinking along those lines. As he planned the contours of the new agency, he drew heavily on the advice of experienced foreign aid hands. He worked especially closely with International Voluntary Services (IVS), a private development agency with operations in nine countries. Within the landscape of international development, IVS was small. Yet its leadership comprised a veritable who's who of community development, including Carl C. Taylor, John H. Provinse, and Stanley Andrews, the former director of the State Department's Point Four aid agency. IVS was, in the most pedestrian of senses, the model for the Peace Corps; IVS staffers were the ones who showed Shriver's team how to set up payrolls for international work, screen recruits, and so forth. It was a model in a loftier sense as well, with its emphases on "people-to-people" contact and learning foreign folkways migrating into the Peace Corps mission.[30] And once the Peace Corps opened its doors to the IVS approach, veterans of the international community development movement rushed in, training Peace Corps volunteers and writing the agency's manuals. A *Community Development Handbook* used by the Corps, for example, featured articles by Louis Miniclier, director of the Community Development Division in the State Department, and by Carl C. Taylor.[31]

Community development was the heart of the Peace Corps' self-image, the organization's "raison d'être," as Miniclier put it.[32] In actuality, community development was only the second-most-frequent job classification in the Corps; more volunteers were listed as teachers.[33] But the classifications were an inexact business, and many volunteers employed as teachers ran community development projects after hours and during the summer. In the same way, volunteers in areas such as agriculture and public health were frequently trained to use community development techniques.[34] Whatever their eventual classification, new recruits imagined themselves in some far-off hamlet, building schools or digging wells with the help of friendly natives, and were often surprised and disappointed if they were assigned desk jobs.[35] As one Peace Corps staffer put it, community development was more than a program area. It was "an attitude, a mystique, a movement central not only to the full spectrum of the Peace Corps programs but to the philosophy of the Peace Corps as well."[36]

*   *   *

ALONG WITH the space program, the Peace Corps was President Kennedy's most popular policy initiative. It was therefore not long after its debut before Eunice Shriver and others began to talk of applying the Peace Corps approach to the domestic problems of the United States.[37] The idea appealed to Robert F. Kennedy, the Attorney General, as well. In November 1962, a few months after the publication of *The Other America*, he convened a cabinet-level committee drawn from various government departments to study, in the words of its director, "the best ways to adapt the overseas Peace Corps concept to this country."[38] Although the Peace Corps posted a representative to the committee, the bulk of its members came from the Labor Department and the Department of Health, Education, and Welfare.[39] And at the center were the men whom Robert F. Kennedy had recruited to the President's Committee on Juvenile Delinquency, one of the three pillars of the War on Poverty.

Juvenile delinquency had gone in the postwar period from a relatively small issue to a central preoccupation within U.S. culture, appearing in such films as *The Wild One* (1953), *Rebel without a Cause* (1955), *Blackboard Jungle* (1955), and *West Side Story* (1961). Part of the interest came from a puzzle about its origins. What had gone wrong with these young men and women, unmoored from the bonds of family and society? Was it their parents, their schools, their peers, or something else? David Hackett, Robert F. Kennedy's high-school friend, was given the job of supervising the Presidential Committee on Juvenile Delinquency, the committee that was supposed to answer the riddle of juvenile delinquency on behalf of the White House. Hackett held no particular theory but, like many others in the Kennedy administration, he trusted the experts.

In particular, Hackett looked to a group of scholars centered on the psychiatrist Leonard Duhl of the National Institute of Mental Health. Duhl had little patience for the prevailing theories that focused on the psychological pathologies of the individual. He suspected mental health problems to be a function of the environment and became curious about effects of urban life on people's psyches. That approach took the problem of juvenile delinquency onto new terrain, turning it from a question of psychology to one of sociology, anthropology, urban planning, and, above all, community life. Duhl formed a group to consider the issue from those angles. Sensing the great distance that separated their approach

141

from mainstream social science, the members of Duhl's group referred to themselves affectionately as the "Space Cadets."

Duhl may have floated in low orbit above the standard social science on juvenile delinquency, but his ideas were not entirely alien. He was a communitarian, concerned with the health of small social solidarities just in the way that an earlier generation of thinkers, including Jacob Levy Moreno, had been. In Duhl's account, it was a revelatory visit to Granville Hicks's small-town home in Grafton, New York—where Duhl visited frequently while dating Hicks's daughter—that had "awakened" him to the possibilities of the community approach.[40] He became an avid reader of Arthur E. Morgan's *Community Service News* and wrote a glowing foreword to a book about international community develop-ment.[41] In it, he proposed that community development strategies might be used at home, as a solution to the problem of juvenile delinquency.

Other Space Cadets had even closer connections to community devel-opment. In Duhl's *The Urban Condition* (1963), an anthology containing the mature thought of the group, Richard Waverly Poston observed that both the countries of the "newly developing world" and U.S. cities suf-fered from a lack of "comprehensive community organization" and sug-gested that the tactics of international community development be brought home.[42] Poston knew a great deal about international community devel-opment since the previous year he had published a key survey of the move-ment, *Democracy Speaks Many Tongues: Community Development around the World* (1962)—the book for which Duhl had written his fore-word. Poston was also in charge of community development instruction at one of the largest Peace Corps training centers, at the University of New Mexico.[43] And within the Space Cadets group, Poston's position was no doubt strengthened by the occasional presence of Louis Miniclier, the director of the Community Development Division of USAID.[44]

Of course, not all of the social scientists who advised Hackett's group had connections to community development. For example, Richard Cloward and Lloyd Ohlin, the authors of the highly influential *Delin-quency and Opportunity* (1960), were entirely domestic and urban in their orientation. But even in their case, it is not hard to draw connec-tions to community development. Ohlin's mentor, whom he drew into the White House discussions, was a Chicago-school sociologist named Leonard Cottrell. Cottrell's main contribution to the debates was his notion of the "competent community" which, he recalled, had come to him while he and Douglas Ensminger toured upstate New York as part of Ensminger's dissertation research in the 1930s.[45] Cottrell then worked closely with sociometrist Jacob Levy Moreno, serving as the President of the Board of the Moreno Institute and as the editor of Moreno's journal, *Sociometry*.[46] All of this drove Cottrell away from a material approach to welfare and toward a sociocultural one. "We can be the best fed, the best housed, the best clad, the best cosmeticized, the most chrome-plated and plastic wrapped people in the world, and still be little more than contented cows," he wrote.[47] The antidote to that bovine existence was, of course, participation in local communities.

In other words, the juvenile delinquency experts who injected ideas about community into the bloodstream of the Kennedy administration had roots in the community development movement. But, of course, even if they hadn't, Hackett and his staff would still have known of international community development since the juvenile delinquency committee moonlighted within the Kennedy administration as the Domestic Peace Corps committee. Both Hackett and his colleague Richard Boone, who headed up the Domestic Peace Corps effort, have insisted in interviews that the Domestic Peace Corps program was central to their developing thoughts about poverty. Hackett described the Domestic Peace Corps work and the juvenile delinquency work as the "two major experiences" that generated enthusiasm within the Kennedy administration for community action.[48] Boone, however, has lamented that historians "never mentioned" the Domestic Peace Corps side of the ledger, focusing instead of juvenile delinquency—and thus obscuring the links to overseas experiences that fed into the War on Poverty.[49]

When they turned to the Peace Corps project, Hackett's staff brought in a parade of experts to Washington to advise them. Boone remembers one of the most articulate and helpful consultants as being Robert A. Roessel, Jr., an anthropologist working on a Navajo reservation.[50] Roessel had been a student of Robert Redfield's at the University of Chicago and, since 1951, had worked as a community developer among the Navajo. Roessel's approach was straight from the community development playbook. "Don't plan *for*, plan *with*," he advised.[51] The advice stuck. "Deep community involvement, above and beyond the traditional 'do good' circles, is essential to the success of the program," read an internal memo of the Domestic Peace Corps committee outlining the program. "Volunteers would live in the areas they serve. In effect, they would be community development workers, 'promotores,' as the Latin Americans call Peace Corps Volunteers."[52]

In January 1963, Hackett's staff submitted its recommendations to the president. Large numbers of domestic corpsmen—hundreds at first, growing to five thousand—would "respond to calls for assistance by American communities." Those corpsmen would act, Kennedy's advisers hoped, like "a fuse," which, once lit, would "explode the latent desire of the American citizen to help out his countryman."[53] President Kennedy submitted a bill to establish the Domestic Peace Corps to Congress in April 1963. The proposal was voted down in the House by Southern congressmen worried that the new agency might act as a force for integration in their districts.[54] But the Domestic Peace Corps idea was nevertheless an important avenue through which ideas about community participation made their way into the Kennedy administration's thinking, and it was reborn, in transformed state, as Volunteers in Service to America (VISTA), a core component of the War on Poverty.

AT THE same time that communitarian ideas migrated into the White House via the Peace Corps, the Domestic Peace Corps, and the juvenile delinquency committee, the Ford Foundation ran its own parallel research into the problems of delinquency and cities. The man in charge, Paul Ylvisaker, was not someone like Shriver, with a longstanding interest in community work. Ylvisaker was an urbanist, mainly interested in problems of large-scale metropolitan governance. Although he acknowledged that community and local institutions might play a role within the larger mechanism of the city, they had never been his focus. Economic development and physical renewal, not communal solidarity, were his top priorities. Or at least, they were until 1960, when Ylvisaker came into direct contact with overseas community projects and began to see matters in a different light.[55]

It appears that Ylvisaker's introduction to community development came at the hands of Bernard Loshbough, a specialist in housing and urban planning from Pittsburgh. Loshbough's trajectory had begun very much like Ylvisaker's. He had regarded urban planning as mainly a material undertaking, a process of "revitalizing" blighted neighborhoods by razing existing buildings and putting new housing stock in their place. But Loshbough's career took an unusual turn in 1951, when Chester Bowles, upon becoming the ambassador to India, recruited Loshbough to join him. Bowles placed Loshbough in charge of the embassy's part in India's community development program. After his stint in government, Loshbough continued to work in India, putting in four years as the

144

deputy representative of the Ford Foundation in India, where he served under Douglas Ensminger. By the time he returned to Pittsburgh, Loshbough had become convinced that community methods were the answer to the United States' urban problems. "It is ironic—perhaps shocking—that an urbanite like myself had to travel 10,000 miles to India to learn that a homegrown product like agricultural extension can likely be adapted for effective use in urban centers," he reflected. "I guess you could call this 'foreign aid'—in reverse."[56]

The Ford Foundation proved to be an ideal conduit for reverse foreign aid, since it worked on both international poverty and domestic urban problems. Ylvisaker's exposure to community development came when Ford sent him to India as part of a team to draft a metropolitan plan for Calcutta. Mostly, the plan dealt with the ordinary business of urban renewal—building a bridge across the Hooghly River, reclaiming land around the city, and so forth. But the Ford team also recommended including an "urban community development" component, presumably related to the experiments that Albert Mayer had been undertaking for Ford in Delhi.[57] Ylvisaker recalled having "profited immensely from the internship" at Calcutta.[58] But he proved his worth as well. The Calcutta project's supervisor, Douglas Ensminger, regarded Ylvisaker as one of his "three chief advisors" on the plan.[59] Another of the advisors whom Ylvisaker named was Bernard Loshbough, back briefly from Pittsburgh.

While the two were in Calcutta, Loshbough explained to Ylvisaker his idea of importing community development into the United States, and the two began "seriously discussing" a grant from Ford to develop the idea.[60] According to an internal foundation report, Ylvisaker "evidenced immediate interest."[61] He felt that Calcutta was undergoing "simply an exaggerated version of the same thing our cities were going through," so transposing policies from one place to another seemed like an obvious move.[62] After returning to the United States in 1961, then, Ylvisaker arranged for Loshbough to receive a third of a million dollars (later increased to $475,000). Loshbough was to apply to Pittsburgh techniques that had been "used successfully in the community development programs in lesser developed nations."[63]

Loshbough launched his Pittsburgh project with a conference, attended by M. L. Wilson and Marshall Clinard, the Ford Foundation's urban community development specialist in Delhi. (Carl C. Taylor, who could not attend, visited Pittsburgh later and expressed "tremendous enthusiasm.")[64] There, Loshbough recounted the origins of the idea. He recalled sitting in his New Delhi office with Wilson, discussing how, despite the vast differences separating Asian villagers from U.S. urbanites, "the processes of getting people to do things are fundamentally the same."[65] Ylvisaker, too, was "very much interested in this technique, having knowledge of its successful application in Asia and other countries," Loshbough explained.[66]

Ylvisaker, Loshbough, and Wilson were not the only ones. Also working on the Calcutta master plan—and Ensminger's third chief adviser—was yet another urban planner, Edward Logue. Like Loshbough, Logue had served in the Bowles embassy in in the early 1950s. As the assistant to the ambassador, Logue had observed "the community development at all levels and participated in it from the smallest detail to the highest policy decision."[67] Upon returning to the United States, Logue decided to launch a community development program in Boston. It was to be, as he described it in a letter to Ensminger, "a New England version of community development."[68] Logue of course saw differences between what he and his colleagues were doing in U.S. cities and what they had done in India, but he was nevertheless struck by the "amazing similarities."[69]

Shortly after its grant to Loshbough, the Ford Foundation under Ylvisaker's direction rounded up all these strands into the larger-scale Gray Areas Program. Between 1961 and 1963, Ford gave $12.1 million to four cities and one state (North Carolina) for "community-development programs" that would be "designed by and with local community leaders, not for them" and that would "encourage and assist neighborhood citizen groups to work for neighborhood improvement and to relate to the community as a whole."[70] The resemblance to Loshbough's work was clear enough. In Logue's case, it was even clearer, since one of the grants, to New Haven, was placed under Logue's supervision.

BY THE end of 1963, then, a good number of well-positioned policymakers were advocating communitarian approaches to poverty, urban problems, and juvenile delinquency. In doing so, they made explicit reference to the U.S. experiences with overseas community development. Those references came naturally, as numerous overlapping filaments connected both Ylvisaker's group and Hackett's to community projects abroad. The two groups were also entangled with each other, both in their personnel and in the pilot projects that they funded.[71] Neither, however, had moved past the experimental stage or had enough time to fully register results. Domestic community development was still in embryo.

It might have remained there, had not President Kennedy's assassination provoked the newly installed Johnson administration to launch an all-out War on Poverty. The decision was made quickly and, because of the sudden political opportunity opened by the assassination, Johnson insisted that it be carried out quickly as well. Lacking the time to carefully craft new policies, members of the administration reached out for seasoned experts. But in a government that had only recently acknowledged the existence of domestic poverty, such men were hard to find. Nevertheless, expertise abhors a vacuum, and the two years of small, tentative steps that Hackett's staff had taken in their work on the abortive Domestic Peace Corps and the juvenile delinquency committee conferred on them great authority, if only relative to the rest of the administration.

As Hackett's staff was sucked from a back office in the White House to the forefront of the new administration's principal domestic policy initiative, its members brought with them their idea that community could conquer poverty. The staffers on the President's Council of Economic Advisers who had been tasked with crafting the War on Poverty had little time to understand the ins and outs of the pilot programs. They took dictation from Hackett and rushed a proposal to President Johnson in late December 1963, just a month into Johnson's presidency, calling for a community development program. Ten demonstration sites were to be chosen, with an eye toward expanding the program quickly if the projects succeeded.

Johnson's advisers came to his ranch to discuss the program over the holidays. They were pleased to see the new president warm to the idea. Johnson recalled his own work in the 1930s with the National Youth Administration, an agency that had, like the TVA and the Bureau of Agricultural Economics, sought to use local action to improve the lives of rural people. Reflecting further, he connected the idea to "one of the oldest ideas of our democracy, as old as the New England town meeting— self-determination at the local level."[72] Johnson must also have registered community development's overseas pedigree, though, because he and his staff considered calling the program Point One, a play on Truman's Point Four.[73] Whatever his thinking, Johnson latched onto community action and insisted that the program be expanded far beyond a few pilot projects. It needed to be instant and national. "Community participation would give focus to our efforts," Johnson later recalled. "The concept of community action became the first building block in our program to attack poverty."[74]

Having decided that the War on Poverty would be a war for community, Johnson named Sargent Shriver as the head of his antipoverty task force. Shriver refused, pointing out that he was already busy with the Peace Corps. Johnson was not a man to give up easily, though, and he insisted that Shriver perform both jobs at once. "You'll have an international Peace Corps—one abroad and one at home," he explained.[75] The head of the most prominent overseas community development agency was to head up its domestic equivalent.

Like nearly every other member of the Kennedy and Johnson administrations, Shriver had little experience with domestic poverty policy. So he called in his own parade of advisers: Oscar Lewis, Michael Harrington, Paul Ylvisaker, and all of Hackett's staff. As his executive secretary, Shriver named Frank Mankiewicz, then the director the Peace Corps in Peru and one of the Corps' staunchest advocates of community development.[76] Mankiewicz dutifully explained the Peace Corps' community development operations in Latin America to the other members of the task force.[77]

Shriver, of course, had no need for such explanations; the relevance of community development to the War on Poverty was obvious to him. "Doing community development in Ecuador is, philosophically and substantially, no different than doing the same thing in some West Virginia hollow," he told an interviewer. "In the Peace Corps one called this process community development; in the war against poverty, we called it Community Action."[78] Mankiewicz agreed. "The Community Action concept really came from the Peace Corps' community development work," he reflected. "In fact we thought about the poor in the U.S., at least in many ways, as an underdeveloped society."[79]

Under Shriver's direction, community action became the centerpiece—though not the whole—of the antipoverty program. In 1964, Congress ratified this arrangement by passing the Economic Opportunity Act, which created a new government agency, the Office of Economic Opportunity (OEO), with Shriver as its head (while remaining in charge of the Peace Corps). The OEO received $800 million—$300 million for community action and the rest for other programs, including the Jobs Corps and VISTA, the latter of which had also been inspired by overseas community development via the Domestic Peace Corps. Under the terms

Power to the people: Sargent Shriver signing grants to community action
agencies in November 1964. Morton D. Engelburg, photog. (Sargent Shriver Personal
Papers, John F. Kennedy Library)

of the Community Action Program, funds would not be spent directly by the federal government but would be granted to community action agencies that could demonstrate that they were seeking to end poverty via the mechanism of community organization. Reformers and antipoverty activists leapt at the chance to receive funding. By June 1965, there were 415 community action agencies in existence; within a year there were over a thousand, most located in large cities.[80]

THE COMMUNITY ACTION PROGRAM was remarkable both for the great hopes that politicians invested in it and for the great speed with which they recoiled from it just a year after it began. After some of the community action agencies became vehicles for militant social protest, community action became, politically speaking, a hot stove. And as the political establishment contemplated its burned fingers, some obvious questions arose. How did the idea to devolve political power to poor communities ever make it through the legislative process? Why didn't anyone foresee what appeared, in retrospect, to have been the predictable consequences?

In Moynihan's telling, the problem was simply that none of the policymakers who designed the program had any prior experience with community strategies. They placed their faith in social scientists, without bothering to think through the political implications of the program. But that interpretation, although popular among historians, is simply incorrect. The architects on the War on Poverty had ample experience with community action because for the preceding fifteen years, the U.S. government and the Ford Foundation had been funding community development projects overseas. So if inexperience was not their problem, why were policymakers so surprised by the radical turn that community action took?

The answer has to do with a crucial ambiguity built into the notion of community development. On the one hand, community schemes in the immediate postwar period had tended overwhelmingly to be conservative in their nature. In India they deferred to local hierarchies of caste and status. In the Philippines it was precisely the counterrevolutionary potential of community development—the possibility that community projects might bind otherwise rebellious peasants to their social superiors—that made it so attractive to the CIA (and, in Vietnam, to the Diem regime). And yet in Kerala, that anomalous communist state in southwest India, community development had turned out differently.

There, the economically heterogeneous "village communities"—so common in the rest of India—did not exist. Community development thus entailed devolving power to very different type of "communities," composed of peasants, students, women's groups, and generally the subordinated classes in society. Keralite community development tapped into a larger counterhegemonic movement, a movement that ultimately turned Kerala from one of the most harshly inegalitarian regions in India to the most egalitarian.

The trajectory of community development thus had to do with the type of community being developed. And when it came to the poor neighborhoods of the United States, their nature was an open question. Were they, as many assumed, "urban villages": bastions of latent neighborhood solidarity, waiting to be activated?[81] Or were they, as others suspected, "dark ghettos": economic prisons of pent-up frustration and rage, waiting to explode?[82] Were they Etawah, in other words, or were they Kerala?

The notion that cities were made up of "urban villages" was in ascent. In the Roosevelt years, those seeking to live "on the human scale" mostly retreated from the cities, with thinkers such as Lewis Mumford, Norman Rockwell, and Granville Hicks abandoning urban life for small towns. Yet starting in the 1940s another option emerged. A class of bohemian artists and professionals, alienated by the high modernist city but unwilling to leave it, carved out pockets of small-scale sociability within the urban landscape. The "brownstoners," as those who left Manhattan for Brooklyn called themselves, latched onto a new unit, the city neighborhood, as a counterforce to modernization. Diverse but communal and bound together by face-to-face contact, the neighborhood was a bridgehead of localism seized in modernist enemy territory.[83]

Ultimately the brownstone vision would come to remake the U.S. urban imagination, resulting in such enduring cultural artifacts as *Sesame Street,* which debuted in 1969. But the ground was already shifting by the beginning of the 1960s, especially after the publication of Jane Jacobs's *The Death and Life of Great American Cities* (1961), which gave memorable voice to the brownstoners' understanding of urban life. Jacobs's book was, above all, a protest against the top-down urban modernization projects pushed by Robert Moses and other city planners. In contrast to their city of gleaming skyscrapers, towering public housing, wide-open parks and plazas, and through-cutting superhighways, Jacobs offered her own, a city of neighborhoods. Small, dense, complex, and organic, the neighborhoods Jacobs described made little physical sense—at least not from the planner's-eye view—but they made great social sense. "Eyes on the street" guaranteed safety, a mixture of side-by-side uses encouraged the kind of iterated social contact that built trust, and the preservation of older architectural forms endowed neighborhoods with a sense of place. Jacobs's neighborhoods were greenhouses for community, for "networks of small-scale, everyday public life."[84]

Jacobs was drawn to ethnic enclaves and evoked their Old World, unassimilated charms with a sympathetic eye. Apart from one offhand description of East Harlem as a "deprived and backward country," though, Jacobs drew no direct comparisons between foreign and domestic spaces.[85] That aspect of brownstone thought would not be rendered explicit until the next year, when one of Duhl's Space Cadets, Herbert Gans, published *The Urban Villagers* (1962). Like Harrington, whose *The Other America* appeared the same year, Gans saw a clear analogy between the urban poor in the United States and the poor abroad. Challenging the prevailing notion that Boston's West End was a slum worthy of razing, Gans argued that the neighborhood was more like a foreign country. It bore "considerable similarity" to the traditional societies of the global South and that, for Gans, was a fine thing.[86] West Enders, living close together, enjoyed "a share in the life that went on around them, which, in turn, made them feel part of the group."[87] Although Gans's work preserved a neutrally scientific tone, it was generally read alongside Jacobs's book (to Gans's frustration) as "a defense of old-fashioned *Gemeinschaft*."[88]

The impression readers gleaned from Jacobs and Gans was of urban neighborhoods as little republics stubbornly clinging to an organic way of life within a larger city that had already given itself over to the technocratic mode of social organization. Such neighborhoods were fragile, imperiled as they were by the high modernists' bulldozers, but they were also sources of hope. If their communal energies could be tapped, perhaps the pathologies of urban life could be solved.

That was, at least, the view that Sargent Shriver took. With foreign villages on his mind, Shriver regarded the poor and largely urban areas of the United States as communities in the making. His vision of community action, Frank Mankiewicz recalled, entailed bringing together the "priest, rabbi, factory owner, and worker" to talk things over.[89] That therapeutic process would benefit the poor but, in Shriver's conception, it would draw on the entire community, which Shriver took to be composed of multiple classes. "I believe in community action as being communal," he argued, "and that's why we should have . . . at the local level of community action, the private sector, those people in the philanthropic area, et cetera."[90] The idea of community action as a consensus-governed process that would draw local powerholders and their subordinates together was, of course, faithful to the model of overseas community development. It was a vision shared by Paul Ylvisaker, David Hackett, and a number of other poverty warriors.[91]

It was also, it appears, a vision shared by President Johnson. When he first heard of community action, Johnson responded enthusiastically. Yet the recordings he made of his conversations during that period reveal that his enthusiasm was based on a particular understanding of the process. Johnson regarded community action as a form of self-help, a way to turn "tax-eaters" into "taxpayers." But Johnson, reflecting on his own experience with the National Youth Administration and perhaps also on the State Department's experience with overseas community development, regarded that process as taking place entirely under the supervision of local politicians. *Community,* for him, meant local government, and *action* meant cooperation with it. It does not seem that Johnson ever considered the possibility that community action might rally the poor against the rich.[92]

Curiously, the sunny "urban villages" image, which saw city neighborhoods as bastions of community life, arose alongside another image of urban life, one that entirely contradicted it. This was the notion of ghetto, a place marked not by adherence to tradition but by social disruption and its attendant trauma. Oscar Lewis's "culture of poverty" argument, based on his anthropological fieldwork in the "slums" (a term that Jacobs and Gans pointedly avoided) of Mexico City, San Juan, and New York City, had taken a grim view of urban poverty.[93] Poor people, in his judgment, had been profoundly damaged by modernizing processes, and the places they lived gave vivid expression to the resulting social pathologies. Lewis's writings on Latinos found an echo in a spate of books that appeared starting in the mid-1960s about black urban life, including *The Autobiography of Malcolm X* (1965), Eldridge Cleaver's *Soul on Ice* (1968), Lee Rainwater's *Behind Ghetto Walls* (1970), and the essays of LeRoi Jones.[94] The prototype of such ghetto realism, however, was Kenneth B. Clark's *Dark Ghetto* (1965).

Clark, who held a Ph.D. in psychology from Columbia University, had already made his mark on social science with a series of doll studies that he and his wife, Mamie Phipps Clark, conducted to test the effects of racism. The coupled showed that many black children exhibited great distress when presented with black dolls, since the children simultaneously considered the dolls unappealing and identified the dolls with themselves. Clark concluded from this that racism had scarred black people's psyches, and he spent most of his later career elaborating on that theme. With funding from the President's Committee on Juvenile Delinquency, Clark founded Harlem Youth Opportunities Unlimited, known as HARYOU, to explore the possibilities for community mobilization among young blacks. But his conclusions, which he expressed in *Dark Ghetto,* were a far cry from Herbert Gans's. "The dark ghetto is not a viable community," Clark warned.[95] Ghettos were not self-sufficient little republics but "social, political, educational and—above all—economic colonies," holding pens for the exploited.[96] This was not the village, in other words, but the prison; references to confinement pervaded the book. Where others had once seen Harlem as a vibrant cultural mecca, Clark saw in it the "tangle of community and personal pathology."[97]

Neither Clark nor Lewis found much to love in the neighborhoods that poverty had made, but neither gave up on the possibility of healing the damage through community action. The difference between their version of community action and the one that Shriver and Johnson endorsed was that theirs was fundamentally combative. The neighborhood community in the dark ghetto was not a well-rounded, cross-class affair. It was a prison population. And its appropriate form of action was not building village democracy but breaking down the ghetto walls. As Lewis saw it, the culture of poverty could only be eradicated when the poor identified with some "larger group," such as a trade union or revolutionary nationalist movement, that sought "basic structural changes in society."[98] Clark felt the same, noting that crime had nearly disappeared in Montgomery when blacks organized around the bus boycott. He even cheered on the urban riots of 1964 as a potentially healthy form of "social defiance."[99] Rioting showed that the denizens of the dark ghetto had not acquiesced to their miserable conditions, although he hoped that they would channel that discontent into more effective forms of protest.

The vision that Clark and Lewis shared of community action as organized defiance also had defenders among the architects of the War on Poverty. It was the President's Committee on Juvenile Delinquency, after all, that had given Clark the money to start HARYOU. Richard Boone, a member of that committee, a sometimes employee of the Ford Foundation, and the man in charge of the Domestic Peace Corps committee, clearly regarded community action as a way to channel revolutionary discontent into oppositional politics. Cloward and Ohlin, the authors of the influential *Delinquency and Opportunity* (1960), appeared to see things in the same light. Pathology, in their view, was the consequence of pernicious structural inequalities, and the point of community action was to overcome that pathology by recognizing and confronting those structures.

But when men like Boone voiced their views, men like Shriver didn't understand them. The problem was not, as Moynihan had proposed, that the architects of the War on Poverty hastily adopted a mode of politics with which they had no prior experience. The problem was that their extensive experience with community action, in the form of overseas community development, conditioned them to interpret critical concepts such as *community* and *participation* in a certain light. They assumed that community meant a geographical unit in which members of the various classes lived side by side and that participation meant bringing the weak and the powerful together into a single, well-connected social whole. They assumed, moreover, that community action would be politically unobjectionable, that its amelioration of poverty would proceed without controversial challenges to entrenched power relations. After all, that is largely how it had worked in the global South for over a decade. And they assumed that inner-city neighborhoods would not differ too much from the foreign villages that they were used to.

The assumptions that Shriver, Ylvisaker, Johnson, and other key figures brought to the table in launching the War on Poverty help explain why they were so surprised by its outcome. The crux was a three-word phrase, "maximum feasible participation," written into the Economic Opportunity Act; community action agencies would have to enroll the maximum feasible participation of the poor in order to receive funding. Most accounts attribute the phrase to Boone, although Mankiewicz remembered it as having emerged in discussions of the Peace Corps.[100] Shriver, for his part, surely associated it with his Peace Corps experience; he understood it to mean cross-class cooperation and compared it to the managers of a factory surveying their workers.[101] But for Boone and some of the other more radical members of the antipoverty task force, "maximum feasible participation" meant that the poor would lead their own movements against the privileged. Two profoundly different meanings, drawn from two different sets of assumptions, were thus tacitly built into the definition of *community action*. In the haste to pass the Economic Opportunity Act, no one who shepherded the bill to passage—in Congress or in the White House—recognized that the ambiguity would prove to be political dynamite.

THE INCENDIARY potential of the "maximum feasible participation" clause became apparent as soon as the Economic Opportunity Act was passed. Urban mayors, as expected, lined up to receive grants from Shriver's Office of Economic Opportunity. But first Philadelphia and then Cleveland, New York, Los Angeles, and San Francisco were turned down when the OEO refused to fund old-style municipal programs that failed to incorporate the poor. Shriver's hope was that, by blocking out the mayors, he could induce new community organizations to form and come forward to claim the hundreds of millions of dollars the government was offering. What came as a surprise to him—and to the legislators who had backed the Economic Opportunity Act—was how many of those community action associations had social protest agendas.

Shriver and his fellow thinkers failed to see that the "urban villages" of their imagination bore a decreasing resemblance to the neighborhoods in which the poor actually lived. The very notion of an urban village had been developed by studies, such as Gans's and Jacobs's, of enclaves of whites, often "white ethnics." By the early 1960s, those were precisely the areas that were disappearing the fastest. A few vocal brownstoners aside, middling whites streamed out of the cities, taking with them political resources, jobs, and a tax base. Residential segregation was quickly killing the sort of economic and social diversity that had afforded places like Boston's West End a flourishing social life even in the absence of economic prosperity. As the supply of urban villages dwindled, areas that had formerly been well-rounded neighborhoods containing a diversity of functions increasingly came to resemble internment camps for the dispossessed. And once poverty was a matter of place, the iterated, intimate, and complex forms of contact between the better-off and worse-off that were a characteristic feature of village life simply vanished. As in Kerala, the social bonds between the poor and the rest had been severed.[102]

As poverty, place, and race fused together, the civil rights movement widened. Unlike in the South, where civil rights was largely (though by no means exclusively) dedicated to dismantling Jim Crow, the civil rights movement in the North and West took up poverty, education, housing, jobs, and residential segregation itself as core concerns, often entering into complicated alliances with Latinos, Indians, and Asians who suffered from similar deprivations.[103] But issues like poverty and education proved dishearteningly slippery, especially compared with the clear-cut violations of citizenship rights that the Southern movement targeted. Even as proponents of racial justice won decisive victories against Jim Crow in the courts and in Congress, the deck was quietly stacked against them in the marketplace, in the schools, and in residential occupancy patterns. The problem no longer seemed to be individual racists or overt discrimination so much as a diffuse "white power structure." And, as the scope of the civil rights movement's diagnosis widened, the movement grew more militant.[104] By the time the Economic Opportunity Act was passed, both Harlem and Rochester, New York, had experienced riots. The next year, more than thirty people in the Watts neighborhood of Los Angeles would die in riots.

Shriver hoped that the federal government could sidestep municipal powerholders and reach directly to the communities where poverty was endemic. What he found, though, was that without urban politicians managing local affairs, there was very little to hold poor people in their accustomed places. Community action agencies organized unions, conducted rent strikes, challenged evictions, monitored police officers, funded gang members, and intervened in electoral politics.[105] Kenneth Clark's community action agency, HARYOU (by then under a different name and management), raised eyebrows when it redirected federal funds to the Black Arts Theater run by the revolutionary poet LeRoi Jones, a man who described his political philosophy at the time as "hate whitey."[106] Boone arranged a grant of nearly a third of a million dollars to a Syracuse organization led by the self-proclaimed radical Saul Alinsky, who spent the government's money organizing tenants' unions, bailing protesters out of jail, and running a voter-registration drive to defeat the incumbent Republican mayor. "We are experiencing a class struggle in the traditional Karl Marx style in Syracuse," protested the director of the city's housing authority, "and I do not like it."[107]

Alinsky was a fitting ally for Boone and a fitting emblem of community action's radical turn. He was a communitarian, with graduate training from the University of Chicago. For decades, Alinsky maintained a correspondence with the French philosopher Jacques Maritain, one of the founders of the personalist philosophical school of which

Diem was so enamored. (Alinsky described Maritain as "my spiritual father and the man I love.")[108] But if Alinsky was a communitarian, he was an unusual one. He wasn't a midwestern farm type but a Jew who had grown up in a Chicago slum, and he was a lifelong radical. The point of community organizing for him had always been to challenge power. He scoffed at the Peace Corps because "it would never be allowed to meddle in the affairs, say, of the United Fruit Company in central America."[109]

It is important to recognize that, although Alinsky had been active since the 1940s, his combative approach to community organizing relegated him to the sidelines of U.S. political life for most of his career. His 1945 book *Reveille for Radicals* awakened few in its intended audience of sleepers. It was only in the 1960s that Alinsky gained any traction. It took a book on the burgeoning urban crisis, which described Alinsky's organizing techniques as "the most important and most impressive experiment affecting Negroes anywhere in the United States," to make Alinsky a national political figure.[110] "My stock split in two," he remembered.[111] Today, Alinsky is regarded as an influential figure on the U.S. left; Hillary Clinton wrote her undergraduate thesis about him, and Barack Obama was trained in (and taught) the Alinsky method of community organizing.[112] Yet it is hard to imagine Alinsky commanding a reputation even nearing that magnitude without the transformation of urban life and the rising civil rights movement that pushed his previously marginal form of community action onto the center stage.

Community action not only emboldened lifelong radicals like Alinsky, it also trained a new generation of them. Even when they were short-lived, community action agencies promoted nonwhites, poor people, and—most notably—women to positions within the bureaucracy, inaugurating new and enduring patterns of activism.[113] Tellingly, it was mainly in the offices of the Oakland OEO-funded poverty centers, where both Huey Newton and Bobby Seale worked, that they wrote the Black Panther Party Platform and Program in the fall of 1966.[114] Nor was the composition of that revolutionary program in government offices all that incongruous, since both the Panthers and the community action agencies drew sustenance from the ambiguous but productive notion of the local community.[115]

It was Newton who took the logic of "community" to its most radical extremes. The Black Panther Party is principally known for its revolutionary nationalism, but in 1970, Newton announced a new doctrine for the Panthers, "intercommunalism." It was a version of internationalism—the search for worldwide solidarity—but instead of taking the nation as the primary unit of affiliation, it took the community. "The communications revolution, combined with the expansive domination of the American empire," was creating a world in which the nation-state was simply irrelevant, reasoned Newton. That new world consisted of two political configurations: a growing U.S.–based empire of global capital and a congeries of embattled communities arrayed against it.[116]

Since globalization had undermined the nation, Newton believed that nationalists should abandon their quest for state power and instead construct a worldwide alliance of autonomous communities. Such communities were to "seize the means of production and distribute the wealth" within their localities, according to his revolutionary program.[117] But the goal of that seizure was not an international alliance of workers, a federation of free nations, or world socialism. It was a "dispersed collection of communities," each "a small unit with a comprehensive collection of institutions that exist to serve a small group of people."[118]

Intercommunalism was community action refashioned into a program for world revolution. Not surprisingly, it, too, relied on a universal notion of poverty, much like that suggested by Oscar Lewis. "We see very little difference in what happens to a community here in North America and what happens to a community in Vietnam," Newton observed.[119] Since both the communities of the global South and the "black community" in the United States (a phrase hardly ever used before 1960 and in constant use thereafter) faced a common enemy—the forces of global capitalism—localist groups such as the Panthers could imagine themselves to be a worldwide revolutionary vanguard, with Oakland as the revolution's epicenter.[120]

IN THE 1960s, Albert Mayer returned to New York, borne back by the tides of antipoverty policy that carried other experts from India to the United States. Nothing he did upon his return would rival the scale and significance of Etawah, but Mayer continued to work, particularly on public housing complexes, which he sought to imbue with a sense of neighborhood community.[121] On one memorable occasion, Mayer's firm was commissioned to redesign a park in a poor neighborhood. Mayer dutifully went about his usual business of meeting with residents to assess local needs. But he was surprised to encounter at one of those meetings "five strapping guys who asserted their views in what can only be called an ominous tone," insisting that he abandon his plans entirely. Mayer acquiesced, though not without great bitterness. The Community Action Program, he concluded, was not yielding genuine community mobilization but "a sort of stand-up knock-down situation with a lot of broken bones, intimidation, general tenseness."[122]

Mayer was not alone in feeling that, whatever the Community Action Program had unleashed, it was not what was intended. With men like Alinsky receiving federal money, accusations quickly piled up that the OEO was using taxpayers' dollars to bankroll a domestic revolution. Congress members objected that a community action agency in Nashville had funded a "Hate Whitey Liberation School" and that an agency in Houston had sought to purchase telescopic rifle sights with OEO funds.[123] Although there was little truth to the more extravagant of such charges, the main thrust was right: the community action agencies *were* a challenge to the status quo.

After the Watts riots, official support for the program evaporated. In late 1965, Charles Schultze, the White House Budget Bureau director, wrote Johnson a memo observing that the OEO had antagonized so many local officials that the Democrats might lose the support of their base in the upcoming midterm elections. "We ought not to be in the business of organizing the poor politically," Schultze wrote to Johnson. "O.K. I agree," the president replied.[124] As the administration gradually removed funding and support for the OEO, its top staff began to resign. In 1966, Jack Conway, head of the Community Action Program, and Richard Boone left to form the Citizens' Crusade against Poverty with Walter Reuther. It was an attempt to handle privately the task the government was backing away from: organizing the poor into direct political action. But the sense that things had gotten out of hand remained. When Sargent Shriver addressed their organization in April, his speech was drowned out by boos. "I will not participate in a riot," Shriver exclaimed before leaving the stage, his speech unfinished.[125]

In 1967, Johnson's draft bill to reauthorize the OEO required that in each locality, the highest-ranking elected official (usually the mayor) be automatically given a place on the board of every community action agency. But that was not enough for Congress, which modified the bill to further require that all community action agencies by supervised by state or local governments. Participation would still be built into the program, but participation with oversight. "They want the rain without the thunder and lightning," griped civil rights leader James Farmer, "the ocean without the terrible roar."[126]

In fact, what the political establishment wanted was participation without insubordination. But that had proved difficult to achieve. The on-the-ground elite that used informal mechanisms to exert social control over the poor in overseas villages was largely lacking in the impoverished neighborhoods of the United States. And so politicians sought to install a new class of Brahmins that could be relied upon to prevent local politics from turning radical. The new Brahmins did not comprise a landed elite as in India or the Philippines—in fact their social ties to the areas they supervised were attenuated—but they served a similar purpose. They prevented participation from leading to a social revolution.

Defanged, the OEO lost much of its momentum. Shriver left the agency in 1968 to become the ambassador to France. His successor, Bertram Harding, was an archetypal manager with little of Shriver's interest in community participation. After Nixon's election, the new president turned to Daniel Patrick Moynihan for advice on how to handle poverty. Moynihan recommended dismantling the OEO entirely. Nixon initially left the agency intact, although he followed Johnson's lead in placing the OEO in the hands of men who, like Harding, had little sympathy for community action. Those included Donald Rumsfeld, Harding's successor as director, and Rumsfeld's special assistant, Dick Cheney. In 1973, Nixon tried to break up the agency and discontinue community action altogether and would have succeeded had not Watergate triggered his resignation. Gerald Ford continued the tradition of maintaining it as a top-down agency until he handed it off in 1981 to Ronald Reagan, who finally abolished it—the only governmental agency that Reagan managed to entirely eliminate.[127]

The federal government's retreat from the Community Action Program did not mean a retreat from the concept of community development altogether. What it meant was that schemes requiring the direct participation of the poor were replaced by programs that mixed "participation" with supervision. The Model Cities program, signed into law by Johnson in 1966, was a sort of Community Action Program from the top down. It still contained participatory mechanisms, but the money went through city officials rather than directly to community groups. Two years later, Robert F. Kennedy and Jacob Javits created, as an amendment to the Economic Opportunity Act, a "Special Impact

Program" to fund Community Development Corporations (CDCs), development agencies designed to create jobs and housing, often by working with local industries. The community action agencies of the early War on Poverty may have died out, but CDCs sprang up by the hundreds in the 1970s.

As community programs continued through the Nixon, Ford, and Reagan years, a pattern emerged. At the same time as the federal government backed away from directly addressing unemployment, inferior housing, and deindustrialization, it turned over responsibility for ameliorating poverty to poor neighborhoods themselves. William Safire expressed the logic as a "national localism," in which the federal government "says to communities, 'Do it your way.' "[128] Thus during the Reagan administration, which saw severe cutbacks in funding for cities and for welfare programs, at least one thousand new CDCs were established.[129] Today there are around four thousand CDCs, responsible for the bulk of housing starts in poor neighborhoods. But as community organizations have had the responsibility for economic development thrust onto their shoulders, their basic composition has changed. The street organizing and social protest that were such a large part of the community action agencies' missions in the 1960s have taken a back seat to tangible outcomes. More and more, the role of the community organization is not that of the town hall but the real estate development office. The executives of CDCs today are often white and hired for their business experience rather than for their ties to the neighborhoods themselves.[130]

BY ONE measure, the centrality of CDCs within today's urban landscape can be scored as a victory for the community development movement. Although their mission to elicit community participation is nearly always tempered by some measure of elite control, the mere fact that the residents of poor areas are *any* part of the equation is an achievement. And the participatory aspects of CDCs should not be minimized. Even though participation can be perfunctory, it is not always so, and advocacy organizations have mastered the art of using formal requirements concerning "community participation" to insert themselves forcefully into decision-making processes, threatening to block developments unless concessions to the poor are made. A tour of poor neighborhoods, with their Malcolm X Boulevards and Frederick Douglass High Schools, gives ample evidence of the power that community activists have claimed over local politics.

The other thing one would notice in making such a tour, though, is how segregated U.S. cities remain and how pernicious the effects of that segregation are. Schools may be named after Frederick Douglass but, because education is funded by local taxation, those schools can claim far fewer resources than their suburban counterparts. Nor is it just education. Income, wealth, crime rates, even basic physical health differ dramatically from place to place. When Michael Harrington published *The Other America* in 1962, readers were taken aback by its claims. Today, they would not be. That the poor and the better-off inhabit different countries is undeniable and obvious.

Huey Newton's hope that the Oaklands of the nation would secede has been, ironically, partially fulfilled. The federal government *has* retreated from the poor areas of the country, devolving policymaking whenever possible to states, cities, and localities. But the rise of community control has come alongside the growth of economic apartheid, which has undermined the value of controlling localities. From the time of the OEO's first community action grant to the present, the share of the national income accruing to the richest 0.1 percent of the population shot up from under two percent to nearly nine percent.[131] Cities, meanwhile, have seen their budgets collapse. How localism can address or reverse such trends is far from clear.[132]

WHAT IS DEAD AND WHAT IS UNDEAD
IN COMMUNITY DEVELOPMENT?

NEW YEAR'S EVE, 1965, caught Carl C. Taylor in a reflective mood, and he sat down to write a series of letters about the state of community development. There were only a handful of people in the world better qualified to hold forth on the topic. In the United States, Taylor had overseen a key division within the USDA's Bureau of Agricultural Economics and had been president of the American Sociological Society. Abroad, he had observed and consulted on community development programs in twenty-one different countries on behalf of the United Nations, the United States, and the Ford Foundation.[1] He also was a board and executive committee member of International Voluntary Services (IVS), the community development agency that served as an important model for the Peace Corps. In fact, one of his letters was to Stanley Andrews, one-time director of the U.S. Technical Cooperation Administration (which was in charge of distributing Point Four aid), who also served on the IVS's board.

Prospects did not appear bright to Taylor, writing on the last day of 1965. "I am afraid that we have not only become institutionalized in our procedures and our administration, but institutionalized in our thinking," he wrote to Andrews.[2] In country after country, community development programs had ossified into top-down bureaucracies, becoming so "mechanized" that "those working at the local levels have become the chore boys of administration rather than the catalyzers and entrepreneurs of local community change."[3] Even the Peace Corps, Taylor added, had become a mass agency, lacking "a real community development understanding."[4] Still worse, the Vietnam War was quickly consuming budgets and displacing the possibility of grassroots development in Asia and Africa.[5]

Taylor knew a great deal about the Vietnam War's heavy toll, since South Vietnam had been one of IVS's primary fields of operation since 1956.[6] Taylor had hoped that IVS's close collaboration with USAID there would pull the U.S. government into development work, but he found instead that the pulling went the other way. The United States was using IVS volunteers as "shock troops, sent into areas of what is thought to be special need, and where no one else will go."[7] At its peak, IVS had more than 160 volunteers in South Vietnam, and at least nine of them died there. The agency's difficulties would soon become so acute that four of its top workers would publicly resign in protest of IVS's complicity with the U.S. war effort. For Taylor, it was a surreal end to a long career. Thirty years after he launched a mission to use communal institutions to protect U.S. farmers from the Depression, he was now forced to mull over his organization's complicity in counterinsurgency campaigns deployed against the peasants of Southeast Asia.

Taylor was far from the only disappointed community developer. Surveying the scene in 1961, one USAID employee lamented that community development was in a "recession." The aid agency had been "strongly infected with 'economism' " and had turned away from community development toward strategies designed to boost GDP. That shift had had "subtle and devastating effects on the morale of the whole community development group in the government."[8] By 1963, the Philippine program was being phased out, and USAID support had been entirely withdrawn from major countries such as India, Iraq, Egypt, Jordan, Iran, South Korea, and Pakistan. Scattered staff remained at their posts in Africa and Southeast Asia, but they, too, were scheduled to be relieved of their duties.[9] The Community Development Division's headquarters was closed later that year. The only foreign country to see an increase in community development aid from the United States after 1963 was South Vietnam.[10]

The real problem that community development faced was not a lack of interest in Washington, although that was palpable, but a lack of interest everywhere else. Community development's persistent inability to generate results, combined with a new sense of urgency triggered by growing populations and looming food crises, had shifted attention away from community building toward the techniques of the Green Revolution. Agricultural technologies, not agrarian communities, commanded investments. Whereas by the late 1950s it was hard to find a developing nation without a community development program of some scope, by the late 1960s it was hard to find a community development program that had not been abolished, defunded, or folded into an agricultural ministry. To the degree that governments continued to use community strategies, they used them not to alleviate poverty but to control poor populations, often within the context of counterinsurgency campaigns.

At the United Nations, previously a bastion of support for community development, the toll was apparent. Eastern European delegates led a series of vigorous attacks on community developers. "You are always talking about process, you are talking about definitions of something that seems vague and general, and we can't exactly put our finger on what it is it's accomplishing," is how Julia Henderson, director of the UN's Bureau of Social Affairs, paraphrased their complaints. "Aren't you avoiding the basic problems of social reform? . . . Can you get real community development where . . . your social structure is so archaic that the people on the bottom are never going to benefit from what you do?"[11] Such questions, Henderson conceded, were increasingly hard to answer.

COMMUNITY DEVELOPMENT had delivered underwhelming or unpredictable results for nearly two decades, and by late 1965, it appeared to have reached its end. That is, at least, how things looked from the standpoint of Carl C. Taylor on New Year's Eve. But that is not how things look now. Today, from the vantage point of the United States, what is noteworthy is how far modernizing ideologies have fallen and how popular communitarian ones are.

Modernizers had never commanded exclusive control over U.S. thought and culture. W. W. Rostow's *Stages of Economic Growth* (1960) is usually read as the apex of modernization theory. Yet it is telling that it was followed, just a year later, by Jane Jacobs's enormously popular anti-modernist tract, *The Death and Life of Great American Cities* (1961). The next year brought another challenge: Thomas S. Kuhn's *The Structure of Scientific Revolutions* (1962), questioning the ability of scientists to generate cumulative advances. Books such as these signaled a subterranean discontent with high modernism. Still, as long as the United States enjoyed global hegemony, unprecedented growth, and political stability, modernization as an ideology made a sort of intuitive sense. Within the metropole, it roughly fit the facts.

The 1970s, however, changed all of that. Economic exhaustion and political turmoil in the United States gave the lie to the notion that all societies were inevitably and happily moving toward a U.S.–style stage of high mass consumption. Worse was the Vietnam War. In addition to depleting U.S. coffers and shattering the domestic political consensus, Vietnam presented the world with the image of a nuclear superpower, governed by the "best and the brightest," unable to overcome an army of peasants equipped with bicycles.[12] The 1973 oil crisis, in which former colonies in the Middle East proved capable of decimating the global industrial economic order, only underscored the message. "We are now living in a never-never land," lamented Secretary of State Henry Kissinger, "in which tiny, poor, and weak nations can hold up for ransom some of the industrialized world."[13]

As the industrial economy failed to deliver on its promises, its costs became more apparent. The same year that Thomas Kuhn published his *Structure of Scientific Revolutions* saw the release of Rachel Carson's *Silent Spring* (1962), the book that is uniformly credited with placing ecological concerns before the public. It did not take long for recognition of the environmental consequences of dams, nuclear power, monocrop agriculture, industrial chemicals, and unrestricted growth to become widespread. In 1970, the organizers of Earth Day surprised even themselves by inducing some twenty million people in the United States to take part in the environmentalist celebration. Taking the hint, Jimmy Carter campaigned against "compulsive dam building" and, upon taking office, prepared a "hit list" of federal water projects for which he hoped to revoke funding.[14] Meanwhile, environmental thinkers began in the late 1960s to issue increasingly dire warnings about overpopulation, the limits of nonrenewable resources, and the carrying capacity of the earth. Alarmingly, the warnings came not just from dyspeptic cultural critics but from scientists themselves, the former handmaidens of modernization.[15]

Under such strain, the intellectual foundations of modernization theory buckled. The cozy assumption that the passage of time would induce all societies to replace traditions with "modernity" lost credibility. The idea of *postmodernity* gained currency and social scientists began to intensively explore—as community developers had been doing for some time—multiple hybrid arrangements of "modern" and "traditional" elements, shattering the link between modernization and development.[16] None of those alternatives individually commanded enough support on its own to replace modernization theory as the center of metropolitan developmentalist thought. But they were enough to render modernization untenable. Developmentalism fractured and coalesced around minimalist projects such as human rights or "basic needs"—placing floors on how much individuals should be allowed to suffer—rather than around full-bodied developmental visions.[17]

The challenges to modernization theory came from many directions at once and, together, they split apart what had been a durable configuration of attributes. Not only did the various components of modernization theory—technology, growth, industry, expertise, centralization, bureaucracy, the state, and secular norms—all encounter stiffer resistance than they had before, they were also breaking away from each other and recombining in new ways. High-tech decentralization, growth-oriented Christian fundamentalism, and the revolt of experts against industrialism all found expression in what Daniel Rodgers has called the "Age of Fracture."[18] The possible permutations were many, and not all proved stable. But as the grand edifice of modernization crumbled, communitarian and localist forms of thought that had lived in modernization's shadow for decades sprang up toward the light. Gerald Ford declared 1976, the bicentennial, to be the "Year of the Neighborhood."[19] The next year, Ford's successor Jimmy Carter invited E. F. Schumacher, the Gandhian economist and author of *Small Is Beautiful* (1973), to the White House for a discussion.

In the midcentury decades, small-group theory had been decidedly ambidextrous in its politics, showing up in the writings of socialists, management theorists, and centrists alike. Communitarianism maintained that ambidexterity throughout the 1970s. On the left, the small community became a bastion of resistance against the liberal establishment. One of the clearest distinctions between the Old Left of the 1930s and the New Left of the 1960s, in fact, concerned the question of scale. Whereas the older leftism centered on trade unions and mass parties, the new generation, enamored with "participatory democracy" and "the beloved community," questioned the very basis for such organizations. "Our monster cities, based historically on the need for mass labor, might now be humanized, broken into smaller communities" and "arranged according to community decision," proposed the Students for a Democratic Society's *Port Huron Statement* (1962).[20] The solidaristic community—*communitas,* as Paul and Percival Goodman named it in a 1947 book that took on new relevance after its republication in 1960—

inspired many tribes of the New Left and the attendant counterculture.[21] It was especially relevant to the radical feminist movement, which regarded consciousness-raising discussion groups as instruments of liberation.[22]

Yet the left had no monopoly on community. The political right, also dissenting from the New Deal establishment, found its own reasons to privilege subnational units. Sometimes that meant a turn to individualism, as celebrated in Milton Friedman's *Capitalism and Freedom* (1962), but just as frequently it meant veneration of the neighborhood and the community. "I am calling . . . for an end to giantism, for a return to the human scale," proclaimed Ronald Reagan in 1975. "It is activity on a small, human scale that creates the fabric of community" and "nurtures standards of right behavior," he explained.[23] The conservative claim to community was firmly staked out two years later in Peter L. Berger and Richard John Neuhaus's *To Empower People* (1977), which proposed neighborhoods, families, churches, and voluntary associations as a middle ground between the "megastructures" of the modern welfare state and the untethered individual.[24] Those "mediating structures," as Berger and Neuhaus called them, became reliable touchstones for Republican speechwriters, never more so than when George H. W. Bush, in his 1989 inaugural address, famously spoke "of a thousand points of light, of all the community organizations that are spread like stars throughout the nation, doing good."[25]

By the 1990s, community had gained footholds on the left and the right and led a campaign to once again seize the center. Serious and well-read works of sociology—among them Alan Wolfe's *Whose Keeper?* (1989), Amitai Etzioni's *The Spirit of Community* (1994), and Robert Putnam's "Bowling Alone" (1995, published as a book of the same title in 2000)—promoted the notion of "civil society" as a necessary balance to both states and markets. There was something familiar in the notion. Although civil society—the wide array of shared norms, informal mechanisms, and voluntary associations that guide human action—was not necessarily a small-scale phenomenon, it nevertheless bore a family resemblance to the idea of the "small group" that animated midcentury thinkers. The new communitarianism, as Etzioni called it, also captured some of groupism's ambivalence about modernization. Wolfe's book began with an examination of the "paradoxes of modernity," and Etzioni explained that communitarianism blended "the virtues of tradition with the liberation of modernity."[26]

Politicians eagerly followed suit. Although "the importance of community" is sometimes no more than a campaign-trail cliché, the reliability with which recent U.S. presidents have adopted communitarian rhetoric is nevertheless extraordinary. Just a year after Bill Clinton's election, reporters noticed that he and his wife had begun to speak in the distinctive cadences of communitarianism (culminating in the 1996 publication of Hillary Clinton's *It Takes a Village*).[27] More substantively, Clinton launched a multi-billion-dollar community empowerment program, closely overseen by Vice President Al Gore, himself a dedicated communitarian.[28] George W. Bush continued the trend by calling on leading civil society experts as advisers. No less an authority than Etzioni himself pronounced Bush's first inaugural address to be "a communitarian text," although that might not have been such a surprise, given that Robert Putnam helped Bush write it.[29] Of course, Bush and Clinton had little on Barack Obama, a native son of the community movement. Obama was a trained community organizer and the prize student of a highly communitarian intellectual milieu—Harvard in the late 1980s— but the ties ran deeper than that. His mother, Ann Dunham Soetoro, was an anthropologist who had worked with the Ford Foundation and USAID to establish microcredit programs in Indonesia.[30]

The most telling sign that the pendulum had swung toward community, however, did not have to do with presidents but with an antipoverty initiative called the Austin Project, launched in 1991. On the surface, it seemed to be standard fare: it promised "comprehensive community development," proceeding via pilot projects, self-help, local leadership, community mobilization, and widespread participation.[31] What was noteworthy was the identity of the man in charge: W. W. Rostow, the prophet of modernization theory and Johnson's national security adviser at the height of the Vietnam War.

The Rostow who led the Austin Project was not the Rostow of the 1950s and 1960s—a triumphant proponent of the values of the United States and the inevitability that other countries would adopt them. It was not the Rostow who believed in the power of modernization theory to plot the destinies of poor nations. It was an altered Rostow, concerned with domestic poverty and given to lamenting the dominance of the "hierarchical, top-down, specialized" style of planning and the threats to "our communal life."[32] In place of planning from above, Rostow suggested communal deliberation, in which "ghetto communities, through credible local leaders, are actively consulted on the character of intervening programs."[33] He even proposed a motto for the Austin Project: "In a democracy those who must carry out a plan should participate in the planning."[34]

IN THE 1990s, Amitai Etzioni hypothesized that there had been a "curl back" in the United States, toward community.[35] Certainly, the demolition of the modernization complex and the rise of various localist and communitarian hybrids there signaled an important intellectual shift. But how widespread was it? Did it extend to the global South? Although this is an area where far more research remains to be done, it is possible to offer a tentative answer. It does not appear that the resurgence of community thinking in the United States was a global trend. Rather, what appeared to Etzioni as a renewal of communitarianism might be better seen, from a broader perspective, to be merely a transposition of its geography.

In the two decades after World War II, the United States was the world's leading industrial power and the greatest beneficiary of its modernizing processes. That was not enough to grant modernists a monopoly on thought and culture—one of the main arguments of the book is that localism persisted during that time—but they did operate from a position of power. It was only in the United States' dealings with the global South, where skepticism about modernization was much more pronounced, that communitarian policymaking came to the fore. In other words, in the twenty years following 1945, it was the global South that provided the impetus for the global community development movement, even as the global North supplied funding and expertise.

By the 1970s, that relationship was flipped on its head. In the United States, communitarian ideologies flowered on the grave of modernization. The global South, by contrast, became *less* fertile ground for community strategies. An older generation of leaders who had come to political maturity under imperial rule and thus maintained an ambivalence about modernization gave way to a new generation for whom the problems of economic production, industrial transformation, and the maintenance of order loomed larger. At a time when the United States acquired an allergy to modernization, Southern leaders developed a newfound taste for it.

When the fracturing of modernization ideology is described, mention is frequently made of the Southern challenge: the demand by the poorer nations of the earth for a redistribution of development's fruits. In

171

contrast to modernization theorists, who assumed that all nations could prosper once they adopted "modern" institutions, prominent Southern economists argued that the poverty of the global South and the wealth of the global North were causally related to each other, that the North was wealthy because it exploited the South. "Dependency theory," as the hypothesis was initially called, emerged from Latin American institutes of economics in the 1950s but enjoyed widespread adoption in the following decades, including among the opponents of modernization theory in the United States.[36]

The sense among dependency theorists that international economic inequalities were not only unfortunate but also unfair was, by the 1970s, shared widely by leaders in the global South. That perception came out clearly when Southern nations joined together in 1974 to address the widening gap between rich and poor countries. It was an auspicious time to revisit the basic terms of the global economy, as the oil embargo begun in 1973 had given the South more bargaining power than perhaps it would ever have. Using their power in the UN's General Assembly—where each country, no matter how small or poor, had one vote—Southern nations passed a resolution proclaiming a New International Economic Order (NIEO). Its twenty principles demanded autonomy for Southern governments over their own resources and economic policies, preferential treatment for poor countries in international trade bargaining, more aid from North to South, and better Southern access "to the achievements of modern science and technology."[37]

What is noteworthy about dependency theory and the NIEO is that, although they challenged the hegemony of the global North and some of the tenets of modernization theory, both implicitly endorsed the modernizers' focus on industrially oriented, state-directed economic growth. In fact, their objection to modernization theory was simply that it failed to recognize the way in which Northern growth came at the expense of Southern growth. Nowhere among the NIEO's twenty principles, which repeatedly affirmed the sanctity of central governments, was there anything that a community developer might take as encouragement.

Indeed, the rise of the NIEO coincided with a pronounced authoritarian trend among Southern governments. According to POLITY IV, a comprehensive dataset rating political conditions in each country, Asia, Africa, and Latin America grew markedly less democratic and more autocratic over the course of the 1960s and 1970s.[38] Even where leaders continued to face fair elections, food crises and the specter of population growth instilled in Southern countries a sense of urgency incompatible with the decentralist, deliberation-centered style of community development. The Stalinist model of brute-force modernization continued to attract adherents well after the Soviet economy faltered (in part because the Soviet Union effectively concealed the conditions of its economy for a remarkably long time). And when Stalinism lost its luster, South Korea's pattern of authoritarian, state-directed capitalism took its place as the agreed-upon model for countries in dire need of growth.[39]

It was not just the complementary relationship between modernization and authoritarianism that kept the urge to modernize alive in the global South after the 1970s. It was also that the global base of industry had moved. Modernization is an ideology for an industrial society, and one reason it lost purchase in the United States is that, by the 1970s, the United States was becoming a postindustrial one.[40] But industry did not vanish, it moved, and the places to which it moved were increasingly located in the global South. That relocation had partly to do with the long-term industrialization campaigns of poor countries, but it had more to do with the increased capital flows and increasing ease of transportation and communication that amplified radically in the 1970s.[41] When globalization shifted the industrial base of the world to the South, it shifted the basis for industrial ideology there, too.

Dams, a frequently invoked symbol of state-directed, top-down development, tell the story well. While Jimmy Carter and other Northern leaders dramatically curtailed dam-building in rich nations, large dams multiplied in the global South. Worldwide, more dams were commissioned in the twenty-year period from 1980 to 1999 than the *thirty*-year one from 1950 to 1979, with many of the new dams going up in China.[42] It was not that the costs of dams were unknown to dam-builders, it was just that industrial development took priority. "I am most unhappy that development projects displace tribal people," explained Indira Gandhi in 1984. "But sometimes there is no alternative and we have to go ahead in the larger interest."[43]

What of environmentalism, which played such an important role in disabling modernization projects and encouraging localism in the United States? In rich nations, which had already banked a century's worth of extraordinary economic growth, environmentalism arrived as a postindustrial ideology, one fitting leaders and citizens equally well. In the South, however, where national growth depended largely on industrial development, governments tended to resist international pressure to accommodate environmentalism. They pointed out the unfairness of rich countries seeking to impose growth-impeding environmental policies on their poorer neighbors. The issue is still not resolved; one of the largest impediments to reaching international accords on environmental policy today is the disagreement about how much of the global burden the governments of poorer economies ought to bear.[44]

The environmentalism of the global South has thus tended not to be the ideology of national leaders but rather to appear as the "environmentalism of the poor": movements of subaltern peoples who have seen few of the benefits of national growth and yet who have paid many of the costs as their lands, health, and livelihoods have been sacrificed to industrial development. Such movements rarely concern themselves with the beauty of nature. They are social justice campaigns, heterogeneous alliances of dam refugees, fisherpeople, indigenous peoples, subsistence farmers, and slumdwellers imperiled by large-scale development projects. These movements are not led by establishment types as they are in the United States—Jimmy Carter and Al Gore. Their leaders, rather, are dissenting figures: Ken Saro-Wiwa of Nigeria, executed by his own government in 1995, or Medha Patkar of India, who has come close to death by drowning and hunger multiple times in her protests against the Sardar Sarovar Dam. For the most part, they are locked in hostile combat with the modernizers who control their governments, and for the most part they are still losing.[45]

THE REAL threat to the top-down developmental state in the global South has not come from insurgent social movements; it has come from the global North. The proclamation of the New International Economic Order, made just as oil-producing countries in the South were crippling industrial economies in the North, proved to be a high-water mark for Southern power. Any fears that Northern leaders might have entertained about a redistribution of the global product, however, were quickly allayed. A debt crisis in the 1980s (fueled, ironically, by the alarmingly easy availability of credit in the 1970s resulting from the surge of petrodollars into the system), placed many Southern governments at the mercy of their Northern creditors. Now it fell to Northern lenders, working through the International Monetary Fund and the World Bank, to set policy in the global South.

When Southern countries' bargaining power peaked in the 1970s, those countries demanded sovereignty over their own economic policies.

Once the tables had turned, Northern countries pressed for the opposite: a massive rollback of Southern states and Southern economic autonomy as a condition for continued loans. The sense among development experts that Southern governments were the problem had been growing since the Berg Report (1981) by the World Bank recommended a sympathetic reconsideration of market strategies.[46] By the 1990s, that impression blossomed into a program, the "Washington Consensus."[47] Backed principally by the International Monetary Fund, the Washington Consensus entailed extending much-needed loans to indebted countries only if the recipient governments would agree to a set of "structural adjustments" that included reducing state expenditures, liberalizing trade, and otherwise reducing the role of public institutions in national life. Whereas in the United States the turn toward the market had come at the hand of elected officials such as Ronald Reagan, in the South it came largely as an ultimatum.

In the United States, the crisis of the liberal state unleashed market ideologies but also, running alongside them, communitarian ones. A similar interplay of markets and civil society emerged among international development experts in the 1990s as hostility toward the developmental state grew. Specifically, developers latched onto the idea of "social capital," as articulated by sociologist James S. Coleman and popularized by Robert Putnam's "Bowling Alone" article.[48] In this vision, development is not just a matter of physical capital—of machines and materials—but requires *social* capital as well: networks of trust, voluntary organizations, and a vibrant associational life. The idea had an all-round appeal. For advocates of markets, social capital suggested a way to provide the necessary social supplements to the market without involving the state. For those on the left, it offered an alternative vision of bottom-up development that emphasized cultural pluralism and grassroots movements. Thus, both markets and social movements, which often stood in clear opposition to one another, were understood to be enhanced by the flourishing of local civil society.[49]

In the late 1990s, the World Bank began to take a strong interest in social capital. Bank economist Christiaan Grootaert proposed in a much-cited 1997 paper that social capital might be the "missing link" in development, the ingredient without which all projects would founder.[50] Grootaert urged the Bank to incorporate "existing associations and organizations" into its development projects and to cultivate "enabling environments" for the growth of local organizations.[51] The Bank took

Grootaert's advice to heart. At the same time as it backed off funding large infrastructural projects such as hydroelectric dams, it channeled great streams of money toward participatory projects that it alternatively described as "community-driven development" and "community-based development." Communal participation is now "a central tenet of development policy," according to the Bank's acting chief economist.[52] In the past decade alone, the Bank estimates that it has loaned or given out roughly $85 billion for community-directed development and the decentralization of governments.[53]

What is surprising about the rapid rise of community-driven development since the 1990s is how little acknowledgment has been given to the community development movement of the midcentury decades. Grootaert's celebrated paper made no mention of it and was hardly exceptional in that regard. Indeed, it appears that midcentury community development has been simply forgotten, aided no doubt by historians' interpretation of the immediate postwar period as a time when top-down modernization commanded a consensus. One economist, while studying the World Bank's work in the field, stumbled upon a master's thesis about midcentury community development and was shocked to discover that there had *been* such a thing. Searching through the scholarly record, he was astonished to find a "vast literature on the topic" from the 1950s and 1960s, but "virtually no references thereafter." What struck him most forcefully were the similarities between midcentury practices and those of today. He found training manuals from the 1940s that, but for the "dated nature" of the photographs, "could well have been from the 1990s."[54]

His observation was astute. There are, of course, clear differences between community-directed development today and the community development of the middle of the twentieth century. Women play a much larger role in the process, as do markets and credit. Nevertheless, for those familiar with the history of community development, today's community projects bear an unmistakable resemblance to their predecessors. Even their shortcomings appear to be identical. After a review of nearly five hundred studies of participatory development and decentralization, Ghazala Mansuri and Vijayendra Rao, two lead economists at the World Bank, found community-directed development to have modest results, benefits that skewed significantly toward local elites, and great difficulty in encouraging the durable formation of egalitarian communities.[55]

176

Those were precisely the problems that killed community development the first time around.

THE FOG of amnesia surrounding the history of community development is regrettable, but it is not surprising. Development experts have little reason to look to the past. The history of development aid has been bleak enough that one rarely wins arguments, much less grants, by stressing the continuities between one's preferred strategy and what came before. The constant circulation of development practitioners from country to country also militates against long memories. Traditionally, it is the job of historians to remind others of the things that have been forgotten. But since historians of development have until very recently told the history of midcentury development as the story of modernization, they have done little to jog developers' memories about community development.

There is another reason community development has been easy to forget: it wasn't noisy in the way that other development strategies were. The quest for community simply did not produce catastrophe on the same scale as the urge to modernize did. It left no crumbling dams, flooded villages, slums filled with refugees, or napalm-scorched forests in its wake. But the tolls of community development, though less spectacular, are no less present. They can be seen in the millions wasted on pointless projects, in the unabated poverty and degradation faced by a large fraction of the world's population, and in the generation of chastened villagers who learned, yet again, not to place their faith in their governments.

Now that community development is once again in vogue, the failures of the midcentury decades merit a moment's contemplation. Are there lessons to learn? Historians, with their deep appreciation for the special particularity of each time and place, are notoriously reluctant to propose that the past "teaches" us anything about the present. But there are nonetheless a few observations that a study of community development's checkered past suggests.

First, though, something that it does *not* suggest. It does not suggest that the modernizers were right all along. Although the best-laid schemes of community developers often went awry, their understanding of the perils of top-down modernization was remarkably prescient. They saw, earlier and more clearly than their contemporaries, the dangers of dams, the antagonistic relationship between expertise and democracy, and the importance of social cohesion to those who live with poverty. Their notion that the intended beneficiaries of development schemes might deserve some say in the planning process was admirable, and their attempt to approach the poor via communal institutions had much to recommend it.

But if one wishes to see poor people participate as organized communities, one cannot treat the notion of community sentimentally. For all the eagerness of community developers to simply defer to naturally occurring communities (and their "natural" leaders), communities do not grow as cleanly or abundantly as that. Where the "community" is, who is in it, and how it works are open—and often contested—questions. Roughly egalitarian groupings with unified interests are likely to be communities capable of accomplishing things of collective benefit to their members. But many of the villages described in this book were unequal and factious places, containing little by way of community spirit. Community developers foundered when, their hearts overruling their heads, they squinted hard until the communities they wished to see blurrily appeared.

Hearts trumped heads all too often in the world of community development. Across the various places where community developers plied their trade, one note is constant: community developers were surprised by the outcomes of the programs they started. In India, the Philippines, and Vietnam, they were puzzled by the inability of village programs to raise living standards. Noting a lack of enthusiastic participation among the "grass roots," they attributed it to excessive bureaucracy and centralization. But genuine popular mobilization, such as the protests in the Japanese internment camps and the militant organizations of the War on Poverty, baffled them as well. Expecting that united communities would busy themselves with self-help, community developers were taken aback by combative social protests. In all cases, the mistaken expectations stemmed from a fantasy that the communities in question were essentially neighborly places that only required a nudge to undertake the therapeutic and cooperative processes of self-improvement.

What community developers overlooked was power: power within communities and power relationships between communities and the larger societies around them. It was the inegalitarian nature of most villages that explained why community programs frequently stalled out (and still do today). And it was the larger structures of power that explained why the few actual grassroots mobilizations that community developers encountered tended to challenge the broader social order. When poor people got the chance to confront impediments to their own flourishing, they rarely limited themselves to group therapy.

The tendency of poor people's movements to search outside themselves for the sources of their impoverishment illustrates an important limit to community action. Simply put, many of the causes of poverty are not local in origin. That is what inner-city U.S. community activists discovered in the 1960s when, examining the causes of their predicament, they found themselves pointing to a distant "white power structure." It is a lesson activists throughout the global South continue to learn as they confront multinational corporations, international financial institutions, and government agencies staffed with foreign experts. What is more, the causes of poverty that *are* local, such as unequal land distribution, are—ironically—extraordinarily difficult to resolve through government-sponsored community action, since the local hierarchies that led to the problem in the first place usually prove fully capable of hijacking community programs.

The principle that motivates community development—that people should have the power to shape the decisions that affect them—is a profoundly democratic one. But it is a leap of logic to assume that principle to be satisfied by encouraging participation in local communities. What if the communities in question are themselves undemocratic? And what if the important decisions are not made locally? Democracy comes in many forms. It is only a sentimental and uncritical view of "community" that would lead one to believe that democracy and local control are the same thing.

THE PROBLEM is not just that communities are rarely up to the task of conquering poverty. It is also that community development's characteristic focus on the small and local is itself evasive. The power of community development to direct attention away from larger structural problems toward small-scale ones was, in fact, precisely why the CIA found it so promising as a counter to rural communism. Community developers, confronted with poverty, ask what the poor can do, locally, to overcome it. But that is rarely the most productive question to ask, since it implicitly places the responsibility for alleviating poverty on the victims of poverty themselves. In the guise of "empowering" the poor, it drops the rich from the equation. And it is the rich who are both the beneficiaries of a skewed system of resource distribution and far more capable of altering that system.

This book has described a running debate between modernizers and communitarians about how to "develop" poor societies. Modernizers, confronted with poor societies, have asked "What can we do for them?" Community developers, by contrast, have asked a different version of that question: "How can we help them help themselves?" But there is another question that members of rich societies might ask, a question that springs neither from the urge to modernize nor the quest for community: "What have we been doing *to* them?"

That question implies a different framework, one that community developers have rarely considered. It raises the possibility of a causal relationship between the wealth of some and the poverty of others. It invites reflection about the past three hundred years of global history and the degree to which empires, markets, wars, and other mechanisms of international control have helped to create a situation in which the richest five percent of households claim 46.4% of the world's income and the poorest quarter of households claim 0.8%.[56] The world now contains 1,426 billionaires, with an aggregate wealth of $5.4 trillion, alongside more than a billion people whose average caloric intake falls short of what the United Nations defines as the minimum daily requirement.[57]

Community developers have little to say about those billionaires, or about the policies of the countries in which they reside. Communitarians' tight focus on the small and local makes it hard to see both the poor and the wealthy in the same frame. But it is worth zooming out for a moment, to examine the problem of poverty with a wide-angle lens. That panoramic perspective is of course not new—critics of capitalism and empire have insisted on its importance for nearly two centuries. Yet it is useful here for the insight it offers into community development. By taking the broader view, one can go beyond asking whether community development "fails" or "succeeds" and consider the larger question of where localist self-help schemes fit into a global economy that is marked by persistent inequality.

Once the frame is enlarged to include both the rich and the poor within it, important aspects of poverty become easier to see. For one, leaving aside the question of how rich countries acquired their wealth in the first place, it is clear that the current distribution of global resources is maintained by an international architecture of trade and finance designed by and for the rich. The International Monetary Fund, for instance, occupies a central position in the management of the world's finances. It is ostensibly a public institution dedicated to the welfare of all, but voting power within it is allocated to countries roughly on the basis of their positions in the world economy. India, with nearly four times the population of the United States, commands fewer than one-seventh of the votes.[58] Similar mechanisms ensure that the richest nations prevail at the UN (where the most powerful countries retain veto power via the Security Council), the World Trade Organization, and the World Bank. Nationally, we aspire to live in democracies. Internationally, we inhabit a plutocracy.

Not surprisingly, rich countries use their power to press their advantage. They erect trade barriers against poor countries while demanding, as the price of loans, that the same poor countries dismantle their own trade barriers. They subsidize agriculture within their own borders and then stand aside as their farmers dump below-market-price produce into Southern markets, crowding poorer agriculturalists out of the marketplace. They demand that Southern nations adopt and enforce stringent protections on intellectual property, driving up the price of medicine and technology for those who need it the most. And they maintain an international trading system that encourages unelected leaders in resource-rich Southern countries to sell off their countries' natural resources for personal gain. The cumulative effect on poor countries of all of these self-interested actions is to create a significant headwind against economic growth.[59]

The motors of global inequality have created a situation where the country in which a person is born—rather than her age, sex, education, or even the wealth of her parents—is by far the greatest determinant of her economic destiny.[60] One of community development's tacit assumptions has been that the poor should improve their lives while standing in place. If, however, we inquire about the possibility that poor people might migrate out of poverty, we confront the fact that, although the world has opened itself to the international flows of ideas, capital, and culture, it remains extraordinarily hostile to the free movement of people. One of the key ways in which those in wealthy countries maintain their wealth, in fact, is by locking foreigners out. Opening borders would both liberalize the global economy and make it more equal.[61] It would also introduce a strong incentive—one that is currently lacking—for rich countries to address global poverty. Were wealthy governments no longer able to simply close their doors on the poor, they would gain an immediate and palpable interest in improving conditions in the global South, if only to ensure that poor people did not come marching across their borders.

Finally, the living conditions of the poor are inextricably linked to the environment. Climate change—resulting in hotter temperatures, fiercer and more frequent storms, rising sea levels, extinctions, and massive disruptions of food and resource provision (which, in turn, trigger violence, disease, and migration)—threatens the poor, who are by definition the most vulnerable, far more acutely than it threatens the rich. That is a particularly queasy matter to contemplate because the overwhelming bulk of economic production and consumption that has *led* to climate change was done on behalf of the rich. Although we used to speak of global warming, somewhat blithely, as a threat to our grandchildren, it is now obviously a menace to the present generation. The heat, storms, and floods have already begun to take their toll. If the oft-expressed consensus of scientists is anywhere close to correct about the scope, rapidity, and likely consequences of future climate change, it seems extraordinarily improbable that humans will avoid a catastrophe within this century that promises to do disproportionate harm to the poor in great numbers.[62]

Global warming vividly illustrates the limits of attacking poverty by encouraging community spirit among the poor. Absent some technological *deus ex machina* capable of rapidly sucking the existing greenhouse gases from our atmosphere or instantly converting the entire world to clean energy—both of which seem very hard to imagine at this late date—the only option remaining to the human species to lessen the extent of the looming crisis is to immediately curtail its consumption of energy.[63] That will require dramatic alterations in the lifestyles of the rich. It will also require confronting powerful interests, particularly energy companies and oil-exporting governments, which have *already* surveyed, acquired, and made plans to sell enough fossil fuel to cumulatively raise global temperatures far above what the majority of governments have agreed on as a viable upper limit.[64]

Cutbacks on the requisite scale are unpleasant to imagine simply for what they imply about future standards of living, but they are also difficult to envision without some sort of international body with coercive capacity to coordinate and enforce them. Such an agency would have to be strong enough to prevent multinational energy companies from selling the oil and gas they already own. It would probably have to dramatically raise the price of fossil fuels, thereby crippling growth-based national economies the world over. This is an issue of profound local relevance, particularly in the places where poor people live, but it is not an issue that appears even remotely likely to yield to state-sponsored community action. The more globally connected the economy has become, the *less* relevant community strategies—especially those funded by governments or the World Bank—are to altering the large structural patterns that create poverty and exacerbate its worst effects.

UNFAIR TRADE rules, border controls, and global warming—none of that is news. Yet it helps to place community development in perspective. If rich countries truly wanted to help poor people and were willing to sacrifice some fraction of their share of global resources to do so, they wouldn't need to bother searching for the correct blend of modernization and communitarianism in their aid programs. They could simply reverse their own self-interested policies. But within a context in which rich nations continue to rig the international system to ensure that wealth accrues disproportionately to certain places, lock poor people out of those places, and then consume resources at a rate that will probably render much of the planet inhospitable, there is something bizarre about the current obsession with helping poor people help themselves. Fostering local solidarity seems beside the point.

And yet, the lure of community development remains strong. Not only wealthy governments, but their well-meaning citizens as well, continue to treat community-building among the poor as a sort of panacea. If large-scale processes are the problem, the logic goes, then the solution must be a return to the small. That line of thinking is sustained by the general sense that industrial societies have never really *tried* localism. Goliath was a poor leader; surely the time has come to give David a chance.

But the rule of Goliath was never as absolute as the partisans of David have insisted. The middle decades of the twentieth century were replete with high modernists, of course, but they contained localists, decentralists, and communitarians as well. Sometimes the modernizers themselves were prone to bouts of communitarianism. It was not King Goliath towering high above a lone David. It was a Goliath-controlled parliament forced to contend with a vocal and often persuasive Davidian minority.

This book has sought to write those Davids back into the story, not as solitary rebels but as serious and sometimes successful participants in politics. In part, bringing the Davids back in is an act of historical recovery, a simple attempt to offer a more accurate account of the past. But it has political stakes as well. To recognize communitarians' place in history is to give up on a fantasy, the fantasy that community is the great untried experiment of the industrial age. It is to treat community with less reverence and with more curiosity, to move it from the altar to the dissection table. Perhaps that is where it belongs. The problems of poverty are no less dire now than they were in the middle of the twentieth century. Solving them will require a clear-eyed understanding of what communities can do—and what they cannot.

NOTES

ACKNOWLEDGMENTS

INDEX

BAE	Bureau of Agricultural Economics, Department of Agriculture (U.S.)
CDC	Community Development Corporation (U.S.)
CDRC	Community Development Research Council (Philippines)
CENIS	Center for International Studies, Massachusetts Institute of Technology (U.S.)
CIA	Central Intelligence Agency (U.S.)
CORDS	Civil Operations and Revolutionary Development Support (Vietnam)
CPA	Community Projects Administration (India)
EDCOR	Economic Development Corps (Philippines)
HARYOU	Harlem Youth Opportunities Unlimited (U.S.)
ICA	International Cooperation Administration (U.S.)
IIRR	International Institute of Rural Reconstruction (Philippines)
IVS	International Voluntary Services (U.S.)
JCRR	Joint Commission on Rural Reconstruction (China)
NAB	National Archives Building, Washington, DC
NACP	National Archives at College Park, Maryland
NAI	National Archives of India, New Delhi
NAMFREL	National Citizens' Movement for Free Elections (Philippines)
NIEO	New International Economic Order
OEO	Office of Economic Opportunity (U.S.)
PACD	Presidential Assistant on Community Development/Presidential Arm on Community Development (Philippines)
PRRM	Philippine Rural Reconstruction Movement

TVA   Tennessee Valley Authority

USAID   U.S. Agency for International Development

USDA   U.S. Department of Agriculture

VISTA   Volunteers in Service to America

WRA   War Relocation Authority (U.S.)

INTRODUCTION

1. See Christina Klein, *Cold War Orientalism: Asia in the Middlebrow Imagination, 1945–1961* (Berkeley: University of California Press, 2003), 87, and *Publishers Weekly* bestseller lists, available at www.booksofthecentury.com. *Lolita* was first published in Paris in 1955 but was not released in the United States until 1958, the same year that *The Ugly American* was.

2. William J. Lederer and Eugene Burdick, *The Ugly American* (New York: W. W. Norton and Company, 1958), 281.

3. Ibid., 267.

4. Ibid., 216.

5. Ibid., 277.

6. There is now an extensive literature on modernization theory and, more generally, the ideology of modernization in the United States. Key works are Robert A. Packenham, *Liberal America and the Third World: Political Development Ideas in Foreign Aid and Social Science* (Princeton: Princeton University Press, 1973); Michael Adas, *Machines as the Measure of Men: Science, Technology, and Ideologies of Western Dominance* (Ithaca: Cornell University Press, 1990); Michael E. Latham, *Modernization as Ideology: American Social Science and "Nation Building" in the Kennedy Era* (Chapel Hill: University of North Carolina Press, 2000); Nils Gilman, *Mandarins of the Future: Modernization Theory in Cold War America* (Baltimore: Johns Hopkins University Press, 2003); David C. Engerman, Nils Gilman, Mark H. Haefele, and Michael E. Latham, eds., *Staging Growth: Modernization, Development, and the Global Cold War* (Amherst: University of Massachusetts Press, 2003); David C. Engerman, *Modernization from the Other Shore: American Intellectuals and the Romance of Russian Development* (Cambridge, MA: Harvard University Press, 2003); Odd Arne Westad, *The Global Cold War: Third World Interventions and the Making of Our Times* (Cambridge: Cambridge University Press, 2005); Michael Adas, *Dominance by Design: Technological Imperatives and America's Civilizing Mission* (Cambridge, MA: Harvard University Press, 2006); Bruce Kuklick, *Blind Oracles: Intellectuals and War from Kennan to Kissinger* (Princeton: Princeton University Press, 2006); Bradley R. Simpson, *Economists with Guns: Authoritarian Development and U.S.–Indonesian Relations, 1960–1968* (Stanford: Stanford University Press, 2008); David Ekbladh, *The Great American Mission: Modernization and the Construction of an American World Order* (Princeton: Princeton University Press, 2009); Larry Grubbs, *Secular Missionaries: Americans and African Development in the 1960s* (Boston:

University of Massachusetts Press, 2009); Nick Cullather, *The Hungry World: America's Cold War Battle against Poverty in Asia* (Cambridge, MA: Harvard University Press, 2010); Michael E. Latham, *The Right Kind of Revolution: Modernization, Development, and U.S. Foreign Policy from the Cold War to the Present* (Ithaca: Cornell University Press, 2011); Inderjeet Parmar, *Foundations of the American Century: The Ford, Carnegie, and Rockefeller Foundations in the Rise of American Power* (New York: Columbia University Press, 2012); and Amanda Kay McVety, *Enlightened Aid: U.S. Development as Foreign Policy in Ethiopia* (Oxford: Oxford University Press, 2012). To that list should be added a neighboring literature, often called "critical development studies," which shares a preoccupation with modernization and technocracy. Critical development studies, however, is less interested in the intellectual trajectory of development thought within the United States and more interested in the malign effects of development practices on the global South. Exemplary works include Wolfgang Sachs, ed., *The Development Dictionary: A Guide to Knowledge as Power* (London: Zed Books, 1992); Arturo Escobar, *Encountering Development: The Making and Unmaking of the Third World* (Princeton: Princeton University Press, 1994); James Ferguson, *The Anti-Politics Machine: "Development," Depoliticization, and Bureaucratic Power in Lesotho* (Minneapolis: University of Minnesota Press, 1994); Timothy Mitchell, *Rule of Experts: Egypt, Techno-Politics, Modernity* (Berkeley: University of California Press, 2002); Tania Murray Li, *The Will to Improve: Governmentality, Development, and the Practice of Politics* (Durham: Duke University Press, 2007); and, arriving at similar conclusions from a different angle of approach, William Easterly, *The Tyranny of Experts: Economists, Dictators, and the Forgotten Rights of the Poor* (New York: Basic Books, 2013). For a review of the literature on modernization and development, see Daniel Immerwahr, "Modernization and Development in U.S. Foreign Relations," *Passport*, September 2012, 22–25.

7. Susan Carruthers, "'Produce More Joppolos': John Hersey's *A Bell for Adano* and the Making of the 'Good Occupation,'" *Journal of American History* 100 (2014): 1086–1113.

8. Robert D. Dean, "Masculinity as Ideology: John F. Kennedy and the Domestic Politics of Foreign Policy," *Diplomatic History* 22 (2002): 58.

9. William J. Caldwell, "Note to Correspondents," 28 August 1957, folder 192, box 7, Max Millikan Papers, Institute Archives and Special Collections, MIT Libraries. Because of their focus on top-down modernization schemes, historians for a time either neglected community development or interpreted it as simply part of the modernization complex. Nevertheless, new work has begun to appear that explores communitarian approaches and challenges the notion that U.S. midcentury developmental practice was exclusively high modernist in character. See Nicole Sackley, "Passage to Modernity: American Social Scientists, India, and the Pursuit of Development, 1945–1961" (Ph.D. diss., Princeton University, 2004); Nick Cullather, "'The Target Is the People': Representations of the Village in Modernization and U.S. National Security Doctrine," *Cultural Politics* 2 (2006): 29–48; Sheyda F. Jahanbani, "'A Different Kind of People': The

Poor at Home and Abroad, 1935–1968" (Ph.D. diss., Brown University, 2009); Jason Pribilsky, "Development and the 'Indian Problem' in the Cold War Andes: *Indigenismo,* Science, and Modernization in the Making of the Cornell–Peru Project at Vicos," *Diplomatic History* 33 (2009): 405–426; Cullather, *Hungry World,* chap. 3; Nicole Sackley, "The Village as Cold War Site: Experts, Development, and the History of Rural Reconstruction," *Journal of Global History* 6 (2011): 481–504; Alyosha Goldstein, *Poverty in Common: The Politics of Community Action during the American Century* (Durham: Duke University Press, 2012); Nicole Sackley, "Cosmopolitanism and the Uses of Tradition: Robert Redfield and Alternative Visions of Modernization during the Cold War," *Modern Intellectual History* 9 (2012): 565–595; Peter Mandler, *Return from the Natives: How Margaret Mead Won the Second World War and Lost the Cold War* (New Haven: Yale University Press, 2013); Edward Miller, *Misalliance: Ngo Dinh Diem, the United States, and the Fate of South Vietnam* (Cambridge, MA: Harvard University Press, 2013); Nicole Sackley, "Village Models: Etawah, India, and the Making and Remaking of Development in the Early Cold War," *Diplomatic History* 37 (2013): 749–778. Even in this new literature, though, there is a tendency to characterize community schemes as "soft" or "alternative" forms of modernization—with Miller's *Misalliance* a notable exception.

10. Robert A. Nisbet, *The Quest for Community: A Study in the Ethics of Order and Freedom* (New York: Oxford University Press, 1953). The "urge to modernize" is a variant of the "urge to mobilize," described in George Yaney, *The Urge to Mobilize: Agrarian Reform in Russia, 1861–1930* (Urbana: University of Illinois Press, 1982).

11. James C. Scott, *Seeing Like a State: How Certain Schemes to Improve the Human Condition Have Failed* (New Haven: Yale University Press, 1998), 335.

12. James C. Scott, *The Art of Not Being Governed: An Anarchist History of Upland Southeast Asia* (New Haven: Yale University Press, 2009).

13. James C. Scott, *Two Cheers for Anarchism: Six Easy Pieces on Autonomy, Dignity, and Meaningful Work and Play* (Princeton: Princeton University Press, 2012), 7. It should be noted that Scott's assessment is not entirely pessimistic. First, his anarchism is not solely a plea for humans to return to small communities. Rather, Scott calls for the injection of flexibility, improvisation, and adaptation—the characteristics of small-scale life—into large-scale institutions. Second, Scott believes that petty acts of insubordination can, if numerous, achieve precisely that end. Scott's anarchism is thus significantly less utopian than the localism of many of his followers and fellow travelers. Nevertheless, there is a strong sense conveyed in Scott's work that the ways of life for which he is arguing are artifacts of the past that face extinction in the present.

14. Dwight Macdonald, "Too Big," 1946, reprinted in *Memoirs of a Revolutionist: Essays in Political Criticism* (New York: Farrar, Straus and Cudahy, 1957), 373.

15. For enlightening meditations on the unique persistence of "techno-hubris" within the United States, see Michael Adas, *Machines as the Measure of Men* and *Dominance by Design.*

16. An evocative reflection on the place of technology in empire can be found in Rudolf Mrázek, *Engineers of Happy Land: Technology and Nationalism in a Colony* (Princeton: Princeton University Press, 2002).

17. Lane E. Holdcroft, "The Rise and Fall of Community Development: 1950–1965" (M.S. thesis, Michigan State University, 1976), 3.

18. Jawaharlal Nehru, "From the Depths of India," *Kurukshetra,* June 1958, 639.

19. Gunnar Myrdal, *The Challenge of World Poverty: A World Anti-Poverty Program in Outline* (London: Allen Lane, 1970), 105.

20. Gerald D. Berreman, "Caste and Community Development," *Human Organization* 22 (1963): 93.

21. Alfred W. McCoy has been a particularly keen observer of this feedback. See Alfred W. McCoy, *Policing America's Empire: The United States, the Philippines, and the Rise of the Surveillance State* (Madison: University of Wisconsin Press, 2009) and Alfred W. McCoy and Francisco A. Scarano, eds., *Colonial Crucible: Empire in the Making of the Modern American State* (Madison: University of Wisconsin Press, 2009). Other useful works in this regard include Laura Briggs, *Reproducing Empire: Race, Sex, Science, and U.S. Imperialism in Puerto Rico* (Berkeley: University of California Press, 2002) and Jennifer S. Light, *From Warfare to Welfare: Defense Intellectuals and Urban Problems in Cold War America* (Baltimore: The Johns Hopkins University Press, 2003). A similar dynamic is explored in David A. Hollinger, "The Protestant Boomerang: How the Foreign Missionary Project Transformed American Culture," Danforth Distinguished Lectures, Washington University in St. Louis, 18–20 November 2013.

22. On the flow of policies from the global South to the United States in the field connected fields of poverty and development, see Christopher T. Fisher, "'The Hopes of Man': The Cold War, Modernization Theory, and the Issue of Race in the 1960s" (Ph.D. diss., Rutgers University, 2002); Jahanbani, "A Different Kind of People"; Goldstein, *Poverty in Common;* Amy C. Offner, "Anti-Poverty Programs, Social Conflict, and Economic Thought in Colombia and the United States, 1948–1980" (Ph.D. diss., Columbia University, 2012), epilogue; and Amrys O. Williams, "Cultivating Modern America: 4-H Clubs and Rural Development in the Twentieth Century" (Ph.D. diss., University of Wisconsin–Madison, 2012), chap. 5.

23. Bill McKibben, "The Era of Small and Many: Reversing the Trend of Generations," *Orion Magazine,* November/December 2011, 10–11. See also Nicco Mele, *The End of Big: How the Internet Makes David the Goliath* (New York: St. Martin's Press, 2013).

24. Hillary Rodham Clinton, *It Takes a Village, and Other Lessons Children Teach Us* (New York: Simon and Schuster, 1996).

25. Ghazala Mansuri and Vijayendra Rao, *Localizing Development: Does Participation Work?* (Washington, DC: The World Bank, 2013), 1. This figure includes money dispensed for the decentralization of governments.

I. WHEN SMALL WAS BIG

1. Walt Disney, quoted in Andrew J. Huebner, "The Conditional Optimist: Walt Disney's Postwar Futurism," *The Sixties* 2 (2009): 228.

2. Quoted in Steve Mannheim, *Walt Disney and the Quest for Community* (Aldershot: Ashgate, 2002), 28.

3. Walt Disney, quoted in Steven Watts, *The Magic Kingdom: Walt Disney and the American Way of Life* (Boston; Houghton Mifflin, 1997), 23. Disney's claim to the contrary, the precise scale to which the parts of Main Street, U.S.A. were built varied, although the entire area was indeed constructed on a reduced scale.

4. EPCOT, the town, was never built, although vestiges of the project can be seen in the Epcot theme park at Disneyworld and in the Disney-developed town of Celebration, Florida. On these issues more generally, see Karal Ann Marling, *As Seen on TV: The Visual Culture of Everyday Life in the 1950s* (Cambridge, MA: Harvard University Press, 1994), chap. 3; Richard V. Francaviglia, *Main Street Revisited: Time, Space and Image Building in Small-Town America* (Iowa City: University of Iowa Press, 1996), chap. 3; Watts, *Magic Kingdom;* Mannheim, *Disney and the Quest for Community;* and Huebner, "The Conditional Optimist."

5. *Time,* 29 March 1954. For an important caution about the extent to which a national interest in science implied a public worship of expertise, see Andrew Jewett, *Science, Democracy, and the American University: From the Civil War to the Cold War* (Cambridge: Cambridge University Press, 2012).

6. *Time,* 12 April 1954.

7. Ira Katznelson, *Fear Itself: The New Deal and the Origins of Our Time* (New York: Liveright Publishing Corporation, 2013), especially chap. 1.

8. Neal Gabler, *Walt Disney: The Triumph of the American Imagination* (New York: Alfred A. Knopf, 2007), 16–17. Watts, *Magic Kingdom,* 4.

9. Nils Gilman, *Mandarins of the Future: Modernization Theory in Cold War America* (Baltimore: Johns Hopkins University Press, 2003), ix–x.

10. Miles Orvell, *The Death and Life of Main Street: Small Towns in American Memory, Space, and Community* (Chapel Hill, University of North Carolina Press, 2012), chap. 1. A very good overview, periodization, and analysis of nineteenth-century intentional communities is to be found in Arthur E. Bestor, Jr., "Patent-Office Models of the Good Society: Some Relationships between Social Reform and Westward Expansion," *The American Historical Review* 58 (1953): 505–526.

11. Mark Twain's *The Adventures of Tom Sawyer* (1876) may be thought to be a counterexample. Small-town proponents in the middle of the twentieth century took it for a warm-hearted exploration of boyhood in a small town (see discussions of Norman Rockwell and *It's a Wonderful Life* above). But that interpretation requires more than a little squinting and is far better sustained by cinematic retellings of the story than by Twain's novel itself. The frequency with which small-town advocates have nevertheless recruited *Tom Sawyer* to their cause suggests a dearth of other options. See Cynthia Griffin Wolff, "*The*

Adventures of Tom Sawyer: A Nightmare Vision of American Boyhood," *The Massachusetts Review* 21 (1980): 637–652.

12. An astute overview of the pastoralist tradition remains Leo Marx, *The Machine in the Garden: Technology and the Pastoral Ideal in America* (New York: Oxford University Press, 1964). See also David Shi, *The Simple Life: Plain Living and High Thinking in American Culture* (Oxford: Oxford University Press, 1985).

13. Frederick Jackson Turner, "The Significance of the Frontier in American History," 1893, in *The Frontier in American History* (New York: Henry Holt and Company, 1920), 30.

14. D. N. Jeans, "Fiction and the Small Town in the United States: A Contribution to the Study of Urbanisation," *Australian Geography Studies* 22 (1984): 266.

15. Carl Van Doren, "Contemporary American Novelists: The Revolt from the Village: 1920," *The Nation*, 12 October 1921, 407–412. See also Anthony Channell Hilfer, *The Revolt from the Village, 1915–1930* (Chapel Hill: University of North Carolina Press, 1969).

16. Sinclair Lewis, *Main Street* (New York: Harcourt, Brace and Company, 1920), 26.

17. Ibid., 265.

18. The theme of urban snobbery is covered well in David M. Kennedy, *Freedom from Fear: The American People in Depression and War, 1929–1945* (Oxford: Oxford University Press, 1999), chap. 1.

19. For details on Lewis and the valorization of the small town in U.S. letters, see Richard Lingeman, *Small Town America: A Narrative History, 1620–The Present* (New York: G. P. Putnam's Sons, 1980), chap. 9; Frank M. Bryan, *Real Democracy: The New England Town Meeting and How It Works* (Chicago: University of Chicago Press, 2004), chap. 2; and Orvell, *Death and Life of Main Street.*

20. Ray Lewis White, introduction to Sherwood Anderson, *Return to Winesburg: Selections from Four Years of Writing for a Country Newspaper* (Chapel Hill: University of North Carolina Press, 1967).

21. Sherwood Anderson, *Home Town: Photographs by Farm Security Photographers* (New York: Alliance Book Corporation, 1940), 4. See also Orvell, *Death and Life of Main Street,* 104–114.

22. E. B. White, "One Man's Meat," *Harper's Monthly Magazine,* 1 June 1938, 556. See also Scott Elledge, *E. B. White: A Biography* (New York: W. W. Norton, 1984).

23. White, "One Man's Meat," 555, 556.

24. Paul H. Appleby, *Big Democracy* (New York: Alfred A. Knopf, 1945), 27.

25. Lewis Mumford, *The Culture of Cities* (New York: Harcourt, Brace and Company, 1938), 382.

26. Granville Hicks, "Is the Small Town Doomed?" unpublished article written for *Woman's Home Companion,* 1956, p. 13, box 104, Granville Hicks Papers, Special Collections Research Center, Syracuse University Library.

27. Norman Rockwell, *Norman Rockwell: My Adventures as an Illustrator* (Garden City, New York: Doubleday and Company, 1960), 302. Rockwell completed a similar set of illustrations for *The Adventures of Huckleberry Finn* in 1940.

28. Ibid., 328, 329. The above discussion is based on Karal Ann Marling, *Norman Rockwell* (New York: Harry N. Abrams, 1997) and William Graebner, "Norman Rockwell and American Mass Culture: The Crisis of Representation in the Great Depression," in Biancamaria Bosco Tedeschini Lalli and Maurizio Vaudagna, eds., *Brave New Words: Strategies of Language and Communication in the United States of the 1930s* (Amsterdam: VU University Press, 1999), 243–261. Rockwell moved only once more in his life, in 1953, from Arlington to Stockbridge, Massachusetts, another small New England town.

29. Marling, *Rockwell,* 97–99.

30. John Updike, *Hugging the Shore: Essays and Criticism* (New York: Alfred A. Knopf, 1983), 770. A helpful, sustained reading of *Shuffleton's Barbershop* can be found in Richard Halpern, *Norman Rockwell: The Underside of Innocence* (Chicago: University of Chicago Press, 2006), 136–147.

31. On the small-town film as a genre see Robert Neuman, "Disneyland's Main Street, U.S.A. and Its Sources in Hollywood, U.S.A.," *The Journal of American Culture* 31 (2008): 83–97.

32. See Thornton Wilder, "Toward an American Language," *Atlantic Monthly,* July 1952, 29–37 and "The American Loneliness," *Atlantic Monthly,* August 1952, 65–69.

33. Educational Theatre Association, Play Survey, 6 February 2013, schooltheatre.org/EdTA/Publications/PlaySurvey.

34. *"It's a Wonderful Life* Tops AFI's List of 100 Most Inspiring Films of All Time," 31 May 2006, www.afi.com/100years/cheers.aspx.

35. Frances Goodrich, Albert Hackett, and Frank Capra, *It's a Wonderful Life: Screenplay* (New York: St. Martin's Press, 1986), 190.

36. Eric Smoodin, "'This Business of America': Fan Mail, Film Reception, and *Meet John Doe,*" *Screen* 37 (1996): 111–128.

37. Elmore M. McKee, *The People Act: Stories of How Americans Are Coming Together to Deal with Their Community Problems* (New York: Harper and Brothers, 1955).

38. Margaret Mead and Muriel Brown, *The Wagon and the Star: A Study of American Community Initiative* (St. Paul: Rand McNally, 1966), 71.

39. The success of the show is discussed and sample episodes are presented in McKee, *The People Act.*

40. Otto G. Hoiberg, *Exploring the Small Community* (Madison: University of Nebraska Press, 1955), 4. A similar movement centered on rejuvenating urban neighborhoods gripped the nation during the war. See Benjamin Looker, "Microcosms of Democracy: Imagining the City Neighborhood in World War II–Era America," *Journal of Social History* 44 (2010): 351–378.

41. Edward A. Shils, "The Study of the Primary Group," in *The Policy Sciences,* ed. Daniel Lerner and Harold D. Lasswell (Stanford: Stanford University Press, 1951), 44.

42. J. L. Moreno, "Preludes of the Sociometric Movement" in *Who Shall Survive?: Foundations of Sociometry, Group Psychotherapy, and Sociodrama,* 2d ed. (Beacon, NY: Beacon House, 1953), xxxiv.

43. Ibid., xxix.

44. J. L. Moreno, *Who Shall Survive?: A New Approach to the Problem of Human Interrelations* (Washington, DC: Nervous and Mental Disease Publishing Co., 1934), 134.

45. Ibid., 338.

46. Moreno, "Preludes of the Sociometric Movement," lxv–lxvi.

47. For information about Moreno's career, *Sociometry,* and the fate of network analysis, see René F. Marineau, *Jacob Levy Moreno, 1889–1974: Father of Psychodrama, Sociometry, and Group Psychotherapy* (London: Tavistock/ Routledge, 1989) and Linton C. Freeman, *The Development of Social Network Analysis: A Study in the Sociology of Science* (Vancouver: Empirical Press, 2004).

48. Moreno was far from the only psychologist to delve into group methods. For a useful overview of the approach and some of its theoretical underpinnings, see Marshall C. Greco, *Group Life: The Nature and Treatment of Its Specific Conflicts* (New York: Philosophical Library, 1950).

49. Jean B. Quandt, *From the Small Town to the Great Community: The Social Thought of Progressive Intellectuals* (New Brunswick: Rutgers University Press, 1970); Thomas Bender, *Community and Social Change in America* (New Brunswick: Rutgers University Press, 1978); William Graebner, *The Engineering of Consent: Democracy and Authority in Twentieth-Century America* (Madison: University of Wisconsin Press, 1987).

50. M. P. Follett, *The New State: Group Organization the Solution of Popular Government* (New York: Longmans, Green and Co., 1918), 3.

51. Follett, *The New State,* 84. See also Jewett, *Science, Democracy, and the American University,* chap. 4.

52. For a distinction made in similar terms, see David Goodman, "Democracy and Public Discussion in the Progressive and New Deal Eras: From Civic Competence to the Expression of Opinion," *Studies in American Political Development* 18 (2004): 81–111.

53. Fred L. Strodtbeck and A. Paul Hare, "Bibliography of Small Group Research," *Sociometry* 17 (1954): 110.

54. Those surveys include George C. Homans, *The Human Group* (New York; Harcourt, Brace, 1950); A. Paul Hare, Edgar F. Borgatta, and Robert F. Bales, eds., *Small Groups: Studies in Social Interaction* (New York: Knopf, 1955); W. J. H. Sprott, *Human Groups* (Baltimore: Penguin, 1958); and Michael S. Olmstead, *The Small Group* (New York: Random House, 1959).

55. William H. Whyte, Jr., "Groupthink," *Fortune,* March 1952, 114.

56. David Riesman, "Individualism Reconsidered," 1951, in *Individualism Reconsidered* (Glencoe, IL: The Free Press, 1954), 28.

57. Stanley Elkins and Eric McKitrick, "A Meaning for Turner's Frontier Thesis," *Political Science Quarterly* 69 (1954): 321–353, 565–602.

58. Lewis Atherton, *Main Street on the Middle Border* (Bloomington: Indiana University Press, 1954), 186.

59. Grace L. Coyle, "Group Work and Social Change," 1935, in *Group Experience and Democratic Values* (New York: The Woman's Press, 1947), 149. See also Gertrude Wilson, "From Practice to Theory: A Personalized History," in *Theories of Social Work with Groups,* ed. Robert W. Roberts and Helen Northern (New York: Columbia University Press, 1976), 1–44 and Albert S. Alissi, "Social Group Work: Commitments and Perspectives," in *Perspectives on Social Group Work Practice: A Book of Readings,* ed. Albert S. Alissi (New York: The Free Press, 1980), 5–35.

60. This view is most famously associated with William F. Whyte, *Street Corner Society: The Social Structure of an Italian Slum* (Chicago: University of Chicago Press, 1943). Gang studies were prominent in the research on small groups and provide some continuity, via Frederic Thrasher's *The Gang: A Study of 1,313 Gangs in Chicago* (Chicago: University of Chicago Press, 1927), with earlier Chicago-school sociology on primary groups. See also Albert K. Cohen, *Delinquent Boys: The Culture of the Gang* (Glencoe, IL: The Free Press, 1955).

61. Ralph Linton, *The Study of Man: An Introduction* (New York: D. Appleton–Century, 1936), chap. 13. On Linton and for an account of how these themes appeared in the natural sciences, see Gregg Mitman, *The State of Nature: Ecology, Community, and American Social Thought, 1900–1950* (Chicago: University of Chicago Press, 1992).

62. Elihu Katz and Paul F. Lazarsfeld, *Personal Influence: The Part Played by People in the Flow of Mass Communications* (Glencoe, IL: The Free Press, 1955), 20; Paul F. Lazarsfeld, Bernard Berelson, and Hazel Gaudet, *The People's Choice: How the Voter Makes Up His Mind in a Presidential Campaign,* 2d ed. (New York: Columbia University Press, 1948), 158.

63. Frank Lloyd Wright, *When Democracy Builds,* rev. ed. (Chicago: University of Chicago Press, 1945), 41; Walter Gropius, *Rebuilding Our Communities* (Chicago: Paul Theobald, 1945), 17. A fine guide to the decentralist trend within urbanist and architectural thought in general remains Svend Riemer, "Escape into Decentralization?" *Land Economics* 24 (1948): 40–48.

64. Katznelson, *Fear Itself,* 13; Michael S. Sherry, *In the Shadow of War: The United States since the 1930s* (New Haven: Yale University Press, 1995).

65. William C. Menninger, "Psychiatric Experiences in the War, 1941–1946," *American Journal of Psychiatry* 103 (1947): 581. Menninger's further reflections on psychiatry and the war, with more reflections on the role of groups, can be found in *Psychiatry in a Troubled World: Yesterday's War and Today's Challenge* (New York: The Macmillan Company, 1948).

66. Samuel Stouffer et al., *The American Soldier,* 2 vols. (Princeton: Princeton University Press, 1949). The theme of the small group in *The American Soldier* is highlighted and discussed in Edward A. Shils, "Primary Groups in the American Army," in *Studies in the Scope and Method of "The American Soldier,"* ed. Robert K. Merton and Paul F. Lazarsfeld (Glencoe, IL: The Free Press, 1950), 16–39.

67. Leo H. Bartemeier et al, "Combat Exhaustion," *The Journal of Nervous and Mental Disease* 104 (1946): 370.

68. Elton Mayo, *The Human Problems of an Industrial Civilization* (New York: Macmillan, 1933), F. J. Roethlisberger and William J. Dickson, *Management and the Worker: An Account of the Research Program Conducted by the Western Electric Company, Hawthorne Works, Chicago* (Cambridge, MA: Harvard University Press, 1939); Richard Gillespie, *Manufacturing Knowledge: A History of the Hawthorne Experiments* (Cambridge: Cambridge University Press, 1991). Today, the Hawthorne studies are used as evidence for the conclusion that the act of observation affects the phenomenon studied, but that is a retroactive interpretation only developed in the 1950s and was not how the original studies were understood.

69. Loren Baritz, *The Servants of Power: A History of the Use of Social Science in American Industry* (Middletown: Wesleyan University Press, 1960); Graebner, *Engineering of Consent;* Jenna Feltey Alden, "Bottom-Up Management: Participative Philosophy and Humanistic Psychology in American Organizational Culture, 1930–1970" (Ph.D. diss., Columbia University, 2012).

70. On the reception of these two intriguing figures, see Jennifer Burns, *Goddess of the Market: Ayn Rand and the American Right* (Oxford: Oxford University Press, 2009) and Angus Burgin, *The Great Persuasion: Reinventing Free Markets since the Depression* (Cambridge, MA: Harvard University Press, 2012).

71. Howard Brick, *Transcending Capitalism: Visions of a New Society in Modern American Thought* (Ithaca: Cornell University Press, 2006); Nelson Lichtenstein, ed., *American Capitalism: Social Thought and Political Economy in the Twentieth Century* (Philadelphia: University of Pennsylvania Press, 2006); Daniel Immerwahr, "Polanyi in the United States: Peter Drucker, Karl Polanyi, and the Midcentury Critique of Economic Society," *Journal of the History of Ideas* 70 (2009): 445–466.

72. F. A. Hayek, "Individualism: True and False," in *Individualism and Economic Order* (Chicago: University of Chicago Press, 1948), 23. For a keen assessment of Hayek's political theory, see Burgin, *The Great Persuasion.*

73. Max Shachtman, *The Fight for Socialism: The Principles and Program of the Workers Party* (New York: New International Publishing, 1946), 164.

74. Dwight Macdonald, *The Root Is Man* (1946; New York: Autonomedia, 1995), 136.

75. Ibid., 148. See also Frank Tannenbaum's small-group rendition of trade unionism in Frank Tannenbaum, *A Philosophy of Labor* (New York: Alfred A. Knopf, 1951).

76. Arthur M. Schlesinger, Jr., *The Vital Center: The Politics of Freedom* (Boston: Houghton Mifflin Company, 1949), 144.

77. Daniel Bell, *The End of Ideology: On the Exhaustion of Political Ideas in the Fifties* (New York: The Free Press, 1960). On the relationship between the turn to the small group and the end of ideology, see Ron Robin, *The Making of the Cold War Enemy: Culture and Politics in the Military-Intellectual Complex* (Princeton: Princeton University Press, 2001), 63.

78. Schlesinger, *Vital Center,* 244, 253.

79. Besides in *The Lonely Crowd* and *Individualism Reconsidered,* Riesman's subtle views on this subject are expressed, in clear form, in a correspondence

197

between Riesman and Robert Nisbet in folder 5, box 2, Robert A. Nisbet Papers, Manuscript Division, Library of Congress.

80. William H. Whyte, Jr., *The Organization Man* (New York: Simon and Schuster, 1956), 12.

81. Whyte, "Groupthink."

82. On Whyte and Riesman's attack on groupism, see Richard H. Pells, *The Liberal Mind in a Conservative Age: American Intellectuals in the 1940s and 1950s* (New York: Harper and Row, 1985), 232–248.

83. Schlesinger, *Vital Center,* 253.

84. Arthur M. Schlesinger, Jr., "The Crisis of American Masculinity," 1958, in *The Politics of Hope* (Boston: Houghton Mifflin Company, 1963), 243–244. On Schlesinger's turn, see K. A. Cuordileone, " 'Politics in an Age of Anxiety': Cold War Political Culture and the Crisis in American Masculinity," *Journal of American History* 87 (2000): 515–545.

85. Mildred Warner, "W. Lloyd Warner: Social Anthropologist," 1980, p. 227, box 4, W. Lloyd Warner Papers, Special Collections Research Center, University of Chicago Library.

86. David Riesman to Granville Hicks, 27 February 1948 and Riesman to Hicks, 16 February 1949, box 51, Hicks Papers. Riesman displayed a similar enthusiasm for Robert Nisbet's *Quest for Community* (1953).

87. Riesman, *Individualism Reconsidered,* 26.

88. Ibid., 32.

89. Ibid., 37.

90. Whyte, *Organization Man,* 400.

91. Ibid., 11.

2. DEVELOPMENT WITHOUT MODERNIZATION

1. David Lilienthal, *TVA: Democracy on the March* (New York: Harper and Brothers, 1944), 11.

2. Lilienthal, *TVA,* 120.

3. David Lilienthal, *Big Business: A New Era* (New York: Harper and Brothers, 1952), 95.

4. David Lilienthal, "The Armament of a Democracy," 1940 speech, quoted in James C. Scott, "High Modernist Social Engineering: The Case of the TVA," in *Experiencing the State,* ed. Lloyd I. Rudolph and John Kurt Jacobsen (Delhi: Oxford University Press, 2007), 25.

5. Lilienthal, *TVA,* 2.

6. Daniel Klingensmith, *"One Valley and a Thousand": Dams, Nationalism, and Development* (Oxford: Oxford University Press, 2007), 1; Benjamin Fong Chao, "Anthropogenic Impact on Global Geodynamics Due to Reservoir Water Impoundment," *Geophysical Research Letters* 22 (1995): 3529–3532.

7. Scott, "High Modernist Social Engineering," 3–52; Paul R. Josephson, *Industrialized Nature: Brute Force Technology and the Transformation of the Natural World* (Washington, DC: Island Press, 2002), chap. 1.

8. David Ekbladh, *The Great American Mission: Modernization and the Construction of an American World Order* (Princeton: Princeton University Press, 2009), 8. See also David Ekbladh, "'Mr. TVA': Grass-Roots Development, David Lilienthal, and the Rise and Fall of the Tennessee Valley Authority as a Symbol for U.S. Overseas Development, 1933–1973," *Diplomatic History* 26 (2002): 335–374.

9. Ekbladh, *Great American Mission*, 57; World Commission on Dams, *Dams and Development: A New Framework for Decision-Making* (London: Earthscan, 2000), 104.

10. David Lilienthal, *TVA: Democracy on the March*, 20th anniversary ed. (New York: Harper and Brothers, 1953), ix.

11. Julian Huxley, *TVA: Adventure in Planning* (Surrey: The Architectural Press, 1943), 7.

12. The case is made famously in Philip Selznick, *TVA and the Grass Roots: A Study in the Sociology of Formal Organizations* (New York: Harper and Row, 1949). A good overview is Richard Lowitt, "The TVA, 1933–45," in *TVA: Fifty Years of Grass-Roots Bureaucracy*, ed. Erwin Hargrove and Paul K. Conkin (Urbana: University of Illinois Press, 1983), 35–65.

13. See Roy Talbert, *FDR's Utopian: Arthur Morgan of the TVA* (Jackson: University Press of Mississippi, 1987).

14. David Lilienthal, quoted in Steven M. Neuse, *David E. Lilienthal: The Journey of an American Liberal* (Knoxville: University of Tennessee Press, 1996), 98.

15. Although the Morgan–Lilienthal feud is a controversial and at times confusing subject, it is hard to credit James C. Scott's claim that Morgan was "the most thoroughgoing exponent of high modernism within the TVA" and that his relentless pursuit of technocratic reform was the cause of dismissal (Scott, "High Modernist Social Engineering," 21). Morgan was a utopian but neither a high modernist nor a technocrat. The rivalry between Morgan and Lilienthal is best approached through Thomas K. McCraw, *Morgan vs. Lilienthal: The Feud within the TVA* (Chicago: Loyola University Press, 1970); Erwin C. Hargrove, *Prisoners of Myth: The Leadership of the Tennessee Valley Authority, 1933–1990* (Princeton: Princeton University Press, 1994), chaps. 2–3; and Neuse, *David Lilienthal*, chap. 5. On the broader competition between Morgan's and Lilienthal's views as each was extended overseas, see Klingensmith, *"One Valley and a Thousand."* Other good treatments of Lilienthal's post-TVA international career are Ekbladh, *Great American Mission* and Amy C. Offner, "Anti-Poverty Programs, Social Conflict, and Economic Thought in Colombia and the United States, 1948–1980" (Ph.D. diss., Columbia University, 2012).

16. In 1943, Morgan founded Community Service, Inc., "to promote the interests of the small community as a basic social institution concerned with the economic, recreational, educational, cultural, and spiritual development of its members." His work after the TVA is well documented in its journal, *Community Service News*. The organization's mission statement can be found in *Community Service News*, January–February 1948, 2 and a useful account of its operations

is Arthur E. Morgan, "The Story of Community Service," *Community Service News,* February 1958, 53–75.

17. Quoted in Kennedy, *Freedom from Fear,* 148.

18. Jess Gilbert, "Agrarian Intellectuals in a Democratizing State: A Collective Biography of USDA Leaders in the Intended New Deal," in Catherine McNicol Stock and Robert D. Johnston, eds., *The Countryside in the Age of the Modern State: Political Histories of Rural America* (Ithaca: Cornell University Press, 2001), 213–239. Although Gilbert's terminology has caught on, I hesitate to use it myself because, for reasons that will be clear later in the chapter, it is not obvious that the "low modernists" were "modernists" at all, at least not when they went abroad. Gilbert and others have written a great deal on the two competing impulses within the New Deal. See Edward S. Shapiro, "Decentralist Intellectuals and the New Deal," *Journal of American History* 58 (1972): 938–957; Jess Gilbert, "Eastern Urban Liberals and Midwestern Agrarian Intellectuals: Two Group Portraits of Progressives in the New Deal Department of Agriculture," *Agricultural History* 74 (2000): 162–180; Olaf F. Larson and Julie N. Zimmerman, "The USDA's Bureau of Agricultural Economics and Sociological Studies of Rural Life and Agricultural Issues, 1919–1953," *Agricultural History* 74 (2000): 227–240; Mary Summers, "The New Deal Farm Program: Looking for Reconstruction in American Agriculture," *Agricultural History* 72 (2000): 241–257; Olaf F. Larson and Julie N. Zimmerman, *Sociology in Government: The Galpin–Taylor Years in the U.S. Department of Agriculture, 1919–1953* (University Park, PA: Pennsylvania State University Press, 2003); Jess Gilbert, "Low Modernism and the Agrarian New Deal: A Different Kind of State," in Jane Adams, ed., *Fighting for the Farm: Rural America Transformed* (Philadelphia: University of Pennsylvania Press, 2003), 129–146; Sarah T. Phillips, *This Land, This Nation: Conservation, Rural America, and the New Deal* (Cambridge: Cambridge University Press, 2007); Jess Gilbert, "Rural Sociology and Democratic Planning in the Third New Deal," *Agricultural History* 42 (2008): 422–438; Jess Gilbert, "Democratizing States and the Use of History," *Rural Sociology* 74 (2009): 3–24; Todd Dresser, "Nightmares of Rural Life: Fearing the Future in the Transition from Country Life to the Family Farm, 1890–1960" (Ph.D. diss., University of Wisconsin–Madison, 2011); and Amrys O. Williams, "Cultivating Modern America: 4-H Clubs and Rural Development in the Twentieth Century" (Ph.D. diss., University of Wisconsin–Madison, 2012).

19. Larson and Zimmerman, *Sociology in Government.* See also Richard S. Kirkendall, *Social Scientists and Farm Politics in the Age of Roosevelt* (Columbia: University of Missouri Press, 1966).

20. Wilson, quoted in Deborah Fitzgerald, *Every Farm a Factory: The Industrial Ideal in American Agriculture* (New Haven: Yale University Press, 2003), 163. See chap. 6 of that book more generally.

21. M. L. Wilson, "Beyond Economics," in U.S. Department of Agriculture, *Farmers in a Changing World: The Yearbook of Agriculture, 1940* (Washington, DC: U.S. Government Printing Office, 1940), 926.

22. M. L. Wilson, *Democracy Has Roots* (New York: Carrick and Evans, 1939), 90, 182.

23. Carl C. Taylor, "Democracy and Group Leadership," 1940, pp. 4, 7, in box 1, Carl C. Taylor Papers, Division of Rare and Manuscript Collections, Cornell University Library. On Taylor and Wilson, see Gilbert, "Agrarian Intellectuals in a Democratizing State"; Gilbert, "Eastern Urban Liberals and Midwestern Agrarian Intellectuals"; Phillips, *This Land, This Nation,* chap. 4; and Dresser, "Nightmares of Rural Life," chaps. 5 and 7.

24. M. L. Wilson, "The Democratic Processes and the Formulation of Agricultural Policy," *Social Forces* 19 (1940), 9, 10.

25. Quoted in Gilbert, "Rural Sociology and Democratic Planning in the Third New Deal," 428.

26. Howard R. Tolley, *The Farmer Citizen at War* (New York: Macmillan, 1943), 138.

27. Wilson, quoted in Andrew Jewett, "The Social Sciences, Philosophy, and the Cultural Turn in the 1930s USDA," *Journal of the History of the Behavioral Sciences* 49 (2013): 408.

28. Material from the Schools of Philosophy lectures was published in the USDA's remarkable 1940 yearbook, *Farmers in a Changing World.*

29. An authoritative account of the Schools of Philosophy experiment can be found in Jewett, "The Social Sciences, Philosophy, and the Cultural Turn." As Jewett explains, though, the interest in democratic small-group discussions as a mechanism for stimulating citizen engagement went beyond the USDA. See David Goodman, "Democracy and Public Discussion in the Progressive and New Deal Eras: From Civic Competence to the Expression of Opinion," *Studies in American Political Development* 18 (2004): 81–111; Robert Kunzman and David Tyack, "Educational Forums of the 1930s: An Experiment in Adult Civic Education," *American Journal of Education* 111 (2005): 320–340; and Gabriel N. Rosenberg, *Breeding the Future: 4-H and the Roots of the Rural Modern World* (Philadelphia: University of Pennsylvania Press, forthcoming).

30. Tugwell's opposition to Wilson and Taylor is covered well in Gilbert, "Agrarian Intellectuals in a Democratizing State" and Gilbert, "Eastern Urban Liberals and Midwestern Agrarian Intellectuals."

31. R. G. Tugwell and E. C. Banfield, "Grass Roots Democracy—Myth or Reality?" *Public Administration Review* 10 (1950): 54.

32. Gilbert, "Democratizing States," 6; Tugwell and Banfield, "Grass Roots Democracy," 55.

33. But see discussions of individual projects in Bureau of Agricultural Economics, *Land Use Planning Under Way* (Washington, DC: USDA, 1940), 12–46 and Arthur F. Raper, *Tenants of the Almighty* (New York: The Macmillan Company, 1943), parts 5–7. For a full survey of the planning committees' achievements, we await Jess Gilbert, *Planning Democracy: Agrarian Intellectuals and the Intended New Deal in Agriculture* (New Haven: Yale University Press, forthcoming).

34. Gilbert, "Eastern Urban Liberals and Midwestern Agrarian Intellectuals," 180.

35. Peter T. Suzuki, "Anthropologists in the Wartime Camps for Japanese Americans: A Documentary Study," *Dialectical Anthropology* 6 (1981): 23–60; Orin Starn, "Engineering Internment: Anthropologists and the War Relocation

Authority," *American Ethnologist* 13 (1986): 700–720; Lane Ryo Hirabayashi, *The Politics of Fieldwork: Research in an American Concentration Camp* (Tucson: University of Arizona Press, 1999); Brian Masaru Hayashi, *Democratizing the Enemy: The Japanese American Internment* (Princeton: Princeton University Press, 2004); and David Price, *Anthropological Intelligence: The Deployment and Neglect of American Anthropology in the Second World War* (Durham: Duke University Press, 2008), chap. 7.

36. Redfield's view but not necessarily his words, reported in E. H. Spicer, "History of the Community Analysis Section," 30 December 1945; Microfilm, M1342, roll 1, p. 3; Community Analysis Reports and Community Analysis Trend Reports of the War Relocation Authority; Headquarters, Community Analysis Section; Records of the War Relocation Authority, Record Group 210 (RG 210); National Archives Building, Washington, DC (NAB).

37. John H. Provinse, *Community Government Manual for Use in Establishing Local Self-Government in Relocation Centers,* 1943; folder: "Community Government (General), May 1942–July 1943," box 400; Subject-Classified General Files, 66.010; Headquarters, Community Analysis Section; RG 210; NAB.

38. An account of the Bureau of Sociological Research, written by its head, can be found in Alexander H. Leighton, *The Governing of Men: General Principles and Recommendations Based on Experience at a Japanese Relocation Camp* (Princeton: Princeton University Press, 1945).

39. Conrad M. Arensberg, "Report on a Developing Community: Poston, Arizona," *Applied Anthropology* 2 (1942): 6.

40. The most thorough account of these councils is Hayashi, *Democratizing the Enemy,* chap. 4.

41. That tendency is helpfully analyzed in Starn, "Engineering Internment."

42. John F. Embree, Community Analytical Report No. 2, "Causes of Unrest at Relocation Centers, 1943; Microfilm, M1342, roll 1, pp. 1, 2, and 4; Community Analysis Reports and Community Analysis Trend Reports of the War Relocation Authority; Headquarters, Community Analysis Section; RG 210; NAB.

43. Arensberg, "Report on a Developing Community," 8.

44. Edward H. Spicer, "Introduction," in Edward Spicer, Asael T. Hansen, Katherine Luomala, and Marvin K. Opler, *Impounded People: Japanese-Americans in the Relocation Centers* (Tucson: University of Arizona Press, 1969), 10; Edward H. Spicer, "Final Report of Washington Community Analysis Section," 18 February 1946; Microfilm, M1342, roll 6, item 248, p. 26; Community Analysis Reports and Community Analysis Trend Reports of the War Relocation Authority; Headquarters, Community Analysis Section; RG 210; NAB.

45. Carey McWilliams, *What about Our Japanese-Americans?* (New York: Public Affairs Committee, 1944), 16.

46. Two exceptions among the white social scientists who worked in the camps were Rosalie Wax and Morris Opler, who criticized the camp administration during and after their employment. See Price, *Anthropological Intelligence,* 157–168.

47. Robert Redfield, "The Japanese-Americans," in *American Society in Wartime,* ed. W. F. Ogburn (Chicago: University of Chicago Press, 1943), 155.

48. Spicer, "Introduction," in *Impounded People,* 1, 2, 16. For Spicer's extended retrospective moral wrestling with the complicity of his group in the internment, see Edward H. Spicer, "Anthropologists and the War Relocation Authority," in Walter Goldschmidt, ed., *The Uses of Anthropology* (Washington, DC: American Anthropological Association, 1979), 217–237.

49. Gilbert, "Eastern Liberals and Midwestern Agrarians," 180.

50. Andrew Wender Cohen, "Smuggling, Globalization, and America's Outward State, 1870–1909," *Journal of American History* 97 (2010): 371–398.

51. On the non-racist aspects of modernization, see Michael Adas, *Machines as the Measure of Men: Science, Technology, and Ideologies of Western Dominance* (Ithaca: Cornell University Press, 1990).

52. The tension between modernization and communitarianism in U.S. foreign policymaking bears a clear resemblance to the related tension within colonial policies between the impetus to "civilize" the colonies and the desire to "protect" native traditions. For perceptive analyses of that alternation, see Thomas R. Metcalf, *Ideologies of the Raj* (Cambridge: Cambridge University Press, 1995); Mahmood Mamdani, *Citizen and Subject: Contemporary Africa and the Legacy of Late Colonialism* (Princeton: Princeton University Press, 1996); and Karuna Mantena, *Alibis of Empire: Henry Maine and the Ends of Imperialism* (Princeton: Princeton University Press, 2010). For the case of the U.S. empire, see Paul A. Kramer, *The Blood of Government: Race, Empire, the United States, and the Philippines* (Chapel Hill: University of North Carolina Press, 2006) and Lanny Thompson, *Imperial Archipelago: Representation and Rule in the Insular Territories under U.S. Dominion after 1898* (Honolulu: University of Hawai'i Press, 2010).

53. Fukuzawa Yukichi, *An Outline of a Theory of Civilization,* trans. David A. Dilworth and G. Cameron Hurst III (1875; New York: Columbia University Press, 2008), 18.

54. Pankaj Mishra, *From the Ruins of Empire: The Intellectuals Who Remade Asia* (New York: Farrar, Straus and Giroux, 2012).

55. Harry S. Truman, inaugural address, 20 January 1949, Miller Center, Presidential Speech Archive, millercenter.org/president/speeches/detail/3350.

56. On Point Four see Gilbert Rist, *The History of Development: From Western Origins to Global Faith,* rev. ed., trans. Patrick Camiller (London: Zed Books 2002), chap. 4; Ekbladh, *Great American Mission,* chap. 3; and Amanda Kay McVety, *Enlightened Aid: U.S. Development as Foreign Policy in Ethiopia* (Oxford: Oxford University Press, 2012), chap. 4.

57. Uma Kothari, "From Colonial Administration to Development Studies: A Post-Colonial Critique of the History of Development Studies," in *A Radical History of Development Studies: Individuals, Institutions, and Ideologies,* ed. Uma Kothari (London: Zed Books, 2005), 47–66; Uma Kothari, "From Colonialism to Development: Reflections of Former Colonial Officers," *Commonwealth and Comparative Politics* 44 (2006): 118–136.

58. Earl S. Pomeroy, "The American Colonial Office," *The Mississippi Valley Historical Review* 30 (1944): 521–532; Julius W. Pratt, *America's Colonial Experiment: How the United States Gained, Governed, and in Part Gave away a Colonial Empire* (New York: Prentice Hall, 1951), chap. 5.

59. McKim Marriott, interview with the author, Chicago, 24 January 2009. David Mandelbaum did fieldwork in India in 1937–1938, but Marriott suspects that Mandelbaum either entered the country clandestinely or negotiated special access.

60. W. E. B. Du Bois, *Color and Democracy: Colonies and Peace* (New York: Harcourt, Brace and Company, 1945), 20.

61. Donna C. Mehos and Suzanne Moon, "The Uses of Portability: Circulating Experts with Technopolitics of Cold War and Decolonization," in *Entangled Geographies: Empire and Technopolitics in the Global Cold War*, ed. Gabrielle Hecht (Cambridge, MA: The MIT Press, 2011), 43–74.

62. This disjuncture between center and periphery in development policy-making is fruitfully explored in Michele Alacevich, *The Political Economy of the World Bank: The Early Years* (Stanford: Stanford University Press and the World Bank, 2009). There, Alacevich observes the tendency of dissenters from the official policy to find themselves far from Washington but close to sites of foreign aid implementation. A similar dynamic can be seen in the British Empire, where imperial plans as articulated in the metropole and imperial actions as undertaken in the colonies turned out to have markedly different orientations. Just as in the United States, the modernizers tended to work the center of imperial policy-making, and those favoring non-modernist and sometimes communitarian forms of development tended to work in the field. See Joseph Morgan Hodge, *Triumph of the Expert: Agrarian Doctrines of Development and the Legacies of British Colonialism* (Athens: Ohio University Press, 2007) and Helen Tilley, *Africa as a Living Laboratory: Empire, Development, and the Problem of Scientific Knowledge, 1870–1950* (Chicago: University of Chicago Press, 2011). On a related tension between "field" policies and metropolitan policies in philanthropic foundations, see Nicole Sackley, "Foundation in the Field: The Ford Foundation's New Delhi Office and the Construction of Development Knowledge, 1951–1970," in *American Foundations and the Coproduction of World Order in the Twentieth Century*, ed. John Krige and Helke Rausch (Göttingen: Vandenhoeck and Ruprecht, 2012), 231–260.

63. "Bio-Data on Arthur F. Raper," 15 February 1965, folder 289, box 7, Arthur F. Raper Papers, Southern Historical Collection, Wilson Library, University of North Carolina at Chapel Hill; Louis Mazzari, *Southern Modernist: Arthur Raper from the New Deal to the Cold War* (Baton Rouge: Louisiana State University Press, 2006); Clifford Kuhn, *At the Crossroads: Arthur Raper, the South, and the World* (Chapel Hill: University of North Carolina Press, forthcoming).

64. Arthur F. Raper, "Rural Sociologists and Foreign Assignments," *Rural Sociology* 18 (1953): 264–266. See also Everett M. Rogers, *Social Change in Rural Society: A Textbook in Rural Sociology* (New York: Appleton-Century-Crofts, 1960), chap. 16; Lowry Nelson, *Rural Sociology: Its Origin and Growth*

in the United States (Minneapolis: University of Minnesota Press, 1969), chap. 11; and Phillips, *This Land, This Nation,* epilogue.

65. Taylor to Henry A. Wallace, 10 March 1959, box 35, Carl C. Taylor Papers.

66. Carl C. Taylor, untitled article about community development, 1966, box 34, Carl C. Taylor Papers.

67. For a more complete accounting of the personnel links between the BAE, WRA, and overseas community development, see Daniel Immerwahr, "Quests for Community: The United States, Community Development, and the World, 1935–65" (Ph.D. diss., University of California, Berkeley, 2011), chap. 2.

68. William J. Caldwell, "Note to Correspondents," 28 August 1957, folder 192, box 7, Max Millikan Papers, Institute Archives and Special Collections, MIT Libraries.

69. Julia Henderson, quoted in International Society for Community Development, Report on Symposium, "The Outlook for Community Development," 8 September 1966, p. 19, folder 12, box 14, Albert A. Mayer Papers, Special Collections Research Center, University of Chicago Library.

70. Philippe de Seynes, "The UN and Community Development," *Community Development Bulletin*, March 1957, 65.

71. Lane E. Holdcroft, "The Rise and Fall of Community Development: 1950–1965" (M.S. thesis, Michigan State University, 1976), 3.

72. David Brokensha and Peter Hodge, *Community Development: An Interpretation* (San Francisco: Chandler Publishing, 1969), 8.

73. For my understanding of Redfield's importance, I am indebted to the work of Nicole Sackley. See her "Passage to Modernity: American Social Scientists, India, and the Pursuit of Development, 1945–1961" (Ph.D. diss., Princeton University, 2004), chap. 2 and "Cosmopolitanism and the Uses of Tradition: Robert Redfield and Alternative Visions of Modernization during the Cold War," *Modern Intellectual History* 9 (2012): 565–595. On Redfield in general, see Clifford Wilcox, *Robert Redfield and the Development of American Anthropology* (Lanham, MD: Lexington Books, 2004).

74. On Redfield's service to the BAE, see folder 8, "USDA," box 36, Robert Redfield Papers, Special Collections Research Center, University of Chicago Library and Robert Redfield, "Rural Sociology and the Folk Society," *Rural Sociology* 8 (1943): 68–71.

75. Important Chicago figures for the history of community development's theory and practice include W. Lloyd Warner, Conrad Arensberg, Edward Spicer, William F. Whyte, John H. Provinse, Frank Lynch, and McKim Marriott. The university was also a training ground for the urban sociologists who designed and implemented the Community Action Program of the War on Poverty, discussed in chapter five: Richard Boone, Saul Alinsky, Lloyd Ohlin, and Leonard Cottrell. See Noel Cazenave, "Chicago Influences the War on Poverty," *Journal of Policy History* 5 (1993): 52–68.

76. Warren I. Susman, *Culture as History: The Transformation of American Society in the Twentieth Century* (New York: Pantheon Books, 1973), chap. 9.

77. Ruth Benedict, *Patterns of Culture* (1934; Boston: Houghton Mifflin Company, 2005), 6.

78. Robert Redfield, *Tepoztlan, a Mexican Village: A Study of Folk Life* (Chicago: University of Chicago Press, 1930), 49.

79. The concept is developed in Robert Redfield, *The Folk Culture of Yucatan* (Chicago: University of Chicago Press, 1941).

80. Redfield, *Tepoztlan,* 134–135.

81. Wilcox, *Redfield,* 5.

82. Stuart Chase, *Mexico: A Study of Two Americas* (New York: The Literary Guild, 1931), 318.

83. Robert Redfield and Alfonso Villa Rojas, *Chan Kom: A Maya Village* (Washington, DC: Carnegie Institution, 1934); Redfield, *Folk Culture of Yucatan.*

84. Robert Redfield, *A Village That Chose Progress: Chan Kom Revisited* (Chicago: University of Chicago Press, 1950), 23.

85. Ibid., 157.

86. Robert Redfield, "Culture Contact without Conflict," *American Anthropologist* 41 (1939): 514–517. An explanation of Redfield's concept of acculturation with some hint of its centrality for his work can be found in Robert Redfield, Ralph Linton, and Melville J. Herskovits, "Memorandum for the Study of Acculturation," *American Anthropologist* 38 (1936): 149–152.

87. Robert Redfield and Milton B. Singer, "The Cultural Role of Cities," *Economic Development and Cultural Change* 3 (1954): 61.

88. Robert Redfield, *The Primitive World and Its Transformations* (Ithaca: Cornell University Press, 1953), 65.

89. Robert Redfield, "Primitive and Peasant: Simple and Compound Society," c. 1956, folder 4, box 66, Redfield Papers.

90. This picture emerged most clearly in M. N. Srinivas, *Religion and Society among the Coorgs of South India* (Oxford: Clarendon Press, 1952), which Redfield and Singer held in particularly high regard.

91. Srinivas, *Religion and Society,* 166.

92. M. N. Srinivas, "A Note on Sanskritization and Westernization," 1956, in *Collected Essays* (Oxford: Oxford University Press, 2002); Simon Charsley, "Sanskritization: The Career of an Anthropological Theory," *Contributions to Indian Sociology* 32 (1998): 527–547.

93. Srinivas's belief that development could be rooted in traditional institutions was further elaborated in two similar volumes by Chicago-school social scientists, each of which served as an important counter to modernization theory: Lloyd I. Rudolph and Susanne Hoeber Rudolph, *The Modernity of Tradition: Political Development in India* (Chicago: University of Chicago Press, 1967) and Milton Singer, *When a Great Tradition Modernizes: An Anthropological Approach to Indian Civilization* (New York: Praeger, 1972). In each, emphasis is firmly placed on the plasticity and, indeed, the "modernity" of traditional institutions. For a critical assessment of the Redfield school's work on India, particularly its acceptance of caste as a benevolent institution, see Jaganath Pathy,

"Underdevelopment of Indian Sociology," *Social Scientist* 4 (1976): 20–31; Mary Hancock, "Unmaking the 'Great Tradition': Ethnography, National Culture and Area Studies," *Identities* 4 (1998): 343–388; and Kamala Visweswaran, *Un/common Cultures: Racism and the Rearticulation of Cultural Difference* (Durham: Duke University Press, 2010), chap. 5.

94. Robert Redfield, "The Future of Civilization," Speech, 17 March 1958, folder 11, box 63, Redfield Papers.

95. Redfield and Singer, "The Cultural Role of Cities," 73. Redfield's position was echoed with striking similarity by Margaret Mead during the relatively brief period in her career when she turned her attention toward the subject of technical assistance. See Margaret Mead, ed., *Cultural Patterns and Technical Change* (Paris: UNESCO, 1953) and Peter Mandler, *Return from the Natives: How Margaret Mead Won the Second World War and Lost the Cold War* (New Haven: Yale University Press, 2013), chap. 7.

96. Nils Gilman, *Mandarins of the Future: Modernization Theory in Cold War America* (Baltimore: Johns Hopkins University Press, 2003), chap. 5.

97. Irwin Sanders, memo, 29 May 1957, folder 192, box 7, Millikan Papers.

98. Ernest E. Neal to Louis Miniclier, 21 February 1957; "Community Development—Vol. 2" folder, box 120; USOM Philippines; Subject Files, 1951–1959; Mission to the Philippines, Executive Office; Technical Cooperation Administration; Records of U.S. Foreign Assistance Agencies, Record Group 469 (RG 469); National Archives at College Park, MD (NACP).

99. Ernest E. Neal to Grace Langley, 23 December 1957, "Community Development—Vol. 3," folder, box 120; USOM Philippines; Subject Files, 1951–1959; Mission to the Philippines, Executive Office; Technical Cooperation Administration; RG 469; NACP.

100. Lucian W. Pye, "Community Development as Part of Political Development," background paper prepared for Endicott House conference, 1957, *Community Development Review,* March 1958, 2.

101. Ibid., 18.

102. Irwin Sanders, *Community Development and National Change: Summary of Conference, Endicott House, December 13–15, 1957* (Washington, DC: International Cooperation Administration, 1958), 25.

103. Ibid., 22–32.

104. Ibid., 40, 41, 57.

105. Ibid., 38.

106. Ibid., 39.

107. Ibid., 5.

108. Louis Miniclier to Max Millikan, 17 December 1957, folder 192, box 17, Millikan Papers.

3. PEASANTVILLE

1. Ellery Foster, "On Learning to Be a Community Organizer," 22 July 1952, folder 470, box 109, Chester Bowles Papers, Yale University Archives.

2. Ellery Foster, "Some Rueful but Relevant Recollections of a Community Development Venture of the United States Government," c. 1952, folder 470, box, 109, Bowles Papers.

3. Foster, "Learning to Be a Community Organizer."

4. Ibid.; Ellery Foster, "A Land to Live in, a Garden with Homes and Work Places," 19 August 1952, folder 470, box 109, Bowles Papers.

5. Ellery Foster, "India's Community Development Problem: A Challenge to Common Sense," 11 August 1952, folder 470, box 109, Bowles Papers.

6. Foster, "Learning to Be a Community Organizer."

7. Ibid.

8. Foster, "Rueful but Relevant Recollections."

9. Ellery Foster, *The Coming Age of Conscience* (Winona, MN: May Sandrock and Milton Foster Memorial Foundation, 1977).

10. S. K. Dey, "Is Partyless Democracy Possible?" *Kurukshetra,* May 1962, 13.

11. For Foster's biography, see "Rueful but Relevant Recollections" and Foster, *Coming Age of Conscience.*

12. On India's archetypal nature and the Indocentricity of developmental thought, see John Kenneth Galbraith, *Economic Development in Perspective* (Cambridge, MA: Harvard University Press, 1962), 10–12 and Hla Myint, "Economic Theory and the Underdeveloped Countries," *The Journal of Political Economy* 73 (1965): 477–491.

13. Max F. Millikan and W. W. Rostow, *A Proposal: Key to an Effective Foreign Policy* (New York: Harper and Brothers, 1957); Edward Shils, *The Culture of the Indian Intellectual* (Chicago: University of Chicago, Committee on South Asian Studies, 1959); and Edward Shils, *The Intellectual between Tradition and Modernity: The Indian Situation* (The Hague: Mouton & Co., 1961). On India's importance to modernization theory and modernization theory's importance to India, see Dennis Merrill, *Bread and the Ballot: The United States and India's Economic Development, 1947–1963* (Chapel Hill: University of North Carolina Press, 1990), chaps. 6–7; David C. Engerman, "West Meets East: The Center for International Studies and Indian Economic Development," in *Staging Growth: Modernization, Development, and the Global Cold War,* ed. David C. Engerman, Nils Gilman, Mark H. Haefele, and Michael E. Latham (Amherst: University of Massachusetts Press, 2003), 199–223; Nicole Sackley, "Passage to Modernity: American Social Scientists, India, and the Pursuit of Development, 1945–1961," (Ph.D. diss., Princeton University, 2004); and David C. Engerman, "Solidarity, Development, and Non-Alignment: Foreign Economic Advisors and Indian Planning in the 1950s and 1960s," in *Die eine Welt schaffen: Praktiken von "Internationaler Solidarität" und "Internationaler Entwicklung,"* ed. Berthold Unfried and Eva Himmelstoss (Wien: Akademische Verlagsanstalt, 2012), 39–58.

14. W. W. Rostow, *Eisenhower, Kennedy, and Foreign Aid* (Austin: University of Texas Press, 1985), chaps. 1, 4, 10–12.

15. It does not appear that Nehru actually uttered the phrase "dams are the temples of modern India," which is so often attributed to him. But he did give a speech in 1954 on dams that has been given the title (perhaps by Nehru but perhaps not) "Temples of the New Age," in which he described the dam as "the biggest

temple and mosque and gurdwara" of the day. Two years later, the *Hindu* reported a comment Nehru made to the Zhou Enlai (intoned "almost as if he were speaking to himself") upon showing Zhou India's dams: "These are the new temples of India where I worship." The frequent rounding up of those two utterance—one public but oblique, the other overheard and private—into a public pronouncement, "dams are the temples of modern India," speaks to the great interest in portraying Nehru as a high modernist, as the sort of person who *would* make such a pronouncement even if he did not actually do so. The 1954 remark is documented in *Jawaharlal Nehru's Speeches,* vol. 3 (New Delhi: Ministry of Information and Broadcasting, Government of India, 1964), 3. On Nehru's 1956 comment to Zhou, see Daniel Klingensmith, *"One Valley and a Thousand": Dams, Nationalism, and Development* (Oxford: Oxford University Press, 2007), 263.

16. Partha Chatterjee, *Nationalist Thought and the Colonial World: A Derivative Discourse?* (Minnesota: University of Minnesota Press, 1986), 100, 150.

17. Ibid., 160, 144. For other important discussions of technocracy and Indian planning in the age of Nehru from a similar perspective, see David Ludden, "India's Development Regime," in *Colonialism and Culture,* ed. Nicholas B. Dirks (Ann Arbor: University of Michigan Press, 1992), 247–288; Partha Chatterjee, *The Nation and Its Fragments: Colonial and Postcolonial Histories* (Princeton: Princeton University Press, 1993), chap. 10; Itty Abraham, *The Making of the Indian Atomic Bomb: Science, Secrecy and the Postcolonial State* (London: Zed Books, 1998); Gyan Prakash, *Another Reason: Science and the Imagination of Modern India* (Princeton: Princeton University Press, 1999), chap. 6; and Itty Abraham, "The Contradictory Spaces of Postcolonial Techno-Science," *Economic and Political Weekly* 41 (2006): 210–217.

18. Ramachandra Guha, *India after Gandhi: The History of the World's Largest Democracy* (London: Macmillan, 2007), 225. Another synthetic work offering the same judgment is Sunil Khilnani, *The Idea of India* (New York: Farrar, Straus and Giroux, 1997), especially chap. 2.

19. Henry Sumner Maine, *Village-Communities in the East and West: Six Lectures Delivered at Oxford* (London: John Murray, 1871), 112.

20. Clive Dewey, "Images of the Village Community: A Study in Anglo-Indian Ideology," *Modern Asian Studies* 6 (1972): 291–328. On Maine and his reception, see also Karuna Mantena, *Alibis of Empire: Henry Maine and the Ends of Imperialism* (Princeton: Princeton University Press, 2010)

21. William Henricks Wiser, *The Hindu Jajmani System: A Socio-Economic System Interrelating Members of a Hindu Village Community in Services* (Lucknow: Lucknow Publishing House, 1936), 52, 136.

22. Gandhi lists his influences in the appendix to *Hind Swaraj* (1909), which remains the fullest source for Gandhian ideology. See *'Hind Swaraj' and Other Writings* (Cambridge: Cambridge University Press, 2009), 118.

23. The relationship between Gandhian ideology and the political support that Gandhi accrued is famously complicated. Especially in places of low literacy where Gandhian thought was refracted through local interpreters, the "vernacular" Gandhi could differ greatly from the official Gandhi, i.e., from the Gandhi of *Hind Swaraj.* Very good examinations of this issue include Shahid Amin,

"Gandhi as Mahatma: Gorakhpur District, Eastern UP, 1921–2" in *Subaltern Studies III: Writings on South Asian History and Society,* ed. Ranajit Guha (Delhi: Oxford University Press, 1984), 1–61; David Hardiman, *The Coming of the Devi: Adivasi Assertion in Western India* (Delhi: Oxford University Press, 1987); and Shahid Amin, *Event, Metaphor, Memory: Chauri Chaura 1922–1992* (Berkeley: University of California Press, 1995). None of those studies, however, suggests that Gandhi's rural followers were enthusiastic modernizers or anything close to it.

24. Gandhi, *Hind Swaraj,* 37.

25. Bharatan Kumarappa, *Capitalism, Socialism or Villagism?,* 2d ed. (1946; Rajghat, Varanasi: Sarva Seva Sangh, 1965), 115. See also J. C. Kumarappa, *Why the Village Movement?: A Plea for a Village Centred Economic Order in India* (Rajamundry: Hindustan Publishing Company, 1936).

26. The projects often cited as precursors in the community development literature are the refugee camp of Faridabad, S. K. Dey's work in Nilokheri, F. L. Brayne's Gurgaon project, the Firka Development Scheme in Madras, Spencer Hatch's Martandam, and the Baroda Rural Development Program under V. T. Krishnamachari. On these schemes and their relation to post-independence community development, see Subir Sinha, "Lineages of the Developmentalist State: Transnationality and Village India, 1900–1965," *Comparative Studies in Society and History* 50 (2008): 57–90 and Nicole Sackley, "Village Models: Etawah, India, and the Making and Remaking of Development in the Early Cold War," *Diplomatic History* 37 (2013): 749–778.

27. The contrast case is Africa, where the British government briefly pursued community development in the late 1940s. See Joanna Lewis, *Empire State-Building: War and Welfare in Kenya, 1925–52* (Oxford: James Currey, 2000), chap. 6.

28. For fuller accounts and sharp analyses of Mayer and his work in India, see Daniel Thorner, "Dropping the Pilot: A Review," *Economic Development and Cultural Change* 7 (1959): 377–380; Alice Thorner, "Nehru, Albert Mayer, and Origins of Community Projects," *Economic and Political Weekly,* 24 January 1981, 117–120; Nick Cullather, "'The Target Is the People': Representations of the Village in Modernization and U.S. National Security Doctrine," *Cultural Politics* 2 (2006): 29–48; Nick Cullather, *The Hungry World: America's Cold War Battle against Poverty in Asia* (Cambridge, MA: Harvard University Press, 2010), chap. 3; and Sackley, "Village Models."

29. Albert Mayer, "A Technique for Planning Complete Communities," *Architectural Forum,* January 1937, 19–36; Thomaï Serdari, "Albert Mayer, Architect and Town Planner: The Case for a Total Professional" (Ph.D. diss., New York University, 2005).

30. Albert Mayer and Associates, in collaboration with McKim Marriott and Richard L. Park, *Pilot Project, India: The Story of Rural Development at Etawah, Uttar Pradesh* (Berkeley: University of California Press, 1958), 6.

31. Jawaharlal Nehru to Albert Mayer, 17 June 1946, folder 1, box 8, Albert A. Mayer Papers, Special Collections Research Center, University of Chicago Library.

32. Clarence S. Stein, Address to the Conference on Economic Development and Housing Abroad, 30 April 1953, folder 37, box 15, Clarence S. Stein Papers, Division of Rare and Manuscript Collections, Cornell University.

33. Mayer, *Pilot Project, India,* 31–32.

34. Ibid., 23. For Nehru's close engagement with the pedestrian details of Mayer's operation, see the Nehru–Mayer correspondence in box 8, Mayer Papers.

35. Mayer, *Pilot Project, India,* 32.

36. Albert Mayer, "Research into Improvement of Rural and Urban Dwellings with Special Reference to Tropical and Underdeveloped Areas," revised draft of United Nations Pamphlet 2, 30 December 1952, pp. 12, 27, and 19, folder 14, box 12, Mayer Papers.

37. Horace Holmes, quoted in Margaret Parton, "Aid to India with Bare Hands," *New York Herald Tribune,* 11 March 1950.

38. Albert Mayer, "Rural Life Analyst," 15 November 1947, folder 4, box 14, Mayer Papers.

39. Rudra Datt Singh would return to India with Opler and become Opler's chief collaborator at Senapur, Cornell's field station for studying Indian village life.

40. Arthur F. Raper, "The Function and Status of Community Development," lecture delivered at a meeting of the Rural Development Seminar in Tehran, 1956, p. 5, folder 232, box 6, Raper Papers.

41. Mayer, *Pilot Project, India,* 277. See chap. 6 in general on Etawah's achievements.

42. K. C. Khanna, "New Techniques in Rural Uplift Being Employed," *Times of India,* 4 May 1955.

43. See columns from 25 March 1952, 9 July 1952, and 18 September 1953, Eleanor Roosevelt Papers Project, www.gwu.edu/~erpapers/myday/. A roundup of coverage of Etawah is given in "News Letter from Albert Mayer," 16 June 1952, folder 1, box 13, Mayer Papers and in Sackley, "Village Models," 765–771.

44. Richard Morse, *Pilot Project in Indian Rural Development* (Cambridge, MA: Harvard Business School, 1952).

45. Chester Bowles to Dean Acheson, 26 September 1952; India; Subject Files, 1951–1953; Office of the Deputy Administrator; Technical Cooperation Administration; RG 469; NACP.

46. Chester Bowles, *Ambassador's Report* (New York: Harper & Brothers, 1954), 198.

47. Ibid., 198–202.

48. Douglas Ensminger, Oral History Transcript, 22 February 1973, p. 9, folder 1, box A, Ford Foundation Archives, New York.

49. Hoffman, paraphrased in S. K. Dey, *Power to the People?: A Chronicle of India, 1947–67* (Bombay: Orient Longmans, 1969), 20.

50. Ensminger, Oral History Transcript, pp. 1–2, folder 13, box A. For a historical account of the Ford Foundation's India office under Ensminger, see Nicole Sackley, "Foundation in the Field: The Ford Foundation's New Delhi Office

and the Construction of Development Knowledge, 1951–1970," in *American Foundations and the Coproduction of World Order in the Twentieth Century*, ed. John Krige and Helke Rausch (Göttingen: Vandenboeck and Ruprecht, 2012), 231–260.

51. Carl C. Taylor, "Sociological Analysis: Two Major Evils," *Kurukshetra*, January 1959, 379; "How Much 'Identification' with the Villagers?" *India Village Service Chronicle*, 14 May 1955, 1.

52. Douglas Ensminger and Carl C. Taylor, "The National Development Program of India with Specific Reference to Its Rural Sector," September 1954, p. 18, Report 614, Ford Foundation Archives.

53. Carl C. Taylor, "Community Mobilization and Group Processes," June 1957, box 34, Carl C. Taylor Papers, Division of Rare and Manuscript Collections, Cornell University Library.

54. R. Jagannathan, "Book Review Programme," n.d., subject file 261, Jayaprakash Narayan Papers, installments I and II, Manuscripts Division, Nehru Memorial Museum and Library, New Delhi.

55. Ensminger, Oral History Transcript, p. 135, folder 21, box B.

56. "The Ranchi Seminar," *Kurukshetra*, January 1957, 7–10. On the general movement of Kurt Lewin's human relations research into Indian government via Ford, see the work of Matthew S. Hull, "Democratic Technologies of Speech: From World War II America to Postcolonial Delhi," *Linguistic Anthropology* 20 (2010): 257–282 and "Communities of Place, Not Kind: American Technologies of Neighborhood in Postcolonial Delhi," *Comparative Studies in Society and History* 53 (2011): 757–790.

57. "A Decade of C. D. Programme at a Glance," *Kurukshetra*, October 1962, 97.

58. Hugh Tinker, "Authority and Community in Village India," *Pacific Affairs* 32 (1959): 366.

59. S. K. Dey to Jawaharlal Nehru, June 1954, reprinted in Dey, *Power to the People?*, 35.

60. Fakhruddin Ali Ahmed, quoted in the proceedings of the First Meeting of the Consultative Council on Community Development and Panchayati Raj, New Delhi, 28 January 1972, file Q-17011/6/70-A8N, Records of the Planning Commission, National Archives of India, New Delhi (hereafter NAI).

61. P. C. Mahalanobis, "Recommendation for the Formulation of the Second Five-Year Plan," 1955, in *Talks on Planning* (Calcutta: Statistical Publishing Society, 1961), 23. For criticisms see P. T. Bauer, *Indian Economic Policy and Development* (London: George Allen and Unwin, 1961).

62. Medha Kudaisya, "'A Mighty Adventure': Institutionalising the Idea of Planning in Post-colonial India, 1947–1960," *Modern Asian Studies* 43 (2009): 939–978.

63. Government of India, Planning Commission, *Third Five Year Plan* (New Delhi: Government of India, 1961), 49.

64. "Agriculture and Community Development" and "Industry and Mining" form united budget categories and are not broken down into their component parts in every plan period. That makes sense in the former case because, as

described above, nearly all agricultural policy was routed through community development agencies.

65. I am dependent for this important argument on Benjamin Zachariah, *Developing India: An Intellectual and Social History, c. 1930–50* (Oxford: Oxford University Press, 2005), chap. 4.

66. K. R. Malkani, *Principles for a New Political Party* (Delhi: Vijay Pustak Bhandar, 1951). Malkani's advocacy for a "biotechnic order" and castigations against "mining civilization" clearly mark his debt to Patrick Geddes (40–41). On Malkani, see Craig Baxter, *The Jana Sangh: A Biography of an Indian Political Party* (Philadelphia: University of Pennsylvania Press, 1969), 59–62. Decentralism is also an important concept in a later major work of Hindu nationalism, Deendayal Upadhyaya's *Integral Humanism* (1965).

67. "Socialist Solution of the Problems of Rural India," c. 1949, p. 7, subject file 243, Narayan Papers, installments I and II.

68. Jayaprakash Narayan, Draft Manuscript of Foreword to *Panchayati Raj as the Basis of Indian Polity,* by Dharampal, n.d., pp. 1–2, file 399, Narayan Papers, installments I and II. A reflection on the same concepts as they have been imported into Indian social science can be found in Carol Upadhya, "The Concept of Community in Indian Social Sciences: An Anthropological Perspective," in *Community and Identities: Contemporary Discourses on Culture and Politics in India,* ed. Surinder S. Jodhka (New Delhi: Sage Publications, 2001), 32–58.

69. Again, I am indebted to Benjamin Zachariah, this time to his biography *Nehru* (London: Routledge, 2004).

70. Arundhati Roy, "The Cost of Living: The Narmada Dam and the Indian State," in *Experiencing the State,* ed. Lloyd I. Rudolph and John Kurt Jacobsen (Delhi: Oxford University Press, 2007), 56.

71. Jawaharlal Nehru, "Social Aspects of Small and Big Projects," 1959, in *Jawaharlal Nehru on Science and Society: A Collection of His Writings and Speeches* (New Delhi: Nehru Memorial Museum and Library, 1988), 172; Ramachandra Guha, "Prime Ministers and Big Dams," *The Hindu,* 18 December 2005.

72. Jawaharlal Nehru, address at the Development Commissioners' Conference, New Delhi, 18 April 1953, in Ministry of Community Development, *Jawaharlal Nehru on Community Development and Panchayati Raj* (New Delhi: Government of India, 1963), 23–24.

73. Nehru, quoted in Dey, *Power to the People?,* 54. A supporting account of the event is offered in Douglas Ensminger, *Rural India in Transition* (New Delhi: All India Panchayat Parishad, 1972), 7.

74. In 1956, the Ministry would be renamed twice more, first as the Ministry of Community Development and Cooperation and later as the Ministry of Community Development and Panchayati Raj, to record its expanded function.

75. "Extract from the speech of Prime Minister in Lok Sabha on 20 November 1957," file 254, Narayan Papers, installments I and II.

76. Tarlok Singh to All State Governments, 12 January 1952; Community Development; International Cooperation Administration; Records of the Agency for International Development, Record Group 286; NACP.

77. Ensminger, Oral History Transcript, p. 3, folder 8, box A. See also p. 1, folder 21, box B.

78. V. T. Krishnamachari, quoted in Gunnar Myrdal, *Asian Drama: An Inquiry into the Poverty of Nations,* vol. 2 (New York: Pantheon, 1968), 870.

79. Ensminger, Oral History Transcript, p. 16, folder 42, box A.

80. Planning Commission, *Report of the Team for the Study of Community Projects and National Extension Service* (New Delhi: Government of India, 1957), 1:7.

81. Ibid., 1:5.

82. Constitution of India, part IV, article 40.

83. Discussions of the democratic decentralization can be found in the summary record of the sixth meeting of the standing committee of the national development council, 12–13 January 1958, file PC/CDN/29/21/57, Records of the Planning Commission, NAI.

84. "States' Agricultural Production Programmes: National Development Council Standing Committee Discussions," 12 January 1958, in ibid.

85. S. K. Dey, *Community Development: A Chronicle, 1954–1961* (Faridabad: Government of India Press, 1962), 113.

86. "A Decade of C.D. Programme at a Glance," *Kurukshetra,* October 1962, 105.

87. John P. Lewis, *Quiet Crisis in India: Economic Development and American Policy* (Washington, DC: The Brookings Institution, 1962), 157.

88. B. R. Ambedkar, *Untouchables, or the Children of India's Ghetto,* unpublished, n.d., in B. R. Ambedkar, *Writings and Speeches,* vol. 5, ed. Vasant Moon (Bombay: Education Department, Government of Maharashtra, 1989), 19.

89. *Constituent Assembly Debates: Official Report* (New Delhi: Lok Sabha Secretariat, 1988), 7:39. Ambedkar's failed attempts to broadcast this view in the United States are discussed in Daniel Immerwahr, "Caste or Colony?: Indianizing Race in the United States," *Modern Intellectual History* 4 (2007): 275–301.

90. See Ronald J. Herring, *Land to the Tiller: The Political Economy of Agrarian Reform in South Asia* (New Haven: Yale University Press, 1983), chap. 5 and Francine R. Frankel, *India's Political Economy, 1947–2004: The Gradual Revolution,* 2d ed. (Oxford: Oxford University Press, 2005).

91. The case is made in Carl C. Taylor, *The Farmers' Movement, 1620–1920* (New York: American Book Company, 1953). On the tendency of BAE leaders to come from Midwestern farm families, see Gilbert, "Eastern Urban Liberals and Midwestern Agrarian Intellectuals."

92. I am indebted to Michael Adas for that formulation.

93. Mayer, *Pilot Project, India,* 337; Ambedkar, *Untouchables, or the Children of India's Ghetto,* 57.

94. Baij Nath Singh, "Factions and What to Do about Them," 1950, reprinted in Mayer, *Pilot Project, India,* 223.

95. Albert Mayer, "Research and Action: The Indian Village," speech, 21 January 1954, folder 21, box 35, Mayer Papers.

96. Ibid.

97. Mayer, *Pilot Project, India,* 282–283.

98. McKim Marriott to Albert Mayer, 3 August 1953, folder 6, box 7, Mayer Papers.

99. [Douglas Ensminger], *A Guide to Community Development* (New Delhi: Ministry of Community Development, Government of India, 1957), 29, 126.

100. Ministry of Community Development and Panchayati Raj, "Village Volunteer Force," December 1962, p. iii, file 103/62—ECS, Ministry of Home Affairs, Emergency Cabinet Secretariat, NAI.

101. Lalit K. Sen and Prodipto Roy, *Awareness of Community Development in Village India: Preliminary Report* (Hyderabad: National Institute of Community Development, 1967), 43.

102. Morris E. Opler, "Political Organization and Economic Growth: The Case of Village India," *International Review of Community Development* 5 (1960): 193–194.

103. Ministry of Community Development and Cooperation, *Report of the Study Group on the Welfare of the Weaker Sections of the Village Community,* 2 vols. (New Delhi: Government of India, 1961).

104. S. K. Dey, paraphrased in Ministry of Community Development and Cooperation, *Main Recommendations and Conclusions* (New Delhi: Government of India, 1960), 57.

105. Dey, quoted in ibid.

106. E. M. S. Namboodiripad, *Kerala: Yesterday, Today, and Tomorrow* (Calcutta: National Book Agency, 1967), 59. See Eric J. Miller, "Village Structure in North Kerala," *The Economic Weekly* (Bombay), 9 February 1952, 159–164; Government of Kerala, *Report of the Administrative Reforms Committee,* vol. 1 (Trivandrum: Government of Kerala, 1958), 28–30; and K. K. Panikkar, *Community Development Administration in Kerala* (New Delhi: S. Chand and Co., 1974), 11–13.

107. *The Complete Works of Swami Vivekananda,* 11th ed., vol. 3 (Calcutta: Advaita Ashrama, 1974), 295; Namboodiripad's *Kerala* provides a useful overview of Kerala as an exception but also see Robin Jeffrey, *Politics, Women, and Well-Being: How Kerala Became a 'Model'* (London: The Macmillan Press, 1992).

108. The Italian microstate of San Marino was ruled by a communist-led coalition from 1945 to 1957. But San Marino's population during that time was between ten and fifteen thousand. Kerala's population in that period, by contrast, ran between ten and fifteen *million.*

109. R. K. Khadilkar, quoted in "Free, Frank and Forthright: Lok Sabha Debate," *Kurukshetra,* September 1957, 17.

110. E. M. S. Namboodiripad, "What Is Wrong with the C.D. Programme?" *Kurukshetra,* 2 October 1962, 29, 30.

111. Patrick Heller, "Moving the State: The Politics of Democratic Centralization in Kerala, South Africa, and Porto Alegre," *Politics and Society* 29 (2001): 153.

112. See Government of Kerala, *Report of the Administrative Reforms Committee.*

113. E. M. S. Namboodiripad, "Note on the Report of the Committee on Panchayati Raj Institutions," in Ministry of Agriculture and Irrigation, Department of Rural Development, *Report of the Committee on Panchayati Raj Institutions* (New Delhi: Government of India, 1978), 163.

114. Patrick Heller, *The Labor of Development: Workers and the Transformation of Capitalism in Kerala, India* (Ithaca: Cornell University Press, 1999).

115. The importance of Kerala has been broadcast especially by Amartya Sen, whose research played a fundamental role in the creation of the Human Development Index. For Sen's vision, including many discussions of Kerala, see Amartya Sen, *Development as Freedom* (Oxford: Oxford University Press, 2000). On Kerala as a model, see also Jeffrey, *Politics, Women, and Well-Being* and Govindan Parayil, ed., *Kerala, The Development Experience: Reflections on Sustainability and Replicability* (New York: Zed Books, 2000).

116. A very good overall account of the limits of community development can be found in S. C. Dube, *India's Changing Villages: Human Factors in Community Development* (Ithaca: Cornell University Press, 1958). Other useful overviews include Adrian C. Mayer, "Development Projects in an Indian Village," *Pacific Affairs* 29 (1956): 37–45; Umrao Singh, *Community Development in India: Evaluation and Statistical Analysis* (Kanpur: Kitab Ghar, 1962); Walter C. Neale, "The Indian Peasant, the State, and Economic Development," *Land Economics* 38 (1962): 281–291; Oscar Lewis, *Village Life in Northern India: Studies in a Delhi Village* (New York: Vintage Books, 1965); Barrington Moore, Jr., *Social Origins of Dictatorship and Democracy: Lord and Peasant in the Making of the Modern World* (Boston: Beacon Press, 1966), chap. 6; Myrdal, *Asian Drama*, vol. 2, chaps. 18 and 26; and Garvin Karunaratne, "The Failure of the Community Development Programme in India," *Community Development Journal* 11 (1976): 95–118.

117. S. C. Dube, "Cultural Factors in Rural Community Development," *The Journal of Asian Studies* 16 (1956): 19–30.

118. People's expenditure as a percentage of government expenditure dropped from 54.6% during the First Plan to 21.3% at the end of the Third Plan. Karunaratne, "Failure of the Community Development Programme," 101.

119. L. C. Jain, with B. V. Krishnamurthy and P. M. Tripathi, *Grass without Roots: Rural Development under Government Auspices* (New Delhi: Sage Publications, 1985).

120. Albert Mayer to Tarlok Singh, 14 March 1955, *Important Letters Issued by Community Projects Administration/Ministry of Community Development and Co-operation,* vol. 2 (New Delhi: Government of India, 1961), 219.

121. Thokurdas Bang and Suresh Ramabhai, "Etawah Project—The Other Side of the Medal," *The Pioneer Magazine Section,* 9 May 1952.

122. Gerald D. Berreman, *Hindus of the Himalayas* (Berkeley: University of California Press, 1963), 291.

123. Dey, *Power to the People?,* 97.

124. Walter C. Neale, "Indian Community Development, Local Government, Local Planning, and Rural Policy since 1950," *Economic Development and Cultural Change* 33 (1985): 681. For a similar account, see Alice Crawford Stone

Ilchman, "Democratic Decentralization and Planning for Rural India" (Ph.D. diss., University of London, 1964).

125. "Changing Women's Attitudes," Field Reports Material "P," 1959, folder 16, box 31, Mayer Papers.

126. Record of discussions of the Emergency Committee of the Cabinet, 17 January 1963, file 103/62—ECS, Ministry of Home Affairs, Emergency Cabinet Secretariat, NAI.

127. Ministry of Community Development and Panchayati Raj, "Village Volunteer Force."

128. Ibid.

129. Rajeshwar Dayal, *Community Development, Panchayati Raj, and Sahakari Samaj* (Delhi: Metropolitan Book Co., 1965), 207.

130. Neale, "Indian Community Development," 687–688.

131. Agricultural Production Team, Ford Foundation, *Report on India's Food Crisis and Steps to Meet It* (New Delhi: Government of India, Ministry of Food and Agriculture and Ministry of Community Development and Cooperation, April 1959), 22, 42.

132. M. J. Coldwell, René Dumont, and Margaret Read, *Report of a Community Development Evaluation Mission in India* (New Delhi: Ministry of Community Development and Co-operation, 1959), 46.

133. Jawaharlal Nehru, quoted in Government of India, Planning Commission, *Report of the Team for the Study of Community Projects and National Extension Service,* vol. 1 (New Delhi: Government of India, 1957), 1.

134. Karunaratne, "Failure of the Community Development Programme," 113.

135. The National Development Council made one such suggestion in 1962. The "Ram Subhag Singh Committee" (the Inter-Departmental and Institutional Coordination for Agricultural Production Working Group) made a similar recommendation the next year.

136. Shastri, quoted in S. K. Dey, "Panchayati Raj in Independent India: Some Personal Reflections," in *Panchayati Raj in Karnataka Today: Its National Dimensions,* ed. George Mathew (New Delhi: Institute of Social Sciences, 1986), 38.

137. Lal Bahadur Shastri, address at Chief Ministers' Conference at New Delhi, 24 June 1964, Group V, SW 32, Lal Bahadur Shastri Papers, Private Archives Division, NAI.

138. These issues are discussed in the proceedings of the Second Meeting of the Consultative Council on Community Development, 7 July 1970, file Q-17011/6/70-A8N, Records of the Planning Commission, NAI.

139. M. S. Haq, *Community Development through Extension* (Allahabad: Chugh Publications, 1979), vii.

140. Chatterjee argues that community development and panchayati raj were part of a Gramscian "passive revolution of capital." On this understanding, Nehru and the Planning Commission deployed communitarian schemes *not* to develop villages as advertised but rather to mollify rural landlords so that the landlords would not resist the state's larger developmental efforts. Thus, the

anti-industrial aspects of community development were but a feint in a larger push toward industrialization. That reading is arguably consistent with the effects of community development, but Sarvepalli Gopal's multivolume biography of Nehru rejects it on the evidence of Nehru's correspondence. (To be fair, it does not appear that Gopal fully comprehends what Gramsci meant by "passive revolution," but his findings nevertheless fail to support the Chatterjee reading.) In my own more limited consultations of the Planning Committee archives and the documentary record left by the Ministry of Community Development, I was also unable to find evidence that India's planners deployed community development cynically. Chatterjee, for his part, has pointed out that his claim does not rest on what the Planning Commissioners *said* but on the inner logic of their positions. In a scolding review, Chatterjee faults Gopal for his superficial reliance on the documentary record. What is needed, argues Chatterjee, is "the cold ray of analysis to penetrate the deceptive layer of contemporary perceptions, and to bring to light the more latent social processes." The difference between Chatterjee and Gopal, in other words, is ultimately not the sort that can be resolved simply by archival research. Partha Chatterjee, *A Possible India: Essays in Political Criticism* (Oxford: Oxford University Press, 1999), 14 and Sarvepalli Gopal, *Jawaharlal Nehru: A Biography*, vol. 3 (London: Jonathan Cape, 1984), 168. The "passive revolution" argument is contained in Chatterjee, *Nationalist Thought and the Colonial World,* chap. 5 and Chatterjee, *The Nation and Its Fragments,* chap. 10.

4. GRASSROOTS EMPIRE

1. "Poland Is Saluted at Copernicus Fete," *New York Times,* 25 May 1943.

2. Pearl Buck's book was *Tell the People: Talks with James Yen about the Mass Education Movement* (New York: The John Day Company, 1945); John C. K. Kiang, ed., *Dr. Y. C. James Yen: His Movement for Mass Education and Rural Reconstruction* (South Bend: published by author, 1976), iv.

3. William O. Douglas, "Toward Greater Vitality," *Today's Health,* May 1973, 57.

4. In a 1959 letter to Marshall Field, DeWitt Wallace refers to the *Digest*'s four articles about Yen as "a record unmatched by any other person." By 1968, the *Digest* had published another two articles about Yen. DeWitt Wallace to Marshall Field, 6 January 1959, Catalogued Correspondents Box, International Institute of Rural Reconstruction (IIRR) Papers, Rare Books and Manuscript Library, Columbia University; Minutes, Annual Meeting of the Board of the Jimmy Yen Rural Reconstruction Movement, 24 September 1968, folder 1, container 601, William O. Douglas Papers, Manuscript Division, Library of Congress. William Lederer's article about community development in the Philippines, which singles out Yen for praise, does not appear to have been published, but a draft of it remains. W. J. Lederer, "The Revolt of Juan de la Cruz," in box 100, IIRR Papers.

5. For Yen's estimation of the scope of his literacy campaign, see Yen to George Marshall, 30 September 1947, box 34, IIRR Papers. The best source on Yen's

remarkable career in China is Charles W. Hayford, *To the People: James Yen and Village China* (New York: Columbia University Press, 1990).

6. Quoted in J. P. McEvoy, "Jimmy Yen and the People's Crusade," *Reader's Digest,* March 1955, 147.

7. Yen, Minutes of the Annual Meeting of the International Committee of the Mass Education Movement, 3 October 1956, folder 1, container 599, Douglas Papers.

8. It is worth noting that by the 1930s, Ford had himself become something of a communitarian, devoting a great deal of his energy to Greenfield Village, a sort of private small-town theme park that sought to blend industrial production with small-scale society. Greg Grandin, *Fordlandia: The Rise and Fall of Henry Ford's Forgotten Jungle City* (New York: Metropolitan Books, 2009), chap. 16.

9. Hayford, *To the People,* 42–43, 141–142.

10. Y. C. James Yen, notes on meeting with Harry Truman, 9 March 1948, box 34, IIRR Papers.

11. "The International Committee of the Mass Education Movement," c. 1951, folder 5, container 598, Douglas Papers.

12. The Joint Commission on Rural Reconstruction (JCRR) received an additional $15 million in 1949. It was only able to spend $9 million of its funds, however, before the Chinese Revolution forced a suspension of its operations. The JCRR retreated to Taiwan, where it became a major force for development. For financial details, see Report of Y. C. James Yen, in Minutes of the Meeting of the American Chinese Committee of the Mass Education Movement, 13 January 1950, folder 4, container 597, Douglas Papers. On the JCRR in Taiwan, see Nick Cullather, "Fuel for the Good Dragon: The United States and Industrial Policy in Taiwan, 1950–1965" *Diplomatic History* 20 (1996): 1–25 and David Ekbladh, "To Reconstruct the Medieval: Rural Reconstruction in Interwar China and the Rise of an American Style of Modernization, 1921–1961," *Journal of American–East Asian Relations* 9 (2000): 169–196.

13. Paul Hoffman, "Most Courageous Comeback in History," *Life,* 5 February 1951, 104.

14. The various versions of the committee were the American-Chinese Committee of the Mass Education Movement, the International Committee of the Mass Education Movement, and the International Mass Education Movement, Inc.

15. Minutes of the Meeting of the International Committee of the Mass Education Movement, Inc., 23 May 1953, folder 5, container 598, Douglas Papers.

16. Dennis Morrow Roth, *The Friar Estates of the Philippines* (Albuquerque: University of New Mexico Press, 1977); Benedict Anderson, "Cacique Democracy in the Philippines: Origins and Dreams," in *Discrepant Histories: Translocal Essays on Philippine Culture*, ed. Vicente L. Rafael (Philadelphia: Temple University Press, 1995), 3–47; Dante C. Simbulan, *The Modern Principalia: The Historical Evolution of the Philippine Ruling Oligarchy* (Diliman, Quezon City: University of the Philippines Press, 2005); Julian Go, *American Empire and the Politics of Meaning: Elite Political Cultures in the Philippines and Puerto Rico during U.S. Colonialism* (Durham: Duke University Press, 2008).

17. James C. Scott and Benedict Kerkvliet, "The Politics of Survival: Peasant Response to 'Progress' in Southeast Asia," *Journal of Southeast Asian Studies* 4 (1973): 241–268; James C. Scott and Benedict J. Kerkvliet, "How Traditional Rural Patrons Lose Legitimacy: A Theory with Special Reference to Southeast Asia" in *Friends, Followers, and Factions: A Reader in Political Clientelism,* ed. Steffen W. Schmidt et al. (Berkeley: University of California Press, 1977), 439–457; Benedict J. Kerkvliet, *The Huk Rebellion: A Study of Peasant Revolt in the Philippines* (Berkeley: University of California Press, 1977).

18. Luis Taruc, *Born of the People* (New York: International Publishers, 1953), 66.

19. Carol M. Petillo, "Douglas MacArthur and Manuel Quezon: A Note on an Imperial Bond," *Pacific Historical Review* 48 (1979): 110–117.

20. Augusto V. De Viana, *Kulaboretor!: The Issue of Political Collaboration during World War II* (Manila: University of Santo Tomas Publishing House, 2003).

21. Kerkvliet, *The Huk Rebellion;* Stephen R. Shalom, "Counter-Insurgency in the Philippines," *Journal of Contemporary Asia* 7 (1977): 153–177; Renato Constantino and Letizia R. Constantino, *The Philippines: The Continuing Past* (Quezon City: The Foundation for Nationalist Studies, 1978), chap. 9.

22. Quoted in Paul M. Monk, *Truth and Power: Robert S. Hardie and Land Reform Debates in the Philippines, 1950–1987* (Clayton, Australia: Centre for Southeast Asian Studies: Monash University, 1990), 20.

23. Jonathan Nashel, *Edward Lansdale's Cold War* (Amherst: University of Massachusetts Press, 2005), 150, 163–173.

24. Edward Geary Lansdale, *In the Midst of Wars: An American's Mission to Southeast Asia* (New York: Harper and Row, 1972), 21.

25. Edward Lansdale, "Civic Action," lecture, 24 February 1961, folder 1269, box 45, Edward Geary Lansdale Papers, Hoover Institution Archives, Stanford University.

26. Lansdale admitted to his biographer that he knew Kelly was "helping [the Huks] out from time to time . . . and carrying messages," but he dismissed this as her "just being fellow townsmates" with the Huks. Cecil B. Currey, *Edward Lansdale: The Unquiet American* (Boston: Houghton Mifflin, 1988), 42.

27. Lansdale, *In the Midst of Wars,* 72.

28. On Lansdale's blend of cultural knowledge and violence, see Nashel, *Lansdale's Cold War,* chap. 1.

29. Ramon Magsaysay, quoted in Frances Lucille Starner, *Magsaysay and the Philippine Peasantry: The Agrarian Impact on Philippine Politics, 1953–1956* (Berkeley: University of California Press, 1961), 28.

30. Lansdale, *In the Midst of Wars,* 37. On the intimate relationship between Lansdale and Magsaysay, see Eva-Lotta E. Hedman, "Late Imperial Romance: Magsaysay, Lansdale and the Philippine-American 'Special Relationship,'" *Intelligence and National Security* 14 (1999): 181–194.

31. Lansdale, *In the Midst of Wars,* 70.

32. Stephen Rosskamm Shalom, *The United States and the Philippines: A Study of Neocolonialism* (Philadelphia: Institute for the Study of Human Issues,

1981), 79–80. The most thorough study of EDCOR, highly sympathetic to the program, is Alvin H. Scaff, *The Philippine Answer to Communism* (Stanford: Stanford University Press, 1955).

33. Simeon Man, "Conscripts of Empire: Race and Soldiering in the Decolonizing Pacific" (Ph.D. diss., Yale University, 2012), 70.

34. Minutes of the Meeting of the International Committee of the Mass Education Movement, Inc., 23 May 1953, folder 5, container 598, Douglas Papers.

35. Ramon Magsaysay, "The Poor Man's Point 4 for the Philippines," 1954, box 38, IIRR Papers.

36. Ibid.

37. Ramon Magsaysay to Y. C. James Yen, 26 April 1954, folder 6, container 598, Douglas Papers.

38. Details on the role of the CIA in the Magsaysay election are drawn from three sources: Lansdale, *In the Midst of Wars;* Joseph Burkholder Smith, *Portrait of a Cold Warrior* (New York: G. P. Putnam's Sons, 1976); and Raymond Bonner, *Waltzing with a Dictator: The Marcoses and the Making of American Policy* (New York: Times Books, 1987). Nick Cullather, however, has argued that the CIA had an exaggerated perception of its own ability to influence Philippine politics and that Magsaysay was beholden less to the United States than he was to the Philippine oligarchy. See his *Illusions of Influence: The Political Economy of United States–Philippines Relations, 1942–1960* (Stanford: Stanford University Press, 1994), especially chap. 4.

39. Quoted in Smith, *Portrait of a Cold Warrior,* 113.

40. On that organization, the Federation of Free Farmers, see Sonya Diane Carter, "The Philippine Federation of Free Farmers (A Case Study in Mass Agrarian Organizations)," in *Social Foundations of Community Development: Readings on the Philippines,* ed. Socorro C. Espiritu and Chester L. Hunt (Manila: R. M. Garcia, 1964), 449–473 and Blondie Po, *Rural Organizations and Rural Development in the Philippines: A Documentary Study* (Manila: Institute for Philippine Culture, 1977). The FFF's program can be found in its *Land to the Tiller* (Manila: Federation of Free Farmers, 1957).

41. Quoted in Monk, *Truth and Power,* 81.

42. For details see Constantino and Constantino, *The Philippines,* chap. 9 and Amando Doronila, *The State, Economic Transformation, and Political Change in the Philippines, 1946–1972* (Oxford: Oxford University Press, 1992), chap. 4.

43. The many components of "barrio fever" are discussed in detail in Jose V. Abueva, *Focus on the Barrio: The Story behind the Birth of the Philippine Community Development Program under President Ramon Magsaysay* (Manila: Institute of Public Administration, University of the Philippines, 1959).

44. For a highly sympathetic overview, see Juan M. Flavier, *Doctor to the Barrios: Experiences with the Philippine Rural Reconstruction Movement* (Quezon City: New Day Publishers, 1970).

45. Smith, *Portrait of a Cold Warrior,* 266–268.

46. Abueva, *Focus on the Barrio,* 192.

47. E. R. Chadwick, progress report no. 26, 2 January 1957, folder S-0175-1701-01, United Nations Archives, New York.

48. His story, and details about the missions to India and the Philippines, are given in Ernest E. Neal, *Hope for the Wretched: A Narrative Report of Technical Assistance Experiences* (Washington, DC: Agency for International Development, 1972).

49. On the portability of village strategies, see Nick Cullather, "'The Target Is the People': Representations of the Village in Modernization and U.S. National Security Doctrine," *Cultural Politics* 2 (2006): 29–48 and Nicole Sackley, "The Village as Cold War Site: Experts, Development, and the History of Rural Reconstruction," *Journal of Global History* 6 (2011): 481–504.

50. From the start of the PACD's operation until fiscal year 1966–1967, 31,109 grants-in-aid projects were completed, at a total cost of 42,406,284 pesos. The PACD paid 15,022,001 pesos, and barrio residents paid 23,200,310 pesos. Figures, drawn from the PACD's official accounting, are given in Chavalit Sukpanich, "The Role of the Presidential Arm on Community Development (PACD) in Nation-Building" (M.P.A. thesis, Centro Escolar University, 1968), 106.

51. Ibid., 106, 113.

52. Presidential Assistant on Community Development, Circular No. 63–26, "The Focus of PACD Operations," 16 September 1963, Filipiniana Books Section, University Library, University of the Philippines, Diliman.

53. Community Development Research Council, annual report 1957–1958, Government Publications Division, National Library of the Philippines.

54. F. Landa Jocano, interview with the author, 1 October 2009, Quezon City; Mary Racelis, interview with the author, 13 October 2009, Quezon City. Both Jocano and Racelis remembered scholars adjusting their topics to fit PACD's interests; Jocano claimed that researchers adapted their conclusions as well, consciously or unconsciously.

55. Gelia T. Castillo, "The Filipino Social Scientist and Rural Development," lecture, 13 March 1974, 3, Filipiniana Collection, University Library, University of the Philippines, Diliman.

56. Racelis, interview.

57. See Emmanuel M. Luna, "Rethinking Community Development in the Philippines: 'Indigenizing' and Regaining Grounds," in *The Philippine Social Sciences in the Life of the Nation,* vol. 1, ed. Virginia A. Miralao (Quezon City: Philippine Social Science Center, 1999), 315–343.

58. Glenn Anthony May, "Father Frank Lynch and the Shaping of Philippine Social Science," *Itinerario* 22 (1998): 99.

59. A fuller account of Lynch's intellectual genealogy would discuss two other Chicago professors, Fred Eggan and W. Lloyd Warner. For their influence on Lynch and their relationship to community development, see May, "Frank Lynch" and Daniel Immerwahr, "Quests for Community: The United States, Community Development, and the World, 1935–65" (Ph.D. diss., University of California, Berkeley, 2011), chaps. 1 and 4.

60. Frank Lynch, "Continuities in Philippine Social Class," lecture, November 1960, Institute of Philippine Culture Collection, Pardo de Tavera Library and Archives, Loyola-Rizal Library, Ateneo de Manila University.

61. Frank Lynch, "Social Class in a Bikol Town" (Ph.D. diss., University of Chicago, 1959), 133.

62. Lynch, "Continuities," 4.

63. Frank Lynch, "Social Acceptance," in *Philippine Society and the Individual: Selected Essays of Frank Lynch, 1949–1976,* ed. Aram A. Yengoyan and Perla Q. Makil (Ann Arbor: University of Michigan, 1984), 23–91.

64. F. Landa Jocano, "Rethinking 'Smooth Interpersonal Relations,'" *Philippine Sociological Review* 4 (1966): 287.

65. May, "Frank Lynch," especially 111–113. Lynch maintained his views about the symbiotic relationship and mutual "attunement" of the higher and lower orders to each other's needs through the 1970s. See Frank Lynch, "Big and Little People: Social Class in the Rural Philippines," 1975, in *Philippine Society and the Individual,* 93–99.

66. Frank Lynch, "Significance of the Nature of the Philippine Community in Community Development Programs," p. 23, May 1960, from "Community Development in the Philippines Seminar," folder 6, box 23, Philippine Studies Program Records, Special Collections Research Center, University of Chicago Library.

67. Jenna Feltey Alden, "Bottom-Up Management: Participative Philosophy and Humanistic Psychology in American Organizational Culture, 1930–1970" (Ph.D. diss., Columbia University, 2012), chap. 7.

68. Ramon P. Binamira, *Community Development: Answer to Communism* (Bangkok: SEATO, 1960), 12.

69. Frances M. Cevallos, "Batangas Governor, Other Officials Go Back to School," *Manila Times Daily Magazine,* 25 June 1958, reprinted in *Community Development: The War against Want, Hunger, Illiteracy, and Disease* (Manila: Presidential Assistant on Community Development, 1958), 80–83.

70. Sukpanich, working with official records of the PACD no longer available in archives, gave the number in 1968 as 4,921,694. A PACD-issued pamphlet from the same year gave the total number of "barrio leaders" who have undergone training as 2,578,894, but it is not clear whether there were other trainees who were not counted as "barrio leaders." See Sukpanich, "The Role of the PACD," 7 and PACD, *The Philippine Community Development Program,* 1968, p. 25, "Community Development" vertical file, Filipiniana Section, Loyola-Rizal Library, Ateneo de Manila University.

71. PACD, "Philippine Community Development: Handbook for Community Development Workers," 1957, 85–86, Filipiniana Section, Library of Social Work and Community Development, University of the Philippines, Diliman.

72. Gelia T. Castillo, Conrado M. Dimaano, Jesus C. Calleja, and Shirley F. Parcon, "A Development Program in Action: A Progress Report on a Philippine Case," *Asian Studies* 2 (1964): 45–46; Shalom, *The United States and the Philippines,* 124–125.

73. Buenaventura M. Villanueva, *A Study of the Competence of Barrio Citizens to Conduct Barrio Government* (Quezon City: Community Development Research Council, 1959), 200, 94.

74. "Barrio Officials, Do your Jobs!," *Weekly Graphic,* 4 April 1962, 16; E. H. Valsan, *Community Development Programs and Rural Local Government: Comparative Case Studies of India and the Philippines* (New York: Praeger, 1970), 217; J. Eliseo Rocamora and Corazon Conti Panganiban, *Rural Development Strategies: The Philippine Case* (Quezon City: Institute of Philippine Culture, 1975), 95.

75. Valsan, *Community Development Programs,* 209, 215.

76. Agaton P. Pal, *The Resources, Levels of Living, and Aspirations of Rural Households in Negros Oriental* (Quezon City: Community Development Research Council, 1963), 254–255; Luz A. Einsiedel, *The Impact of the Community Development Women and Youth and Lay Leadership Institutes of the PACD* (Quezon City: Community Development Research Council, 1966), 12; Agaton P. Pal and Robert A. Polson, *Rural People's Response to Change: Dumaguete Trade Area, Philippines* (Quezon City: New Day Publishers, 1973), 241.

77. The anecdote is told, among other places, in Gelia T. Castillo, "A New Look at Old Concepts in Development: A Minority Report," *Solidarity* 3 (May 1968): 1–19.

78. Castillo et al., "Development Program in Action," 58.

79. Ibid., 64–65. See also Gelia T. Castillo, *How Participatory is Participatory Development?: A Review of the Philippine Experience* (Makati: The Philippine Institute for Development Studies, 1983).

80. Rocamora and Panganiban, *Rural Development Strategies,* 140.

81. Agricultural incomes at constant 1966 prices had declined from 462 pesos per family to 400 pesos. No measure was available to the researchers for total rural incomes, however. Pal and Polson, *Rural People's Response to Change,* 153, 165, 240.

82. David C. Korten, "Community Organization and Rural Development: A Learning Process Approach," *Public Administration Review* 40 (1980): 482.

83. Napoleon G. Rama, "EEA vs. PACD," *Philippines Free Press,* 1 June 1963, 14.

84. Sukpanich, "The Role of the PACD," 106. Although part of this drop was surely the result of Macapagal's lack of relative lack of interest in the PACD, another part stemmed, as described above, from the PACD's new focus on working through barrio councils.

85. "Glancing Back," *PACD Newsette,* August–September 1967, 20.

86. Nick Cullather, *The Hungry World: America's Cold War Battle against Poverty in Asia* (Cambridge, MA: Harvard University Press, 2010), 170.

87. Asian Development Bank, *Asian Agricultural Survey* (Tokyo: University of Tokyo Press, 1969), 31–32.

88. Ferdinand E. Marcos, "The Miracle of the Decade," *PACD Newsette,* January 1969, 4.

89. "Incentives Awards," *PACD Newsette,* January–February 1971, 3.

90. Ferdinand E. Marcos, "Liberation of Our Barrios," 17 July 1969, in *Presidential Speeches,* vol. 2 (n.p., 1978), 324.

91. Aquino, quoted in Manuel F. Almario, "Battle for the Barrios," *Weekly Graphic,* 29 May 1968, 12.

92. On Marcos's use of the PACD institutional machinery for the centralization of power, see Rocamora and Panganiban, *Rural Development Strategies* and Po, *Rural Organizations and Rural Development.*

93. H. W. Brands, *Bound to Empire: The United States and the Philippines* (Oxford: Oxford University Press, 1992), 277.

94. Constitution of the Philippines, 1973, Article II, Section 10.

95. Gabriel Kaplan, "How Can the Private Sector Protect Itself against the Risks of the Cold War?," p. 4, lecture, 13 October 1965, box 4, Gabriel Kaplan Papers, Division of Rare and Manuscript Collections, Cornell University Library.

96. Ibid., 12–13.

97. Abueva, *Focus on the Barrio,* 149n.

98. Meeting of the IIRR board, minutes, 22 June 1967, in folder 6, container 600, Douglas Papers.

99. Y. C. James Yen to William O. Douglas, 13 June 1962 and William O. Douglas to Henry Heald, 29 June 1962, in folder 1, container 600, Douglas Papers.

100. International Mass Education Movement, annual meeting report, 17 January 1964, folder 4, container 600, Douglas Papers.

101. Ibid.

102. Stephen Shalom has alleged that Yen's Philippine Rural Reconstruction Movement took CIA funds but, following his citation to its source, Abueva's *Focus on the Barrio,* yields no information on that score. Shalom, *The United States and the Philippines,* 104.

103. Smith, *Portrait of a Cold Warrior,* 272.

104. Robert Alexander Karl, "State Formation, Violence, and Cold War in Colombia, 1957–1966" (Ph.D. diss., Harvard University, 2009), chap. 7. On Ensminger's involvement see Louis Miniclier to Robert E. McCoy, 18 October 1962, folder 2, carton 30, Paul S. Taylor Papers, Bancroft Library, University of California, Berkeley. Kaplan's post-Philippines career is also discussed in Satoshi Nakano, "Gabriel L. Kaplan and U.S. Involvement in Philippine Electoral Democracy: A Tale of Two Democracies," *Philippine Studies* 52 (2004): 149–178.

105. Gabriel L. Kaplan, *New Horizons for the Art of Community Development* (Arlington: The Community Development Counseling Service, c. 1962), box 2, Kaplan Papers.

106. Franklin D. Roosevelt, 1943 address to Pacific War Council, quoted in Mark Philip Bradley, *Imagining Vietnam and America: The Making of Postcolonial Vietnam, 1919–1950* (Chapel Hill: University of North Carolina Press, 2000), 76. On the Philippines–Vietnam connection more broadly, see Bradley, *Imagining Vietnam and America* and Man, "Conscripts of Empire," chap. 2.

107. Edward G. Lansdale, "Civic Activities of the Military, Southeast Asia," 13 March 1959, folder 32, carton 30, Paul S. Taylor Papers.

108. Filipino–Vietnamese exchanges are discussed in Rufus Phillips, interviewed by Ted Gittinger, 4 March 1982, Association for Diplomatic Studies and Training, Foreign Affairs Oral History Project, hdl.loc.gov/loc.mss/mfdip .2004phi03 and in Man, "Conscripts of Empire," chap. 2.

109. Ngo Dinh Diem, *The Emergence of Free Viet-Nam* (Saigon: Presidency of the Republic of Vietnam, Press Office, 1957), 11.

110. Neil Sheehan, *A Bright Shining Lie: John Paul Vann and America in Vietnam* (New York: Random House, 1988), 138.

111. The case is made persuasively in Edward Miller, "Vision, Power and Agency: The Ascent of Ngo Dinh Diem, 1945–54," *Journal of Southeast Asian Studies* 35 (2004): 433–458 and Edward Miller, *Misalliance: Ngo Dinh Diem, the United States, and the Fate of South Vietnam* (Cambridge, MA: Harvard University Press, 2013). The following section relies heavily on Miller's revisionist account of U.S. relations with the Diem regime.

112. Emmanuel Mounier, *Personalism,* trans. Philip Mairet (1950; New York: Grove Press, 1952).

113. Miller, *Misalliance,* 43–46.

114. Edward Garvey Miller, "Grand Designs: Vision, Power and Nation Building in America's Alliance with Ngo Dinh Diem, 1954–1960" (Ph.D. diss., Harvard University, 2004), 220; Philip E. Catton, *Diem's Final Failure: Prelude to America's War in Vietnam* (Lawrence: University Press of Kansas, 2002), 46.

115. Ngo Dinh Diem, *President Ngo Dinh Diem on Democracy* (Saigon: Presidency of the Republic of Vietnam, Press Office, 1957), 11.

116. Ngo Dinh Diem, *Toward Better Mutual Understanding,* vol. 1, 2d ed. (Saigon: Presidency of the Republic of Vietnam, Press Office, 1958), 21.

117. Ngo Dinh Diem, *Toward Better Mutual Understanding,* vol. 2 (Saigon: Presidency of the Republic of Vietnam, Press Office, 1958), 32.

118. Miller, *Misalliance,* 182.

119. The resettlement schemes included the Cai San project, the Land Development Program, and the Agroville program (the official title of which was "Rural Community Development"). They are discussed in Catton, *Diem's Final Failure,* chap. 3 and Miller, *Misalliance,* chap. 5.

120. [Ngo Dinh Nhu], "Discussion Paper: From Strategic Hamlets to Self Defense Village," n.d., folder 5, box 2, Vladimir Lehovich Collection, Virtual Vietnam Archive, Texas Tech University.

121. Miller, *Misalliance,* 236. Compare that with David Ekbladh's claim that the strategic hamlets were "set on a modernization footing" and exemplified a modernization ideology rooted in the TVA or Latham's very similar argument that the strategic hamlet program sought to turn "'traditional' peasants" into "'modern' citizens." David Ekbladh, *The Great American Mission: Modernization and the Construction of an American World Order* (Princeton: Princeton University Press, 2009), 201; Michael E. Latham, *Modernization as Ideology: American Social Science and "Nation Building" in the Kennedy Era* (Chapel Hill: University of North Carolina Press, 2000), 178.

122. On the Mekong project, see Ekbladh, *Great American Mission,* chap. 6

123. Rufus Phillips, *Why Vietnam Matters: An Eyewitness Account of Lessons Not Learned* (Annapolis, MD: Naval Institute Press, 2008), 103.

124. Avelina B. Asuncion, "Practice of Community Development," *Social Work* 2 (1957): 70.

125. Y. C. James Yen to William O. Douglas, 31 October 1969, in folder 1, container 106, Douglas Papers. Positions held by IIRR trainees included Undersecretary of the Ministry for Ethnic Minorities, Training Director, Field Operations Director, and Provincial Governor.

126. James McAllister, "The Lost Revolution: Edward Lansdale and the American Defeat in Vietnam, 1964–1968," *Small Wars and Insurgencies* 14 (2003): 1–26.

127. Phillips, *Why Vietnam Matters* offers a detailed account of the loss of the war by reference to the "triumph of the bureaucrats."

128. "Check the Brain Drain," *PACD Newsette,* October 1967, 12.

129. For this interpretation of Westmoreland, see Eric Bergerud, "The Village War in Vietnam, 1965–1973," in *The Columbia History of the Vietnam War,* ed. David L. Anderson (New York: Columbia University Press, 2011), 262–296 and Gregory A. Daddis, review of *Westmoreland: The General Who Lost Vietnam,* by Lewis Sorley, *Parameters* 41 (2011): 99–105.

130. "Major Describes Move," *New York Times,* 7 February 1968, 14.

131. John A. Nagl, foreword to U.S. Army and U.S. Marine Corps, *The U.S. Army/Marine Corps Counterinsurgency Field Manual* (Chicago: University of Chicago Press, 2007), xvii.

132. This dynamic is discussed in Alfred W. McCoy, *Policing America's Empire: The United States, the Philippines, and the Rise of the Surveillance State* (Madison: University of Wisconsin Press, 2009), part 2, especially chap. 17.

133. Walden Bello, Herbert Docena, Marissa de Guzman, and Mary Lou Malig, *The Anti-Development State: The Political Economy of Permanent Crisis in the Philippines* (Diliman: University of the Philippines, Diliman and Focus on the Global South, 2004).

134. Philippine Overseas Employment Administration, 2009 Stock Estimate of Filipinos Overseas, www.poea.gov.ph/stats/statistics.html; Asian Institute of Management Policy Center, Pinoy Youth Barometer Project, reported in "Four of Ten Filipino Students Want to Migrate Abroad," *Asian Pacific Post,* 2 April 2013, www.asianpacificpost.com.

135. 2010 figures, Maddison Project Database, January 2013 update, Groningen Growth and Development Centre, www.ggdc.net/maddison/maddison-project /home.htm.

5. URBAN VILLAGES

1. John F. Kennedy, Yale University Commencement Speech, 11 June 1962, Miller Center Speech Archive, millercenter.org/president/speeches/detail/3370.

2. Maddison Project Database, January 2013 update, Groningen Growth and Development Centre, www.ggdc.net/maddison/maddison-project/home.htm.

3. Michael J. Piore, "Keynes and Marx, Duncan and Me," in *Social Fairness and Economics: Economic Essays in the Spirit of Duncan Foley,* ed. Lance Taylor, Armon Rezai, and Thomas Michl (New York: Routledge, 2013), 22.

4. Paul Gray, "Required Reading," *Time,* 8 June 1998, 111.

5. Michael Harrington, *The Other America: Poverty in the United States* (New York: The Macmillan Company, 1962), 12.

6. See Daniel Horowitz, *The Anxieties of Affluence: Critiques of American Consumer Culture, 1939–1979* (Amherst: University of Massachusetts Press, 2004).

7. John Kenneth Galbraith, *The Affluent Society* (Boston: Houghton Mifflin Company, 1958), 323.

8. Harrington, *The Other America,* 159.

9. I am indebted to Sheyda Jahanbani and to her dissertation, "'A Different Kind of People': The Poor at Home and Abroad, 1935–1968" (Ph.D. diss., Brown University, 2009), for clarifying the importance of a unified category of poverty in this period. A briefer version of the argument is contained in her "One Global War on Poverty: The Johnson Administration Fights Poverty at Home and Abroad, 1964–1968," in *Beyond the Cold War: Lyndon Johnson and the New Global Challenges of the 1960s,* ed. Francis J. Gavin and Mark Atwood Lawrence (Oxford: Oxford University Press, 2014), 97–117. For a broader theoretical overview of this issue, see the discussion of "monoeconomics" and "polyeconomics" in Albert O. Hirschman, "The Rise and Decline of Development Economics," in *Essays in Trespassing: Economics to Politics and Beyond* (Cambridge: Cambridge University Press, 1981), 1–24.

10. Biographical details are from Susan M. Rigdon, *The Culture Façade: Art, Science and Politics in the Work of Oscar Lewis* (Urbana: University of Illinois Press, 1988).

11. Oscar Lewis, *Life in a Mexican Village: Tepoztlán Restudied* (Urbana: University of Illinois Press, 1951).

12. Oscar Lewis, "Group Dynamics in a North-Indian Village: A Study of Factions," c. 1954, Report 8288, Ford Foundation Archives, New York; Oscar Lewis, review of *Pilot Project, India,* by Albert Mayer, *American Anthropologist* 61 (1959): 534–536; and Oscar Lewis, *Village Life in Northern India: Studies in a Delhi Village* (New York: Vintage Books, 1965).

13. Oscar Lewis, *Five Families: Mexican Case Studies in the Culture of Poverty* (New York: Basic Books, 1959), 2.

14. Oscar Lewis, *La Vida: A Puerto Rican Family in the Culture of Poverty— San Juan and New York* (New York: Random House, 1965), xlv.

15. Lyndon Baines Johnson, State of the Union, 8 January 1964, Miller Center, Presidential Speech Archive, millercenter.org/president/speeches/detail /3382.

16. Daniel Patrick Moynihan, "What Is 'Community Action'?" *Public Interest,* Fall 1966, 5.

17. Daniel Patrick Moynihan, *Maximum Feasible Misunderstanding: Community Action and the War on Poverty* (New York: The Free Press, 1969), 6.

18. William Ryan, *Blaming the Victim* (New York: Pantheon Books, 1971). On the reception of the Moynihan report, see Daniel Geary, "Racial Liberalism, the Moynihan Report, and the *Daedalus* Project on 'The Negro American,'" *Daedalus* 140 (2011): 53–66.

19. In the book, Moynihan refers offhandedly to community action as "the Peace Corps concept brought home" but has very little else to say. Moynihan, *Maximum Feasible Misunderstanding*, 72.

20. See Richard Blumenthal, "Community Action: The Origins of a Government Program" (B.A. thesis, Harvard University, 1967); Peter Marris and Martin Rein, *Dilemmas of Social Reform: Poverty and Community Action in the United States* (London: Routledge and Kegan Paul, 1967); Kenneth B. Clark and Jeannette Hopkins, *A Relevant War against Poverty: A Study of Community Action Programs and Observable Social Change* (New York: Metropolitan Applied Research Center, 1968); James L. Sundquist, *Politics and Policy: The Eisenhower, Kennedy, and Johnson Years* (Washington, DC: The Brookings Institution 1968), chap. 4; Moynihan, *Maximum Feasible Misunderstanding;* Allen J. Matusow, *The Unraveling of America: A History of Liberalism in the 1960s* (New York: Harper and Row, 1984); Michael B. Katz, *The Undeserving Poor: From the War on Poverty to the War on Welfare* (New York: Pantheon Books, 1989); Nicholas Lemann, *The Promised Land: The Great Black Migration and How it Changed America* (New York: Alfred A. Knopf, 1991); Jill Quadagno, *The Color of Welfare: How Racism Undermined the War on Poverty* (Oxford: Oxford University Press, 1994); James T. Patterson, *America's Struggle against Poverty, 1900–1994* (Cambridge, MA: Harvard University Press, 1994); Gareth Davies, *From Opportunity to Entitlement: The Transformation and Decline of Great Society Liberalism* (Lawrence: University of Kansas Press, 1996); Michael L. Gillette, *Launching the War on Poverty: An Oral History* (New York: Twayne Publishers, 1996); Alice O'Connor, *Poverty Knowledge: Social Science, Social Policy, and the Poor in Twentieth-Century U.S. History* (Princeton: Princeton University Press, 2001); Sidney M. Milkis and Jerome M. Mileur, eds., *The Great Society and the High Tide of Liberalism* (Amherst: University of Massachusetts Press, 2005); and Noel A. Cazenave, *Impossible Democracy: The Unlikely Success of the War on Poverty Community Action Programs* (Albany: State University of New York Press, 2007).

21. See chapter 2, note 18.

22. Jahanbani, "A Different Kind of People"; Alyosha Goldstein, *Poverty in Common: The Politics of Community Action during the American Century* (Durham: Duke University Press, 2012); Amy C. Offner, "Anti-Poverty Programs, Social Conflict, and Economic Thought in Colombia and the United States, 1948–1980" (Ph.D. diss., Columbia University, 2012), epilogue; and Amrys O. Williams, "Cultivating Modern America: 4-H Clubs and Rural Development in the Twentieth Century" (Ph.D. diss., University of Wisconsin–Madison, 2012), chap. 5.

23. John F. Kennedy, inaugural address, 20 January 1961, Miller Center, Presidential Speech Archive, millercenter.org/president/speeches/detail/3365.

24. Max F. Millikan, "Memorandum on an International Youth Service," pp. 6, 21, and 30, December 1960, box 1, Max Millikan Papers, John F. Kennedy Presidential (JFK) Library.

25. Fritz Fischer, *Making Them Like Us: Peace Corps Volunteers in the 1960s* (Washington, DC: Smithsonian Institution Press, 1998), 9–10; Michael E. Latham, *Modernization as Ideology: American Social Science and "Nation Building" in the Kennedy Era* (Chapel Hill: University of North Carolina Press, 2000), chap. 4; Christopher T. Fisher, "'The Hopes of Man': The Cold War, Modernization Theory, and the Issue of Race in the 1960s" (Ph.D. diss., Rutgers University, 2002), 99–100; David Ekbladh, *The Great American Mission: Modernization and the Construction of an American World Order* (Princeton: Princeton University Press, 2009), 192. All four works interpret the Peace Corps as part of the modernization complex, although the point is made most forcefully in Latham's *Modernization as Ideology*. There, Latham argues that the Peace Corps' community development work was of a piece with modernization theory in that its principal goal was "to alter local social life and accelerate modernization at the town or village level" (122). It would be impossible to argue with Latham's contention that the Peace Corps sought to alter the places it targeted. But the mere desire to change conditions does not entail an urge to modernize and, as this chapter argues, there is reason to think that the Peace Corps entertained other, non-modernizing models of development.

26. Quoted in Scott Stossel, *Sarge: The Life and Times of Sargent Shriver* (Washington, DC: Smithsonian Books, 2004), 205.

27. Sargent Shriver to John F. Kennedy, Report to the President on the Peace Corps, c. 1961, reference box 8, President's Office Files, Departments and Agencies, Papers of President Kennedy, JFK Library.

28. Eunice Kennedy and Sargent Shriver, Prospectus for Committee on Juvenile Delinquency, 1947, quoted in Stossel, *Sarge*, 99–102.

29. The views of both Sargent Shriver and Eunice Kennedy Shriver on these matters are discussed in Jahanbani, "A Different Kind of People," chap. 4.

30. Information on IVS has been derived from the following sources: a telephone interview with former IVS volunteer Gene Stoltzfus, 14 July 2009; Paul A. Rodell, "John S. Noffsinger and the Global Impact of the Thomasite Experience," in *Back to the Future: Perspectives of the Thomasite Legacy to Philippine Education,* ed. Corazon D. Villareal (Manila: American Studies Association in the Philippines, 2003), 63–79; Paul A. Rodell, "International Voluntary Services in Vietnam: War and the Birth of Activism, 1958–1967," *Peace and Change* 27 (2002): 225–244; Jessica Breiteneicher Elkind, "The First Casualties: American Nation Building Programs in South Vietnam, 1955–1965" (Ph.D. diss., UCLA, 2005); and the Carl C. Taylor Papers, Division of Rare and Manuscript Collections, Cornell University Library.

31. Andres S. Hernandes, *Community Development Handbook: A Guide to Community Development Practice for Peace Corps Volunteers,* c. 1962–1963, "Training Materials (U.S.), 1," box 2, Kirby Jones Papers, JFK Library.

32. Louis Miniclier, "Community Development as a Vehicle of U.S. Foreign Aid," *Community Development Journal* 4 (1969): 11.

33. Statement of Jack Vaughn before the Foreign Operations Subcommittee of the House Appropriations Committee, 19 April 1967, box 20; Records of Jack Vaughn, Director; Records of the Peace Corps, Record Group 490 (RG 490); NACP.

34. Fischer, *Making Them Like Us*, 149; Jonathan Zimmerman, *Innocents Abroad: American Teachers in the American Century* (Cambridge, MA: Harvard University Press, 2006), 147.

35. Fischer, *Making Them Like Us,* especially chap. 5.

36. The Peace Corps, *Community Development from Village to City: Charting the Course of Human Progress,* c. 1968, box 17, "Fogarty, Gertrude: Pamphlets, Community Planning Opportunities in the Peace Corps," Peace Corps Collection, JFK Library.

37. "Position Report: The Need for a National Service Program to Meet Critical Needs of Disadvantaged Persons and Groups in the United States—First Draft," September 1962, p. 1, 24; "DPC," box 1; Subject File of the Office of the Director, 1961–1966; RG 490; NACP and Jahanbani, "A Different Kind of People," 224–225.

38. David Hackett, interviewed by John W. Douglas, 21 October 1970, p. 79, Oral Histories, JFK Library.

39. On the history and composition of the committee, see William R. Anderson to Lester Hill, 12 June 1963, folder group 999-17, box 213, White House Central Files, Subject File, JFK Library.

40. Leonard J. Duhl to Granville Hicks, 30 October 1949, "Leonard J. Duhl" folder, box 18, Granville Hicks Papers; Leonard Duhl, interview with author, 20 July 2011, Oakland, CA. See also, in the same place in the Hicks papers, letters from Duhl to Hicks on 15 December 1949 and 6 January 1955.

41. Letter from Leonard J. Duhl, *Community Service News,* January–March 1955, 2; Leonard J. Duhl, foreword to Richard Waverly Poston, *Democracy Speaks Many Tongues: Community Development around the World* (New York: Harper and Row, 1962).

42. Richard W. Poston, "Comparative Community Organization," in *The Urban Condition: People and Policy in the Metropolis,* ed. Leonard J. Duhl (New York: Basic Books, 1963), 313.

43. Alyosha Goldstein, "Civic Poverty: An Empire for Liberty through Community Action" (Ph.D. diss., New York University, 2005), 132.

44. Miniclier is listed as a member in Duhl, ed., *Urban Condition,* xv. A shorter membership list upon which Miniclier's name does not appear, presumably corresponding to more central figures in the group, can be found in "List of Sp. C," carton 1, Leonard J. Duhl Papers, Bancroft Library, University of California, Berkeley.

45. Leonard S. Cottrell, Jr., "The Competent Community," speech delivered 15 March 1971, box 2, Leonard S. Cottrell, Jr., Papers, American Philosophical Society, Philadelphia.

46. See Leonard S. Cottrell, Jr., 7 June 1967, "Sociometry: 1937–1955–1967," "Personal File" folder, box 7, Cottrell Papers.

47. Leonard S. Cottrell, Jr., "The Competent Community: A Long Range View," c. 1965, p. 2, box 2, Cottrell Papers.

48. David Hackett, interviewed by John W. Douglas, 21 October 1970, p. 87, Oral Histories, JFK Library.

49. Richard Boone, quoted in "Poverty and Urban Policy," 1973, p. 226, Oral Histories, JFK Library. See also Hackett's comments along similar lines on p. 223.

50. Richard Boone, quoted in ibid., 245.

51. Richard Boone, quoted in Elizabeth Cobbs Hoffman, *All You Need Is Love: The Peace Corps and the Spirit of the 1960s* (Cambridge, MA: Harvard University Press, 1998), 195. Roessel's thoughts on planning with versus planning for, which were firmly in place by the early 1950s, can be found in Roessel's reports from that time, reprinted in Robert A. Roessel, Jr., *Indian Communities in Action* (Tempe: Arizona State University Bureau of Publications, 1967).

52. "Proposal for a Pilot Project: National Service Corps," c. 1963, p. 3, "DPC," box 1; Subject File of the Office of the Director, 1961–1966; RG 490; NACP.

53. "A Report to the President from The President's Study Group on National Voluntary Services," 14 January 1963, FG 999-17, box 213, Subject File, White House Central Files, JFK Library.

54. Jahanbani, "A Different Kind of People," chap. 4.

55. For good accounts of Ylvisaker's work at the Ford Foundation, see Alice O'Connor, "Community Action, Urban Reform, and the Fight against Poverty: The Ford Foundation's Gray Areas Program," *Journal of Urban History* 22 (1996): 586–625 and Karen Ferguson, *Top Down: The Ford Foundation, Black Power, and the Reinvention of Racial Liberalism* (Philadelphia: University of Pennsylvania Press, 2013), chap. 2. Ferguson's account, however, differs from the one offered here in stressing the continuities between Ylvisaker's earlier interest in metropolitan government and his later interest in community strategies.

56. Bernard E. Loshbough, "Rural Extension Techniques Getting Try in Pittsburgh Self-Help Renewal Area," *Journal of Housing,* May 1963, 202. On Loshbough, see also Williams, "Cultivating Modern America," chap. 5.

57. Bernard E. Loshbough, "A Proposal for a US-AID Program for Calcutta," 22 May 1964, p. 3, Report 9238, Ford Foundation Archives.

58. Paul N. Ylvisaker to Douglas Ensminger, 28 March 1962, folder 5, box 5, Paul N. Ylvisaker Papers, Harvard University Archives.

59. Douglas Ensminger to George F. Gant, 17 October 1962, folder 568, box 158, Edward J. Logue Papers, Yale University Archives.

60. Bernard E. Loshbough to Paul N. Ylvisaker, 6 June 1961, PA 61–222, Ford Foundation Archives.

61. Richard M. Catalano, "ACTION-Housing Urban Extension Program," April 1964, p. 3, Report 8422, Ford Foundation Archives.

62. Paul N. Ylvisaker, interview by Charles T. Morrissey, 27 September and 27 October 1973, folder 15, box 5, Ylvisaker Papers.

63. ACTION-Housing, "Application for a Grant from the Ford Foundation for a Test Demonstration of Urban Extension to be Carried out in Four Neighborhoods in the Pittsburgh Area," 25 September 1961, p. ii, PA 62-160, Ford Foundation Archives.

64. Marshall Clinard, a Chicago-trained urban sociologist, also believed that Ford's work in India could be imported to the United States. "On many occasions, when I have read through the material [on urban development in India]," he wrote to Loshbough, "I have thought that perhaps some of it has implications for the American scene and perhaps even our specific techniques could be adapted." Clinard to Loshbough, 12 May 1961, PA 62-160, Ford Foundation Archives. For Taylor's reaction, see Carl C. Taylor to Bernard Loshbough, 23 October 1963, box 14, Carl C. Taylor Papers.

65. ACTION, "Urban Extension: Proceedings of the Pittsburgh Urban Extension Conference," 1961, p. 4, PA 61-222, Ford Foundation Archives.

66. Ibid.

67. Edward Logue to Mitchell Sviridoff, 29 January 1953, folder 109, box 29, Logue Papers.

68. Edward Logue to Douglas Ensminger, 16 January 1956, folder 43, box 25, Logue Papers. In the same letter, Logue suggested that S. K. Dey, India's Minister of Community Development, might want to study Logue's work in Boston.

69. Edward Logue to Jeanne Lowe, 30 April 1957, in folder 418, box 59, Logue Papers.

70. Ford Foundation, *American Community Development: Preliminary Reports by Directors of Projects Assisted by the Ford Foundation in Four Cities and a State* (New York: Ford Foundation, 1964), 4.

71. Alice O'Connor, "Community Action," 612–613.

72. Lyndon Baines Johnson, *The Vantage Point: Perspectives of the Presidency, 1963–1969* (New York: Holt, Rinehart and Winston, 1971), 74.

73. Ibid.

74. Ibid., 75.

75. Quoted in Stossel, *Sarge*, 349. It also seems likely that Johnson chose Shriver as a way of pulling control of community action away from Shriver's brother-in-law Robert Kennedy.

76. For Mankiewicz's views on the subject, see Frank Mankiewicz, "An Explanation of Community Development as It Is Practiced by the Peace Corps in Latin America," General Staff Meeting, 11 August 1964, box 14, Subject File of the Office of the Director, 1961–66; RG 490; NACP.

77. Frank Mankiewicz, interview with the author, Washington, DC, 21 July 2010.

78. Transcript, Sargent Shriver Oral History Interview I, by Michael L. Gillette, 20 August 1980, p. 10, AC 05-24, Lyndon Baines Johnson Presidential (LBJ) Library, Austin, TX. Shriver's enthusiasm for community action and the connections he made between it and the Peace Corps have often been passed over because, as many accounts of the antipoverty task force report, Shriver at first resisted the idea of community action, exclaiming "It will never fly." But as Shriver subsequently explained, his resistance was not to the idea of community action but to the notion that the antipoverty program would consist entirely of community action. As someone with long experience with the practice, Shriver doubted that a purely participatory program could work were it not backstopped by efforts in employment, education, and other areas. Compare Adam Yarmolinsky's

account in "Poverty and Urban Policy," 1973, p. 234, Oral Histories, JFK Library with Shriver's response in Shriver, Oral History Interview I, 36.

79. Transcript, Frank Mankiewicz Oral History Interview I, by Stephen Goodell, 18 April 1969, p. 12, LBJ Library.

80. Matusow, *The Unraveling of America,* 245.

81. Herbert J. Gans, *The Urban Villagers: Group and Class in the Life of Italian-Americans* (New York: The Free Press of Glencoe, 1962).

82. Kenneth B. Clark, *Dark Ghetto: Dilemmas of Social Power* (New York: Harper and Row, 1965).

83. Suleiman Osman, *The Invention of Brownstone Brooklyn: Gentrification and the Search for Authenticity in Postwar New York* (Oxford: Oxford University Press, 2011).

84. Jane Jacobs, *The Death and Life of Great American Cities* (New York: Random House, 1961), 119.

85. Ibid., 307.

86. Gans, *Urban Villagers,* 100. Gans compares his account of the "urban renewal" of the West End to Daniel Lerner's canonical book about modernization, *The Passing of Traditional Society* (1958).

87. Ibid., 21.

88. Herbert J. Gans, *The Urban Villagers: Group and Class in the Life of Italian-Americans,* expanded ed. (New York: The Free Press, 1982), xi. For a discussion of the complicated relationship between *The Urban Villagers* and Jacobs, *The Death and Life of Great American Cities,* see Osman, *Brownstone Brooklyn,* chap. 5. While she was researching her book, Jacobs toured Boston with Gans as her guide. Alice Sparberg Alexiou, *Jane Jacobs: Urban Visionary* (New Brunswick: Rutgers University Press, 2006), 68.

89. Mankiewicz, interview with the author.

90. Transcript, Sargent Shriver Oral History Interview II, by Michael L. Gillette, 23 October 1980, p. 12, AC 05-25, LBJ Library.

91. A very good source on the ideological differences between the various factions of poverty warriors with respect to the ideal of cross-class consensus is Blumenthal, "Community Action: The Origins of a Government Program," especially around 26.

92. Guian A. McKee, "'This Government Is with Us': Lyndon Johnson and the Grassroots War on Poverty," in *The War on Poverty: A New Grassroots History, 1964–1980,* ed. Annelise Orleck and Lisa Gayle Hazirjian (Athens: University of Georgia Press, 2011), 31–62.

93. The culture of poverty thesis, delivered first as a paper as a paper in a scholarly conference in 1958, is articulated in Lewis, *Five Families;* Lewis, *Children of Sánchez;* Oscar Lewis, "The Culture of Poverty," *Society* 1 (1963): 17–19; and Lewis, *La Vida.*

94. Daniel Matlin, *On the Corner: African-American Intellectuals and the Urban Crisis* (Cambridge, MA: Harvard University Press, 2013), 43 and 281n. See also Carlo Rotello, *October Cities: The Redevelopment of Urban Literature* (Berkeley: University of California Press, 1998), chap. 8.

95. Clark, *Dark Ghetto,* 27.

96. Ibid., 11.

97. Ibid., 106. The discussion of Clark in this paragraph and the one that follows relies heavily on Matlin's illuminating account in *On the Corner,* chap. 1.

98. Lewis, *La Vida,* xlviii, lii. It is important to recognize that Lewis reversed his position with regard to the culture of poverty over the course of the 1960s and 1970s, in response to its popularity with the political right, which found in it a justification for abandoning welfare programs, and to challenges from Lewis's fellow anthropologists, who found the notion of transregional "culture" of poverty incoherent. For an excellent discussion of the fate of Lewis's theory, see Rigdon, *The Culture Façade.*

99. Clark, *Dark Ghetto,* 15.

100. On the origins of that infamous phrase, see Gillette, *Launching the War on Poverty,* 77–83 and "Poverty and Urban Policy," 1973, Oral Histories, JFK Library. Mankiewicz's recollections are registered in Cobbs Hoffman, *All You Need Is Love,* 194.

101. Transcript, Sargent Shriver Oral History Interview II, by Michael L. Gillette, 23 October 1980, p. 10, AC 05-25, LBJ Library.

102. Residential segregation and the changing patterns and politics of urban life have become important themes in recent historical writing. Key works include Kenneth Jackson, *Crabgrass Frontier: The Suburbanization of the United States* (Oxford: Oxford University Press, 1985); Thomas J. Sugrue, *The Origins of the Urban Crisis: Race and Inequality in Postwar Detroit* (Princeton: Princeton University Press, 1996); Robert O. Self, *American Babylon: Race and the Struggle for Postwar Oakland* (Princeton: Princeton University Press, 2003); Matthew D. Lassiter, *The Silent Majority: Suburban Politics in the Sunbelt South* (Princeton: Princeton University Press, 2006); Thomas J. Sugrue, *Sweet Land of Liberty: The Forgotten Struggle for Civil Rights in the North* (New York: Random House, 2008); and Osman, *The Invention of Brownstone Brooklyn.*

103. Self, *American Babylon;* Sugrue, *Sweet Land of Liberty.*

104. An excellent articulation of the "power structure" thesis and its importance for civil rights can be found in Stokely Carmichael and Charles V. Hamilton, *Black Power: The Politics of Liberation in America* (New York: Random House, 1967).

105. See Matusow, *Unraveling of America,* chap. 9 and Orleck and Hazirjian, eds., *The War on Poverty.*

106. Amiri Baraka, preface to *The LeRoi Jones/Amiri Baraka Reader,* ed. William J. Harris (New York: Thunder's Mouth, 1991), xiii.

107. Quoted in Matusow, *Unraveling of America,* 248.

108. Bernard Doering, ed., *The Philosopher and the Provocateur: The Correspondence of Jacques Maritain and Saul Alinsky* (Notre Dame: University of Notre Dame Press, 1994), xxvi.

109. Alinsky, quoted in Sanford D. Horwitt, *Let Them Call Me Rebel: Saul Alinsky—His Life and Legacy* (New York: Alfred A. Knopf, 1989), 526.

110. Charles E. Silberman, *Crisis in Black and White* (New York: Random House, 1964), 318.

111. Alinsky, quoted in Horwitt, *Let Them Call Me Rebel,* 450.

112. Peter Slevin, "For Clinton and Obama, a Common Ideological Touch-stone," *Washington Post*, 25 March 2007.

113. Self, *American Babylon*, chaps. 5–6; Cazenave, *Impossible Democracy*; Sugrue, *Sweet Land of Liberty*, chap. 11; Orleck and Hazirjian, eds., *The War on Poverty*.

114. Self, *American Babylon*, 226.

115. On community as a key theme within the black power movement more broadly, see Howard Brick, *The Age of Contradiction: American Thought and Culture in the 1960s* (New York: Twayne Publishers, 1998), 104–113.

116. Huey P. Newton, "Intercommunalism," 1971, in *The Huey P. Newton Reader*, ed. David Hilliard and Donald Weise (New York: Seven Stories, 2002), 188.

117. Huey P. Newton, "Speech Delivered at Boston College: November 18, 1970," in *The Newton Reader*, 170.

118. Newton, "Intercommunalism," 187.

119. Newton, "Speech at Boston College," 170. See also "Uniting against a Common Enemy" (1971) in *The Newton Reader*, 234–240.

120. On intercommunalism in general, see David Hilliard and Lewis Cole, *This Side of Glory: The Autobiography of David Hilliard and the Story of the Black Panther Party* (Boston: Little, Brown and Company, 1993), 320–321 and Self, *American Babylon*, chap. 8. An important discussion of the resilience of localist politics can be found in Thomas J. Sugrue, "All Politics Is Local: The Persistence of Localism in Twentieth-Century America," *The Democratic Experiment: New Directions in American Political History*, ed. Meg Jacobs, William J. Novak, and Julian Zelizer (Princeton: Princeton University Press, 2003), 301–326. Between 1960 and 1972, the frequency with which the phrase "black community" appeared in U.S. books (as a percentage of all two-word phrases) rose over five-hundredfold and has remained in currency since, according to Google Books' Ngram Viewer (books.google.com/ngrams).

121. On Mayer's work in New York City in the 1960s, see Samuel Zipp, *Manhattan Projects: The Rise and Fall of Urban Renewal in Cold War New York* (Oxford: Oxford University Press, 2010), chap. 7.

122. Albert Mayer, "A New Level of Local Government Is Struggling to Be Born," *City*, March/April 1971, 62. In a similar vein, see also Richard Waverly Poston's reaction to an OEO-funded project on New York's Lower East Side to empower gang members: *The Gang and the Establishment* (New York: Harper and Row, 1971).

123. Cazenave, *Impossible Democracy*, 156.

124. Stossel, *Sarge*, 411.

125. Ibid., 458.

126. James Farmer, quoted in M. S. Handler, "Farmer Dropping Literacy Project," *New York Times*, 4 July 1966. Farmer was paraphrasing Frederick Douglass's 1857 speech on emancipation in the British West Indies.

127. On the final years of the OEO, see Lemann, *The Promised Land*. For a response, highlighting the continued success of community action, see Robert F. Clark, *Maximum Feasible Success: A History of the Community*

Action Program (Washington, DC: National Association of Community Action Agencies, 2000).

128. Quoted in Sugrue, *Sweet Land of Liberty,* 522.

129. On the growth of CDCs, see Neal R. Peirce and Carol F. Steinbach, *Corrective Capitalism: The Rise of America's Community Development Corporations* (New York: Ford Foundation, 1987).

130. A helpful review of these trends is Keith Getter and Leonardo Vasquez, "Out Front and in Sync," *Shelterforce,* Winter 2007, 9–13. See also Nicholas Lemann, "The Myth of Community Development," *New York Times Magazine,* 9 January 1994.

131. Thomas Piketty and Emmanuel Saez, "Income Inequality in the United States, 1913–1998," *Quarterly Journal of Economics* 118 (2003): 1–39; September 2013 update of figures available at elsa.berkeley.edu/~saez/TabFig2012prel.xls.

132. On the mismatch between grassroots politics and large-scale economies, see Sugrue, *Sweet Land of Liberty,* chap. 14 and Ferguson, *Top Down.*

EPILOGUE

1. Carl C. Taylor, untitled article about community development, 1966, box 34, Carl C. Taylor Papers, Division of Rare and Manuscript Collections, Cornell University Library.

2. Carl C. Taylor to Stanley Andrews, 31 December 1965, box 37, Carl C. Taylor papers.

3. Ibid.

4. Ibid.

5. Carl C. Taylor to Dr. and Mrs. Howard Beers, 31 December 1965, box 37, Carl C. Taylor papers.

6. On IVS in Vietnam, see Don Luce and John Sommer, *Viet Nam: The Unheard Voices* (Ithaca: Cornell University Press, 1969); Paul A. Rodell, "International Voluntary Services in Vietnam: War and the Birth of Activism, 1958–1967," *Peace and Change* 27 (2002): 225–244; and Jessica Breiteneicher Elkind, "The First Casualties: American Nation Building Programs in South Vietnam, 1955–1965" (Ph.D. diss., UCLA, 2005).

7. Carl C. Taylor to Stanley Andrews, 31 December 1965, box 37, Carl C. Taylor papers.

8. William Y. Elliott, "Community Development and the New AID Approach," 15 October 1961, folder 1371, box 49, Edward Geary Lansdale Papers, Hoover Institution Archives, Stanford University.

9. Louis Miniclier, "Community Development as a Vehicle of U.S. Foreign Aid," *Community Development Journal* 4 (1969): 9–10.

10. Lane E. Holdcroft, "The Rise and Fall of Community Development: 1950–1965" (M.S. thesis, Michigan State University, 1976), 27.

11. Julia Henderson, "United Nations' Community Development Programs," in International Society for Community Development, Report on Symposium, "The Outlook for Community Development," 8 September 1966, p. 21, folder 12, box 14, Mayer Papers.

12. For an excellent account of the challenge posed by Vietnam to the United States' modernizing ambitions, see Michael Adas, *Dominance by Design: Technological Imperatives and America's Civilizing Mission* (Cambridge, MA: Harvard University Press, 2006), chap. 6.

13. Quoted in Daniel J. Sargent, "The United States and Globalization in the 1970s," in *The Shock of the Global: The 1970s in Perspective,* ed. Niall Ferguson, Charles S. Maier, Erez Manela, and Daniel J. Sargent (Cambridge, MA: Harvard University Press, 2010), 49.

14. Quoted in Paul E. Scheele, "President Carter and the Water Projects: A Study in Presidential and Congressional Decision-Making," *Presidential Studies Quarterly* 8 (1978): 349.

15. An authoritative overview of the environment and environmentalism is J. R. McNeill, *Something New under the Sun: An Environmental History of the Twentieth-Century World* (New York: W. W. Norton and Company, 2000). Helpful accounts of the post-1970s environmentalism and its challenge to modernization, developmentalism, and liberalism are Keith Woodhouse, "A Subversive Nature: Radical Environmentalism in the Late-Twentieth-Century United States" (Ph.D. diss., University of Wisconsin, 2010) and Stephen Macekura, "Of Limits and Growth: Global Environmentalism and the Rise of 'Sustainable Development' in the Twentieth Century" (Ph.D. diss., University of Virginia, 2013).

16. See, for example, Joseph Gusfield, "Tradition and Modernity: Misplaced Polarities in the Study of Social Change," *American Journal of Sociology* 72 (1967): 351–362 and Lloyd I. Rudolph and Susanne Hoeber Rudolph, *The Modernity of Tradition: Political Development in India* (Chicago: University of Chicago Press, 1967). The reliance of both Gusfield and the Rudolphs on the research of M. N. Srinivas and Chicago-school anthropologists highlights the connections between post-modernization understandings of development and those urged in the 1950s by community developers. See chapter 2, note 93 of this book.

17. On human rights as a minimalist ideology, see Samuel Moyn, *The Last Utopia: Human Rights in History* (Cambridge, MA: Harvard University Press, 2010); a similar case can be made for the "basic needs" approach to which Robert McNamara committed the World Bank in 1976. This account of the twilight of modernization theory draws on Nils Gilman, *Mandarins of the Future: Modernization Theory in Cold War America* (Baltimore: Johns Hopkins University Press, 2003), chap. 6; David Ekbladh, *The Great American Mission: Modernization and the Construction of an American World Order* (Princeton: Princeton University Press, 2009), chap. 7; and Michael E. Latham, *The Right Kind of Revolution: Modernization, Development, and U.S. Foreign Policy from the Cold War to the Present* (Ithaca: Cornell University Press, 2011), chap. 6. A very good analysis of the retreat of modernization theory is James Ferguson, *Global Shadows: Africa in the Neoliberal World Order* (Durham: Duke University Press, 2006), chap. 7.

18. Daniel T. Rodgers, *Age of Fracture* (Cambridge, MA: Harvard University Press, 2011).

19. Suleiman Osman, *The Invention of Brownstone Brooklyn: Gentrification*

and the Search for Authenticity in Postwar New York (Oxford: Oxford University Press, 2011), 232. On the rise of localism in the wake of modernization, see also Benjamin Looker, "Visions of Autonomy: The New Left and the Neighborhood Government Movement of the 1970s," *Journal of Urban History* 38 (2012): 577–598.

20. Tom Hayden, *The Port Huron Statement: The Visionary Call of the 1960s Revolution* (1962; New York: Thunder Mouth Press, 2005), 142.

21. Percival Goodman and Paul Goodman, *Communitas: Means of Livelihood and Ways of Life,* rev. ed. (New York: Vintage Books, 1960).

22. Rosalyn Baxandall, "The New Politics of Participatory Democracy Viewed through a Feminist Lens," in *The Great Society and the High Tide of Liberalism,* ed. Sidney M. Milkis and Jerome M. Mileur (Amherst: University of Massachusetts Press, 2005), 270–288. On participatory groups and the left in general, see Howard Brick, *The Age of Contradiction: American Thought and Culture in the 1960s* (New York: Twayne Publishers, 1998), chap. 5; Francesca Polletta, *Freedom Is an Endless Meeting: Democracy in American Social Movements* (Chicago: University of Chicago Press, 2002); and Francesca Polletta, "How Participatory Democracy Became White: Culture and Organizational Choice," *Mobilization* 10 (2005): 271–288.

23. Quoted in Frank Bryan and John McClaughry, *The Vermont Papers: Recreating Democracy on a Human Scale* (White River Junction, VT: Chelsea Green Publishing, 1989), 23.

24. Peter L. Berger and Richard John Neuhaus, *To Empower People: The Role of Mediating Structures in Public Policy* (Washington, DC: American Enterprise Institute for Public Policy Research, 1977).

25. George H. W. Bush, Inaugural Address, 20 January 1989, Miller Center, Presidential Speech Archive, millercenter.org/president/speeches/detail/3419. Overviews of the communitarian and decentralist dimensions of conservatism can be found in William A. Schambra, foreword to Robert Nisbet, *Quest for Community: A Study in the Ethics of Order and Freedom* (San Francisco: Institute for Contemporary Studies, 1990) and Jeff Taylor, *Politics on a Human Scale: The American Tradition of Decentralism* (Lanham, MD: Lexington Books, 2013), chaps. 6–8.

26. Alan Wolfe, *Whose Keeper?: Social Science and Moral Obligation* (Berkeley: University of California Press, 1989), 20; Amitai Etzioni, *The New Golden Rule: Community and Morality in a Democratic Society* (New York: Basic Books, 1996), viii. On the newfound interest in civil society in the United States in the 1990s, see E. J. Dionne, ed., *Community Works: The Revival of Civil Society in America* (Washington, DC: Brookings Institution Press, 1998). The interest in civil society is related to a slightly earlier turn among moral and political philosophers—including Alasdair MacIntyre, Michael Sandel, Charles Taylor, and Michael Walzer—to communitarianism, a trend reviewed in Daniel Bell, "Communitarianism," *Stanford Encyclopedia of Philosophy,* Fall 2013 ed., plato.stanford.edu/archives/fall2013/entries/communitarianism.

27. Michael Kranish, "Communitarianism: Is Clinton a Convert?" *Boston Globe,* 22 May 1993.

28. For an illustration of Gore's fairly in-depth engagement with the issues and ideas surrounding community development, see Al Gore, "A National Commitment to Community Development," *Shelterforce,* March/April 1994.

29. Dana Milbank, "Needed: Catchword for Bush Ideology; 'Communitarianism' Finds Favor," *Washington Post,* 1 February 2001.

30. David Moberg, "Obama's Community Roots," *The Nation,* 16 April 2007; Michael R. Dove, "Dreams from His Mother," *New York Times,* 10 August 2009; and James T. Kloppenberg, *Reading Obama: Dreams, Hope, and the American Political Tradition* (Princeton: Princeton University Press, 2011).

31. Martin H. Gerry, Coordinating Director of the Austin Project, "The Austin Project: A Stylized Overview," appendix to W. W. Rostow, "The Austin Project, 1989–1993: An Innovational Exercise in Comprehensive Urban Development," Yale University, Fall 1993, Seminar on Inner City Poverty, www.utexas .edu/depts/ic2/pubs/ssicp.pdf, 23.

32. W. W. Rostow and Elspeth D. Rostow, "Reflections on How to Bring People in the Disadvantaged Communities into the Mainstream," *Proceedings of the American Philosophical Society* 126 (1992): 371; Rostow, "The Austin Project," 12.

33. Rostow and Rostow, "Reflections," 367.

34. Ibid., 372. I am grateful to Nils Gilman for alerting me to this phase in Rostow's career.

35. Etzioni, *New Golden Rule, 59.*

36. Helpful overviews include Fernando Henrique Cardoso, "The Consumption of Dependency Theory in the United States," *Latin American Research Review* 12 (1977): 7–2; Gabriel Palma, "Dependency: A Formal Theory of Underdevelopment or a Methodology for the Analysis of Concrete Situation of Underdevelopment?" *World Development* 6 (1978): 881–924; and Cristóbal Kay, "Reflections on the Latin American Contribution to Development Theory," *Development and Change* 22 (1991): 31–68.

37. United Nations General Assembly, "Declaration on the Establishment of a New International Economic Order," 1 May 1974, A/Res/S-6/3201. On the NIEO see Gilbert Rist, *The History of Development: From Western Origins to Global Faith,* rev. ed., trans. Patrick Camiller (London: Zed Books, 2002), chap. 9 and Richard Jolly et al, *UN Contributions to Development Thinking and Practice* (Bloomington: Indiana University Press, 2004), chap. 5.

38. Polity IV Project, 10 June 2013 update, www.systemicpeace.org/polity /polity4.htm. The above conclusion was based on comparing the average "policy2" variable for all countries in Asia, Latin America (including the Caribbean), and Africa in 1963 to the same average for the same countries in 1977. On a scale from –10 to 10, with –10 indicating a country that is maximally autocratic and minimally democratic and 10 indicating the reverse, the scores of the countries in question dropped from –2.25 to –4.69 over the fifteen-year period.

39. For a useful overview of the relationship between centralized states and capitalist growth in the global South, see Atul Kohli, *State-Directed Development: Political Power and Industrialization in the Global Periphery* (Cambridge:

Cambridge University Press, 2004). On the Korean and Soviet models, see Bruce Cumings, *Korea's Place in the Sun: A Modern History* (New York: W. W. Norton, 1997), 321–325.

40. On the relationship between industrial production and modernization as an ideology, see David Harvey, *The Condition of Postmodernity: An Enquiry into the Origins of Cultural Change* (Cambridge, MA: Blackwell, 1989).

41. On capital flows, see Barry Eichengreen, *Globalizing Capital: A History of the International Monetary System,* 2d ed. (Princeton: Princeton University Press, 2008), chap 5. For an illuminating account of the material processes of globalization, see Marc Levinson, *The Box: How the Shipping Container Made the World Smaller and the World Economy Bigger* (Princeton: Princeton University Press, 2006).

42. Patrick McCully, *Silenced Rivers: The Ecology and Politics of Large Dams,* enlarged ed. (London: Zed Books, 2001), xxviii.

43. Indira Gandhi to Baba Amte, 30 August 1984, quoted in Smitu Kothari, "Whose Nation?: The Displaced as Victims of Development," *Economic and Political Weekly* 31 (1996): 1476.

44. Macekura, "Of Limits and Growth," especially chaps. 3 and 7.

45. Ramachandra Guha, *Environmentalism: A Global History* (Oxford: Oxford University Press, 2000), chap. 6; Joan Martinez-Alier, *The Environmentalism of the Poor: A Study of Ecological Conflicts and Valuation* (Northampton, MA: Edward Elgar Publishing, 2002); Jacques Leslie, *Deep Water: The Epic Struggle over Dams, Displaced People, and the Environment* (New York: Farrar, Straus and Giroux, 2005); and Rob Nixon, *Slow Violence and the Environmentalism of the Poor* (Cambridge, MA: Harvard University Press, 2013).

46. The World Bank, *Accelerated Development in Sub-Saharan Africa: An Agenda for Action* (Washington DC: International Bank for Reconstruction and Development, 1981).

47. John Williamson, "What Washington Means by Policy Reform," in *Latin American Adjustment: How Much Has Happened?,* ed. John Williamson (Washington, DC: Institute for International Economics, 1990), 7–20.

48. James S. Coleman, "Social Capital in the Creation of Human Capital," *American Journal of Sociology* 94 (1988): supplement S95–S120; James S. Coleman, *Foundations of Social Theory* (Cambridge, MA: Harvard University Press, 1990); Robert D. Putnam, *Making Democracy Work: Civic Traditions in Modern Italy* (Princeton: Princeton University Press, 1994); Robert D. Putnam, "Bowling Alone: America's Declining Social Capital," *Journal of Democracy* 6 (1995): 65–78; and Robert D. Putnam, *Bowling Alone: The Collapse and Revival of American Community* (New York: Simon and Schuster, 2000). For a critical assessment of the rise of social capital and its use in development, see John Harriss, *Depoliticizing Development: The World Bank and Social Capital* (Delhi: LeftWord, 2001).

49. Kristian Stokke and Giles Mohan, "The Convergence around Local Civil Society and the Dangers of Localism," *Social Scientist* 29 (2001): 3–24; Giles Mohan and Kristian Stokke, "Participatory Development and Empowerment: The Dangers of Localism," *Third World Quarterly* 21 (2000): 247–268.

50. Christiaan Grootaert, "Social Capital: The Missing Link," in *Expanding the Measure of Wealth: Indicators of Environmentally Sustainable Development* (Washington, DC: The World Bank, 1997), 94–113.

51. Ibid., 108.

52. Martin Ravallion, foreword to Ghazala Mansuri and Vijayendra Rao, *Localizing Development: Does Participation Work?* (Washington, DC: The World Bank, 2013), ix.

53. Mansuri and Rao, *Localizing Development,* 1.

54. Howard White, "Politicising Development?: The Role of Participation in the Activities of Aid Agencies," in *Foreign Aid: New Perspectives,* ed. Kanhaya L. Gupta (Boston: Kluwer Academic Publishers, 1999), 112.

55. Mansuri and Rao, *Localizing Development.* See also Ghazala Mansuri and Vijayendra Rao, "Community-Based and -Driven Development: A Critical Review," *World Bank Research Observer* 19 (2004): 1–39.

56. Thomas Pogge, "Are We Violating the Human Rights of the World's Poor?" *Yale Human Rights and Development Law Journal* 14 (2011): 22. Based on data supplied by Branko Milanovic of the World Bank's Development Research Group.

57. Luisa Kroll, "Inside the 2013 Billionaires List: Facts and Figures," *Forbes,* 25 March 2013; Food and Agriculture Organization of the United Nations, *The State of Food Insecurity in the World* (Rome: FAO, 2009).

58. Current IMF voting power is at www.imf.org/external/np/sec/memdir /members.aspx.

59. Ha-Joon Chang, *Kicking away the Ladder: Development Strategy in Historical Perspective* (London: Anthem, 2002); Oxfam International, *Rigged Rules and Double Standards: Trade, Globalisation, and the Fight against Poverty* (Oxford: Oxfam International, 2002); Thomas Pogge, *World Poverty and Human Rights* (Cambridge: Polity Press, 2002); Thomas Pogge, *Politics as Usual: What Lies behind the Pro-Poor Rhetoric* (Cambridge: Polity Press, 2010).

60. Branko Milanovic, *The Haves and Have-Nots: A Brief and Idiosyncratic History of Global Inequality* (New York: Basic Books, 2011), 120–123.

61. A possibility explored in Martin Wolf, *Why Globalization Works,* Yale Nota Bene Press edition (New Haven: Yale University Press, 2005), 85–87. Ayelet Shachar discusses problems introduced by the outright abolition of borders and suggests a number of middle-ground solutions, including the unbundling of citizenship rights and the establishment of an inheritance tax on the winners of the "birthright lottery." Ayelet Shachar, *The Birthright Lottery: Citizenship and Global Inequality* (Cambridge, MA: Harvard University Press, 2009).

62. Intergovernmental Panel on Climate Change, *Climate Change 2013: The Physical Science Basis* (Stockholm: IPCC, 2013). For a useful synthesis of recent scientific research on the environmental consequences of various levels of global warming, see Mark Lynas, *Six Degrees: Our Future on a Hotter Planet* (Washington, DC: National Geographic, 2008).

63. For a clear and bracing discussion of this situation, see William Barnes and Nils Gilman, "Green Social Democracy or Barbarism: Climate Change and

the End of High Modernism," in *The Deepening Crisis: Governance Challenges after Neoliberalism,* ed. Craig Calhoun and Georgi Derluguian (New York: Social Science Research Council and New York University Press, 2011), 43–66.

64. Bill McKibben, "Global Warming's Terrifying New Math," *Rolling Stone,* 19 July 2012.

ACKNOWLEDGMENTS

This book contains some sharp words about the ways in which various thinkers have made a fetish of "community." But it was itself the product of a sustaining community of colleagues, teachers, students, and friends. It takes a village to write a monograph, so let me now, with gratitude, make a census of that happy hamlet's principal inhabitants.

Thinking Small began at the University of California, Berkeley. They say that scholarship is a lonely pursuit, but it never felt that way at Berkeley. I am grateful to the entire history department for that, and especially to four fellow-tillers in the broad field of development studies who watched this project from seeding to harvest. Over beers, on bicycle rides, and in rickshaws, I came to count on Ariel Ron, Ben Oppenheim, Mike Levien, and Dan Buch to share their infectious enthusiasm, offer frank opinions, and patiently explain things to me.

I've also had the good fortune to study with some of the best teachers in the business. Anders Stephanson sparked an interest in U.S. foreign relations, and C. A. Bayly (now Sir Christopher) and Francesca Orsini introduced me to India. David Szanton generously oriented me in the Philippines, loaning out half of his Filipiniana library in the process. In the realm of development, it would be hard to imagine a better guide than Peter Evans. And it would be harder still to think of a better model for how to be a historian than Robin Einhorn. Thanks are due, above all, to David Hollinger. I would be, frankly, embarrassed to enumerate all of the thousand small ways in which this book bears the Hollingerian imprint. I will just say that, without him, it would have been a much more boring book or, more likely, not a book at all.

But a book it is, and as it waddled its way toward publication, it was urged along by sympathetic bystanders. They cajoled and prodded, sometimes with not-entirely-hidden exasperation, as it tripped over itself, spun in circles, and took frequent rest breaks. Their motives in all of this remain unclear to me, but the standard injunction against making dental inspections of donated horses applies. So I will just offer my heartfelt, slack-jawed thank-yous to the people who inexplicably took the time to read my drafts and listen to my ideas with sympathy and care.

I am grateful, then, to Michael Adas, Michele Alacevich, Richard Cándida Smith, Todd Dresser, Naomi Lamoreaux, Gabe Rosenberg, Daniel Sargent, and a group of anonymous reviewers for reading the entire manuscript at a tender moment in the book's adolescence and making trajectory-altering comments. Participants in the Agrarian Studies Seminar at Yale and the Tamiment Cold War Seminar at NYU gave portions of this book the "I know this hurts now but you'll (possibly) feel better later" treatment, which improved the resultant chapters considerably. At Northwestern, Ken Alder, Michael Allen, Kathleen Belew, Henry Binford, Kevin Boyle, Gerry Cadava, Caitlin Fitz, Chuck Hayford, Laura Hein, Rajeev Kinra, Simeon Man, Kate Masur, Susan Pearson, Mike Sherry, Helen Tilley, and Keith Woodhouse proved to be not only shout-it-from-the-rooftops stupendous colleagues but also inadvisably obliging about allowing me to bother them with drafts and questions. Warnings, suggestions, references, careful readings, corrections, provocations, and general aid and encouragement came from Ryan Acton, Jenna Feltey Alden, Hannah Appel, Brooke Blower, Eliah Bures, Angus Burgin, Nick Cullather, Prachi Deshpande, David Ekbladh, David Engerman, Grahame Foreman, Dan Geary, Jess Gilbert, Nils Gilman, David Henkin, John Immerwahr, Samantha Iyer, Sheyda Jahanbani, Andy Jewett, Robert Johnston, Michael Latham, Sam Lebovic, Stephen Macekura, Peter Mandler, Rebecca Marchiel, Kate Marshall, Dan Matlin, Glenn May, Rebecca McLennan, Amanda McVety, Ed Miller, Tom Meaney, Amy Offner, Tore Olsson, Suleiman Osman, Sarah Phillips, Mary Racelis, Bill Rankin, Biju Rao, Scott Saul, Daryl Michael Scott, Tim Shenk, Lynsay Skiba, Jonathan Spies, Anders Stephanson, Corinna Unger, Amrys O. Williams, and the International Development in History seminar at Columbia University. A crisp salute and knowing wink go to my co-conspirators in panelifying, Michele Alacevich and Gabe Rosenberg.

To Andrew Kinney, Vetoer of Perfectly Good Title Ideas, is due an indiscriminate firehose spray of gratitude. Though one hesitates to quantify these things, it is fair to say that his keen editorial judgment and dedicated hard work de-awfulized this book by at least twenty percent. I am also grateful to Andrew's colleagues at Harvard University Press for preparing and marketing the book, to Lisa Roberts for designing its cover, and to Kitty Wilson for her judicious copyediting. Eliah Bures, Michael Falcone, Andrew Kinney, Scott Saul, and Brock Winstead supplied titles for the book and its chapters. Tom Meaney would have made that honor roll, too, had not A. Kinney objected (see above) to publishing a book called *Gemeinshafted*.

Every crime requires accomplices, and I would like to acknowledge a special set of them for their love, support, and disinclination to testify. Scott Armstrong, Gloria Bruce, Kathy Byrnes, Ragnhild Handagard, James Hudspeth, Adam Immerwahr, John Immerwahr, Stephen Immerwahr, Stephanie Johnstone, Luke Leafgren, Jon Katz, Sam Means, Ivy McDaniel, Lindsay Noll, Ben Oppenheim, Liz Oppenheim, Andy Ozment, Anna Piller, Wendy Seider, Teya Sepinuck, Jonathan Spies, and Charlie Ward—thank you.

Author's royalties from this book go to 350.org, an organization dedicated to restoring the quantity of carbon dioxide in the atmosphere to a level below 350 parts per million.

www.ingramcontent.com/pod-product-compliance
Ingram Content Group UK Ltd.
Pitfield, Milton Keynes, MK11 3LW, UK
UKHW032202260325
456773UK00002B/59